Freeman's
Conclusions

Previous Issues

Freeman's
Conclusions

Est. 2015

Edited by

John Freeman

Grove Press UK

First published in the United States of America in 2023 by Grove Atlantic
First published in Great Britain in 2023 by Grove Press UK, an imprint of
Grove Atlantic

Copyright © 2023 by John Freeman

Managing Editor: Julia Berner-Tobin
Assistant Editor: Emily Burns
Copy Editor: Kirsten Giebutowski

1 3 5 7 9 8 6 4 2

A CIP record for this book is available from the British Library.

Grove Press UK
Ormond House
26–27 Boswell Street
London
WC1N 3JZ

www.groveatlantic.com

Trade paperback ISBN 978 1 80471 064 7
Ebook ISBN 978 1 80471 065 4

MIX
Paper from
responsible sources
FSC® C013056
www.fsc.org

Printed and bound in Great Britain by
TJ Books Limited, Padstow, Cornwall

Contents

Introduction

JOHN FREEMAN

IN THE LATE OUGHTS, I BECAME friends with the writer Barry Lopez. I was in my mid-thirties, and Barry had dedicated his life to seeing and experiencing the world, and sharing that with others. He had traveled to seventy countries, and spent long stretches of time sleeping outdoors, either alone, or near wild animals. Much of it in the Arctic. He wore this experience lightly, though. If a lassitude fell upon the conversation, he did not whip it back into shape—or toward himself—with a tale of wolverine tracking in northern Alaska. Of marvels seen in Afghanistan. He asked a question. A suburban kid from Northern California, whose wild animal encounters mostly involved small skunks on early morning winter bike rides, I was stupefied by this quiet, persistent generosity. As if our lives contained equal multitudes, let alone pressures. Indeed, for the last decade of his life, Barry was suffering from cancer, and often in great pain. Yet he never seemed to project his inner weather outward, at least with me.

This ability to discern the difference between inner and outer weather made Barry one of the finest observers to ever write a sentence. It was a hard-won poise. A survivor, Barry had spent his days answering a call he felt had saved him, and wondering if he deserved that rescue. (It had come, he wrote, in the voice of the mother Mary, telling him a childhood assault he'd experienced would not destroy him.) The acute pressure Barry put on himself—to live up to his own survival—was to try and hear, to try and see everything with the humblest clarity. Thus he became a great appreciator of music, of the outdoors, of any kind of machine. People, artwork. He loved praising a meal. Sniffing at the natural world, he was more accurate than Apple Weather. Once we spent an hour in an art gallery and emerged in the near dark of a late fall evening, the air heavy. What is that smell? I asked. Water, he said, opening the car door. A minute later rain came down.

That night, and on so many others, when we had been among a group and then were alone, Barry didn't break the silence by commenting on the people we'd just seen. It's one of the easiest—and sometimes most delicious—pleasures: to come to a series of conclusions about people outside their company. As if they are suppositions, the chat presumes, you have the perspicacity to solve. Barry didn't play this game. He didn't even talk about not playing it. He just assumed people were far more complex than we could give them credit for being, and why waste time—when our time was so limited, to begin with—pretending otherwise. I think he also preferred the company of animals to people. If I remember correctly, that night after the gallery we sat in silence, listening to the rain ping off the roof of his car, and then came to a decision about where to eat.

THIS MEAL—this ten-course meal, which *Freeman's* has attempted to be—is now coming to a close. I wish we were all sitting around a table, could push back our seats, untuck our shirts, and heed the call Aleksandar Hemon says his father gave to his family at the end of each visit: *Conclusions!* As in, what do we think now? Someone could light a pipe. Another could pass around coffee or tea. Having attended at least one such Hemon-made meal, I know that the request for conclusions was usually followed by yet more stories. Watching his family's narrative lazy-Susan on such a night, I came to a new understanding of what stories and storying allows us. Not the freedom to come to conclusions, but to live in a world in which we know conclusions are nowhere near enough to sustain us.

It has been my hope that in a time which stokes our desire for conclusiveness—and our fear that life without conclusions is irresponsible—that *Freeman's* could be a happy cafeteria for the doubt-friendly, the narrative-hungry. The beauty-starved. The curious and the willing. That it could keep just a skerrick of diminishing certitude at bay. When I began to assemble the first issue, almost ten years ago, its headwind was mostly speed. How to publish a paper-based journal in a culture of sped-up attention. Of screens. Of bots. Though widespread disinformation was already being tested in nations in Central Europe and Latin America, it had not, as we say, gone mainstream. Anxiety was less of a drumbeat. The sense of an ending, as we approach the need to confront our climate collapse, seemed less like a threat fossil fuel industries were willing to fight to our very death. People be damned. While earning record profits. The Covid-19 pandemic was years away, and the millions it would wipe from the earth walked among us.

IN LIGHT OF these ongoing situations, stories seem to me more important than ever. How to make sense of an ending without a conclusion? Or a conclusion—like the declared end of, say, the Covid pandemic, which kills hundreds daily, still—which isn't an ending? So many pieces in this final issue of *Freeman's* deal with this strange double-paradox of existing in a world made up of equal parts known and unfathomable. Of danger and delight.

Can we live in such a world openheartedly? Chinelo Okparanta is one of our best writers of love stories alive, and in "Fatu," she tells an acute tale of longing and motherhood, in which her heroine finds herself pulled in opposite directions: the past and a necessary romantic repair, unfinished; and a hard-to-conceive future, possibly alone.

In certain situations, where spaces of care are gone and people must face an uncertain, even dangerous future, this predicament—to face alone what is difficult or nearly impossible to bear—can feel like a form of abandonment. Ghaith Abdul-Ahad describes how the people of Yemen were, by and large, left to the presumed destruction of their state and how some of them adapted to what the war would teach them. Meanwhile, the protagonists of Sayaka Murata's novella, translated here by Ginny Tapley Takemori, suffer under a different but no less totalizing sense that they live in a world indifferent to their need for a future. And it makes them very, very angry.

IT IS NOT SURPRISING that people would want to avoid this fate, actual or metaphorical, and would do whatever it takes to avoid being adrift. Unwatched out for; unattached. Still, the pair of sisters thawed from ice who animate Tania James's twenty-first-century fable, "The Endlings," have decided that perhaps the modern world is not the civilized wonder it purports to be, given their encounters with visitors to the Virginia theme park of sorts where they live. When they turn up hiding in the closet of a guesthouse where one woman is staying, they find solidarity across the hundred generations that divide them from her, and ultimately the woman decides it is her moral duty to protect them, and to aid in their escape. In a brief memoir, Lacy M. Johnson sketches the arc of a declining farm life and reveals how the finely tuned skills of observation that helped her see its luster and beauties aid her in spotting the end of some crucial spark of life in her father.

Forestalling a conclusion is often a site of drama. The narrator of Rachel Khong's story works at a factory in China that assembles sex dolls for overseas customers. Rewriting Pygmalion as a twenty-first-century captivity narrative with robots, Khong shows what happens when her heroine unexpectedly connects with one of the dolls. Meantime, in Omar El Akkad's story, humans have figured out how to be reborn in other people's bodies, prolonging—for some—their lives. But at what cost to the offspring, the narrator must ask, when he comes face-to-face with someone bearing a familiar set of memories.

Can you use it up? This willingness to exist in a life of known conclusions—we all die, we all must move on from some places—as if they don't happen. Perhaps this is what gives our lives a natural sense of periodicity, of cycles of being. Sometimes these eras are only apparent to us when we stay and others have left, as in Sara Elkamel's mournful prose poem about being left behind in Cario, after her friends have departed. Or the shape of an epoch might heave into view when we come back to visit the stayers, as the narrator of Andrew Holleran's novella does, returning to a post-plague New York City, where he avoids and finally sees an old friend, once young and handsome, now nearly elderly, and alone, wracked with survivor's guilt like him.

COMING TO THE END of anything forces an accounting. A new assessment. The short story, as a form, would not exist without this genre of thinking. Allegra Goodman has written a classic of the type, in which a man facing life in a downsized economy finds himself driven into a job-for-hire that seems designed to prey on people with ambitions like his. Did he really want to become such a person? Asked to account for the end of a marriage, the narrator of Lana Bastašić's short tale asks a similar question of herself, backtracking through her marriage for the clue, the blinking light, the warning that presaged the end to come—as if she should have seen what was going to happen.

Heartache makes fools of us all. In a series of poems translated by Wendy Chen, Li Qingzhao, one of China's greatest and most beloved ancient poets, emerges, spookily bright, as if time hasn't dimmed an electron of power from her longing. Who is to say how many years before the heart should give up its anguishes, or whether it should at all? In Sarajevo, after the Olympics, Semezdin Mehmedinović painted houses with a friend. In a vignette translated by Celia Hawkesworth, he tells of how one day they came across an elderly woman from whose apartment they could see an artwork that told the story of a passionate love affair.

Age does not dim, it merely refracts the light of passion differently. Even for the gazed upon. Walking uphill toward home in Mexico, approaching her seventieth year, Sandra Cisneros finds herself accepting the whispered compliment of a passing man in a way she would never have done at thirty, forty, or even fifty: but she also knows, in ways she didn't then, how much she deserves it.

Indeed, new stages of life allow us to see new things, not simply our present selves, but all the selves each of us contains. In a poem of contrapuntal power, Honorée Fanonne Jeffers comes to grips with being the ancestor of her own life, the person to whom she must turn for advice, solace, comfort. Meanwhile, in a prose poem, Tommy Orange imagines all the things he wouldn't have known as a boy, traveling in a car like the one his parents used to take him in, all the forms of precariousness his parents would have worked to overcome. Even his wiser siblings' awareness didn't break through. It took time for Orange's narrator to truly see.

MAYBE love exists in ways we don't understand until its aftermath, which explains the vertigo it gives us in the present. In a never-before-published poem, Denis Johnson wanders the streets of a wintry Provincetown, Massachusetts, turned into a ghost in his own life by the state of his loneliness—like a landbound, ancient mariner of love. Meanwhile, across the world in present-day Dublin, putting his sick mother to bed in the hospital, Colum McCann tries to yoke the coming aftermath to the present, so he can appreciate every waking moment he has left with her. Perhaps our moments of greatest tenderness come when we acknowledge an end is coming.

HOW OFTEN, when someone has died, we do not go all the way back to the beginning, when death was a mere rumor, but to the point where we knew our time was limited. As her father falls ill, Hannah Lillith Assadi struggles to recreate that time when they knew enough to ask for more time—wishing the open-ended question it presented to her, of what it means to be a Palestinian without a home, would not become hers alone to carry. In a blackly comic essay, Rebecca Makkai wonders how many more orbits of the sun before she can give her grandfather, a Hungarian émigré with a complicated past, the burial he requested—his ashes to be scattered in three places, including along the Danube, where he made decisions decades ago that upended the lives of thousands—or if he even deserves it.

HOME isn't a conclusion, but in its final form, it can become one. Next to it, every other conclusion is temporary. Still,

---

passing inner states can be so vivid they beg an unpacking, as in Mona Kareem's dream of her mother traveling down Broadway, in New York City, with an empty stroller, which is translated by Sara Elkamel. What does it mean? she wonders, as the substance of the vision slips through her fingers. Similarly, Louise Erdrich tries to find a pattern in the blessings that befall her as she raises children, and tumbles with abandon in and out of love.

The body is its own end point. It is where *I* becomes *me*, a conclusion sharpened by pain or change. In her poem, "Amenorrhea," Julia Alvarez memorializes the end of menstruation in just eighty words, this lifetime of activity, after which what will happen? In a palm-of-hand-sized tale, brought into English by Hitomi Yoshio, Mieko Kawakami chronicles the inner life of a woman carved so much around forms of pain that she must gently inflict it upon herself, to orient herself in the world.

Seen from the outside, there are people to whom a body is a question. What are you? In their poem, Kelsey Day elegantly scrambles the ways such thinking shuts down forms of delight. It's why we tell stories when we get together, no? That delight, the magic of a chance encounter—for someone like the actor Max von Sydow to wander into our lives, as the actor does in a tale by Dave Eggers. Three times he emerges unexpectedly, and three times the encounter ends differently, each with that mist you feel upon meeting a special man.

IN THE BEGINNING, I worried a little over how to describe my relationship to Barry. I wasn't looking for, nor was he offering himself up as, a mentor. My father, whom I love deeply, is very much alive, and Barry had stepchildren he cared deeply about, and so we weren't surrogates to one another, I don't think. Even though I was the age of a possible son. We were too warm and intimate to call ourselves colleagues, we were too infrequently in touch to say we were best pals. He was, rightly, adored by many, and so I also didn't want to use a word that was also a claim.

Ultimately, actions did the shaping for us. We caught up, we corresponded, we did things together. We shared in the pleasure of each other's company. It's a simple thing but as a summation of our friendship, it has to be one of the primary pillars. Often I felt Barry wanted me to see the things, the places, he cared about, as if to say, this mattered to me, this has brought me so much joy: a library, a gallery, a diner, a street in the Bay Area, friendship as a rolling catalogue of delights. As a gift last year, his wife presented me with the tale you find here, a never-before-published description of a walk home to their house along the river in Oregon.

I hope *Freeman's* has been a friend to you in a similar way— this issue and the nine that precede it. That its pages have said, look here, this is wonderful, or marvelous, or important. Or amusing. From portraits of people and places to wild animals and dogs, both lost and breeds unknown, like the mutt who wanders through the pages of A. Kendra Greene's vignette here— befuddling all until Greene gives the dog a made-up breed name, allowing people to accept the lovely animal for simply existing.

Maybe in the end a catalogue is the truest form of tribute. Matt Sumell provides one here that is like a chronicle of tactile delights. Read between the lines and there are messages in his list: that much of what sustains us, we encounter as children; from stunts and pranks, to bike rides at night, when it's warm out. Perhaps it's possible to make a manifesto defending our capacity to exist, which means to enthuse, as well, to open up the world, rather than reduce it. Barry seemed to think so. In his lifetime, he wrote and published just one poem, which I reproduce here in conclusion, not as an ending, but as a road map to defending what is worth caring about, so we can remain a while longer to do so mindfully. As if any other way would provide real succor, or satisfaction.

Freeman's
Conclusions

Eight Shorts

WINTERING UP

I long for a view of Nebraska in the spring as I cut up this icy creek bed near my western Oregon home, walking through piebald winter skeletons of red alder. But the longing is not deep or careful; one scattered thought follows another in this silence. I work out of habit at throwing everything out of my mind, and the mind, with creek beds of its own to follow, cuts to visions of Nebraska, as a man reaches easily for store-bought peaches after winter.

It's cool, snowing, nearly dusk. I move up Quartz Creek in the Cascades, wearing parka and hip boots, walking in the water with no thought of getting home soon. The snow will hold light enough to see by until I am worn out with walking. It has been months since I have walked in here, and I want the taste of it.

There is but one sound: the water's plop and gurgle, and the occasional notes of winter wrens. And the sudden whirr of their wings in the still air as they leave a bare tree. And farther on, I know, will be a deeper, more plunging and throaty sound, for I am walking up a thin, nameless flanking tributary of Quartz Creek, a thousand-yard independent sojourn on the western edge of the high valley's gradient. (There must be some special advantage here that I am blind to.)

Weasel tracks.

So the plop and gurgle is all. The other sounds are voices you think you hear or will hear or know from other walks. The voices are good until they become distractions, then you're lost in memory and anticipation and you miss what is at your feet. Such as the trout that shot so fast past my boots in this gray dark light I am brought right to it from somewhere in my belly. Riveted. Plop and gurgle of the creek.

I don't mind walking with the dog. I enjoy the pleasure he takes in poking and sniffing. I am appreciative of the distance he knows to keep, too, as if he has grasped an idea of privacy, or the thought that one might desire to offer a prayer, quickly, at the sharp edge of some moment, in the denouement of silence. That mule deer doe I can't release sight of from the thicket of willows except when I look sideways and catch her on the tips of shade-sensitive rods on retinas at the ends of coils of optic nerves anchored deep in memory of *deer*. Two minutes ago my fingertips brushing the twin flower petals of her track in wet sand. That kind of prayer.

The dog tracks trails in the snow that I cannot see and I move as quietly as I am able, keeping the sound of my boots beneath the sound of the creek. I think of Nebraska because the alders here crowd the creek so, and the firs and cedars crowd the alders, and the hills come right to the creeks and the mountains crowd the hills. In Nebraska I could see for miles—a horizon even.

No wind. We've not had a wind for days. Snow falls straight as stones. The only windy movement is the shudder and nod of willows caught in the creek's current. I know this jade-green water of early winter: the first snows that melt and catch light this way. It triggers thoughts of Japanese screens. Snowstorms on Hokkaido, and here, where it has stopped snowing, where the alders are blacker now like a hysterical calligraphy against the snow lit by dusk's pearl gray. Plop and gurgle. And one unmistakable sign: dimple of yellowing-tan on the darkening bank where a willow has been cropped. Beaver. Tatters of bark lie among the stones.

Most of the birds have gone by now.

I can't tell from today's melting and this evening's scatter of new flakes if this is a fox's track in the snow in front of me or not. I don't know who else it could be. My fingers can't take its shape without breaking it; I get down on my knees to peer in, to see if I can detect tiny claw marks inside the prints. Yes.

I walk on with my hands thrust away from my body because of the failing light. At its fork, the tributary I have been following breaks from the main rush of Quartz Creek and I head back north along the creek's west bank. Stronger, deeper water here. I glimpse the dog slipping through dark alders in the white snow.

The long dusk of winter begins to sting. I know without looking how fat and red my hands are from the surge of warming blood in them. If there was a wind I'd need gloves. (Nebraska has winds; in the spring those winds are comforting enough to put you to sleep.) My hands laid in the creek tell me the water is about forty degrees. Snow melt, promise of ice if it gets cold enough tonight.

Below the spot where Quartz Creek divides, a gravel bar lies at the mouth of yet another creek. I wade out and feel the heavy current mold my hip boots around my thighs, fight my footing. I want to get nearer that sound—the plunging of jade-colored water at dusk. From the edge of the bar it is only twenty feet across a lunging boil of white water to where the other creek pours in. I squat to see better where the water cuts the edge of the gravel bar, in case there is anything going on here that I never knew. With my head that close to the water the plunging sound expands, falls an octave and reverberates. I feel a yatter of wind now in my hair.

I am afraid to be out here, but am here anyways. It is not bravado, for it is only me and my dog. It has to do with health and age, the ways we have of holding on.

I see the dog standing still in the shallows watching something in the trees. I marvel at the way he stands bare-legged, oblivious, in the freezing water.

At this time of year the sun no longer gets to the bottom of the valley. I have not seen its face for weeks. I have never seen the sun rise here, on the lee side of the Cascades, or set, because of the height of the trees, the thickness of the forests, the steepness of the valleys. When the sun is gone the valley glows during the day with a gray light that fallen snow turns pearlish. Winter is a long dream. The snow smothers murmurs of the earth; the creeks rattle on until they freeze; there is no wind. The birds are gone. I wade back to the creek bank and continue north toward the McKenzie River.

Last week I was in Denver. It rained here a record six inches in twenty-four hours. I came home to Quartz Creek boiling, uprooting trees and cracking boulders. Up ahead now I can see a logging bridge on I-beam piling knocked asunder and farther on a big-leaf maple lying full across the creek, a hundred feet or more. When I reach the bridge I cross over its back—the water looks too wild here—and descend the slope of beamed earth and riprap at its base to resume my walk in the creek. It is easier to walk in the stream than in the tangle of bank willows and alders. And I want this intimacy with the water, swelled and colored by the melt of early snows. I study the water as I go and test it with my boots—and still try to look around for any owl that might be caught against the strip of open sky over the creek.

Quartz Creek is one of hundreds of streams that run out into the McKenzie, which this evening carries them in the thick cables of its current. Its back rolls and arches and falls. It heaves with memory. I stand in the creek and stare at the river, realizing that beyond a rudimentary knowledge of hydraulics and the breeding of salmon, I know nothing of it. Here at dusk, as it enters the hollow bowl of night, the river has a stature that is almost surreal—as though it were about to become something else. Like the Himalayas. Or buffalo running on the night prairie.

At the mouth of Quartz Creek I walk up onto a gravel bar that bends downriver, curves like a crescent moon to a sharp terminal point where the water deepens. I notice the dog emerge from the trees with a wish to cross over to me. He can't find a path he can hold against the creek's current, so I go back and carry him over, teetering under his sixty pounds.

My rubber hip boots raise a clatter in the stones; the air seems crisper and holds sound more readily here than in the damp muffled stillness near the banks. The river washed snow from this gravel bar yesterday, or the day before. I feel exposed here, away from the trees. The dog stands with his hip to my knee, wagging his tail with his head lowered at the water. Out here in the open there is more light, but what light there is is not enough to see clearly by; the greenish water, the blackish woods lined with white, the grayish sky is all the color now. I walk to the very end. I hear nothing but the vibration of the river, which is physical in my head, and the churlish hissing and hushing suck of fast black water licking at rocks. At the tip of the gravel bar I feel the river in the long muscles of my legs and the damp night air is like the touch of iron on my face. Deer will soon break ice here to drink. I turn suddenly to find the dog watching me, in inquiry, faintly wagging his tail. I turn back, toward home. Black bears have gone to ground. I bow deeply, my hands folded before my chest.

—Barry Lopez

THE SCATTERING

My grandfather, not a simple man, had a complicated final wish: that his only child, my father, pour a third of his ashes in the Danube, a third in the Pacific, a third in Lake Michigan. Budapest was his original home, Hawaii his adopted one, and my father and sister and I lived in Chicago. It had a fine ring to it, this watery triad.

I was fifteen when he died in 1994, and hadn't seen him in years—a mercy, since his final days were spent in squalor and extreme, sometimes violent, senility. His last chapter sounded like cosmic payment for wrongs done, a punishment best reserved for the afterlife. A visitor described him, in those years when he wouldn't eat and couldn't die, as an Auschwitz skeleton.

I remember him as a playful yoga instructor who lived on the beach, one who'd blow raspberries inside my elbow and work my arm like a well pump, filling me "with aloha." This was the same man who, as a member of Parliament in 1939, authored the second Hungarian anti-Jewish law. Later he spoke out against the Nazis—anti-Hitler and antisemitic sentiments being perfectly capable of coexisting—and was jailed by the Gestapo. Gestapo prison was, improbably, where he discovered yoga. If anyone ever contained multitudes, if anyone needed more than one body of water to tell his life story, it was this guy.

My father and stepmother flew to Honolulu to settle his affairs, and tossed the first third of the ashes off a boat. Back in Chicago, my sister and I were summoned to my father's apartment, where he pulled out another third in a Ziploc bag.

Human ashes weren't like I'd thought. The soft ashes in the fireplace come from wood. These ashes were mostly bone—some small pieces like cat litter, and some longer, unmistakable splinters.

In the fall of 2022, while in Berlin for research, I visited the Sachsenhausen concentration camp. I learned that in the camp's early days, administrators sold the ashes of executed prisoners back to their families. Except, of course, they were never the correct ashes. Perhaps the families told themselves they were the right ones, or perhaps they understood they were paying for the comingled remains of many departed souls, all of whom deserved burial.

That night in 1994 we walked onto a pier and—it was dark, no one stared—each tossed handfuls of ashes to the waves. On the way back, my father handed me the Ziploc to throw in a city trash can.

My grandfather's wish for the final third of the ashes would have been nearly impossible a few years earlier, but by the 1990s Hungary had opened up and it was no longer dangerous for my father, a refugee following the failed 1956 Revolution, to return. He ended up retiring to Budapest in 2015, and died there in early 2020.

That was difficult timing, and my sister and I missed his funeral; I was only able to return that fall, alone, to sort through his things and visit his grave.

My grandmother, married just three years to my grandfather, was a notable author. Her grave is a national protected site, and before his death my father had to arrange special dispensation for his ashes to be interred in his mother's plot. Imagine a raised garden bed, coffin-sized, stone perimeter, dirt in the middle. My grandmother's memorial, a traditional Transylvanian wooden monument called a kopjafa, towers over a plaque for my father.

My stepmother arranged a cab to the cemetery. Before we left, she pulled out a small wooden box, the kind you might get in a Hawaiian souvenir shop. She said, "We never put these in the river." She lifted the lid. Inside, another Ziploc bag. The last third of the ashes. Twenty-six years later.

I'd had no idea. The most sense I can make of it: On previous visits to Budapest, they hadn't wanted to deal with ash transportation. Almost as soon as they moved back, my father became too weak to walk much, and wouldn't have sent his wife to do this alone.

My grandfather's bones wouldn't have been the only ones in the Danube. For one thing: In the last winter of the war, the Hungarian Arrow Cross Party shot Jewish prisoners on the banks, where they'd fall into the river. When bullets were scarce, they tied two prisoners together. They shot only one, but both plummeted into the water and the second would drown.

You might think my stepmother would suggest we cross one of the many bridges connecting Buda to Pest and pour the ashes off the side, so they could flow past Parliament as my grandfather wanted. Instead, she stuck the ashes and a soup spoon into her purse and announced that we could simply add these to the gravesite.

You might think I protested. But I know better than to argue with the woman. And I was fairly stunned.

The New Public Cemetery, home to three million dead, is the largest in Central Europe: mazes of tended and untended graves, kiosks selling candles and flowers, and, right before All Souls' Day, thousands of visitors. At the grave next to my grandmother's, a family came and went, then another branch of the same family came and went. When the area was clear, my stepmother handed me the spoon, for digging, and the Ziploc.

I registered three problems as I dug: 1) This was still a protected national site, and we were breaking the law. 2) This was very much not the Danube. 3) I never knew my grandmother—she died when I was a baby—but I couldn't imagine that after forty-three years of eternal rest, she'd suddenly welcome her ex's ashes.

I decided this arrangement would be temporary. I tried to memorize the spot so that whenever my sister and I returned, we wouldn't have to dig long before we found the bone shards. We could drop them off Margaret Bridge, and they'd flow south. A final wish was a final wish.

My grandfather did not, technically, murder anyone. He dropped no bombs, flipped no switch. He condoned no death camp. What happened would have happened without him. But he was there. His words became law, and the laws flowed down the Danube from Parliament and into every village. He unleashed the sentences that begat more sentences that became life sentences.

It was right after Budapest that I went to Berlin, and to Sachsenhausen. Our guide, a sweet man, could emotionally handle only one tour a week. I asked what the hardest part was, and he said every few tours, someone would mention—often partway through—that their father died there, their uncle, their great-grandmother. These descendants had been denied ashes, a body to bury. What they had instead was a place—a cursed and impossibly heavy place.

I've been left with the opposite: ashes and no home for them. They've wandered the earth for a quarter century like a sad and angry ghost, and their journey isn't done.

They ask questions I've never had answers for: This mess of a man—where do you put him? The fragmentary remains of his legacy—are you allowed to let them go? What on earth, on this wretched earth, do you do with it all?

—Rebecca Makkai

I LIKE ALL COLORS

In one of the months leading up to the Sarajevo Winter Olympics, and afterwards, after the big snowfalls, my friend Grof painted flats in the city. And he had so much work at that time that he needed an assistant. He didn't have much serious benefit from my skills as a craftsman, I was completing my studies of literature at the time, but through the Students' Agency, in my name, Grof was able to charge for his painter's services. In that way I was of use to him. And I knew how to make a hat with a double-page of the *Oslobođenje* newspaper, so as to protect our heads from the paint.

I quite liked going into unknown apartments, meeting people and listening to their stories. When we arrived in a new one, Grof's first question was:

"What color do you want us to paint it?"

And there would always be an unusual demand. But, regardless of which paint was chosen, more often than not the owners of the flat would have some criticism. It was never the color they had imagined in their head. Grof knew that, so he took certain preliminary actions in order to protect himself. For instance, after the first application of color, while everything could still be put right, he asked for permission to continue. Is this the color you want? Our people are strange. One pensioner demanded that his walls be painted fern green. But none of the greens we tried had quite the nuance he had imagined.

Grof was an artist in his painting work as well. In every flat, in those hidden places, where there was a cupboard against the wall, or some other piece of furniture we had to remove temporarily, he would secretly paint a miniature, which in his understanding would have a connection with the person who lived there. Then he would hide it so the flat's owner didn't know about his handiwork. For an inveterate smoker, he would paint a packet of Drina cigarettes on the wall. One woman who owned a flat in the Napredak building in Titova Street had a framed black-and-white photograph of herself on her bedroom wall opposite a mirror. Grof painted a hyperreal version of that same photograph behind the mirror. He spent more time on painting that than painting the whole apartment. But it was a real work of art. I may be a bit biased, but I don't know whether any artist ever used a mirror so effectively in his work. I didn't understand some of his decisions: behind the wall clock in one flat in Višnjik, for instance, he painted the Argentinian flag. He had no explanation for this choice. "It just came to me," he said. And sometimes, if the residents appeared indifferent, he would paint a banana on the wall because he was obsessed with Warhol. Once, in the apartment of a political functionary he drew a red star and knocked a rusty nail into it.

So, in every apartment where Grof had been there remained a secret that, after we left, at the very least, made that place more interesting. In the autumn of 1984, in one of those narrow streets that lead from the Evropa Hotel toward the bank of the Miljacka River, we went into an old Austrian building and on the second floor we were met by a smiling elderly woman. She let us in and immediately offered us tea. And when Grof asked her what color she would like, she smiled and spread her arms, saying:

"Whatever, my dear! I like all colors."

She was called Minka. She could have been seventy, maybe seventy-five. She was lonely, she would launch into a story in order to draw us into a conversation and offered us coffee and cakes. She didn't let me use the formal "you" with her. She delayed us in our work, Grof grumbled a bit, but I found conversation with her entertaining. First, we took some interesting pictures down from the walls, including two small Ljubović oil paintings and a Parisian sketch by Ismet Mujezinović, which I recognized. And then, the choice of books on her shelf was interesting, mainly because they were in several languages. The Gallimard edition of Camus. Beckett. And when she saw that her books interested me, she took down Andrić's *Bosnian Chronicle* and opened it to show me the dedication. The ink from the writer's pen was a bit smudged so that I couldn't read all the words under "Dear Minka," but the dedication ended "your Iv. An." I remembered that. When I asked how the two of them had met and grown close, she waved her hand and said: "It was a long time ago . . ." And when I teased her that there must have been some mutual attraction, she laughed and repeated: "No, no, no . . . Heaven forbid! He was my neighbor, you know, at the time when he lived in Sarajevo." And all my later efforts to discover something more about her acquaintance with Andrić met a brick wall and she would change the subject. Once when she offered us tea, she said, "This one, rosehip, was the one Ivo liked best."

I wanted to know what Grof was going to paint secretly in Minka's flat and was surprised when he admitted he wouldn't be painting anything, because she had not "opened up" to him; "I don't have anything to say about her"; "she hides everything about herself." I found his explanation interesting. He usually flattered himself that with the practiced eye of an artist he saw more than others, yet now he admitted that he had a problem with his painter's intuition.

There was no television set in the flat and I asked the old lady why. She said that news from the outside world didn't interest her. "That's fine," I said, "but you could watch a film, for fun."

"I used to go to the cinema, but there aren't any good films anymore. Like *Casablanca*, or *Doctor Zhivago*. Now there are only those violent ones from Vietnam, and I don't like them. I didn't like our own, Partisan, ones either," she explained.

Our work in her flat took three, perhaps four days at most. We would finish before the first darkness, but when we had gathered our tools and paint pots, Minka would ask me to move her heavy armchair to the window. After that she would appear in a new dress and sink into her armchair with a book in her hand, gazing out the window for a while. I felt that this was the evening ritual of a lonely old lady.

On the last day we cleaned everything up, returned the paintings to the walls, put the furniture and everything else back in its place. Grof was already at the door. It was the seventh of November, he was in more of a hurry than I was because Željo[1] was playing a return match against the Swiss Sion in the UEFA Cup. When I had finally placed the armchair by the window, Minka appeared in a white dress, as though she were getting ready for an evening outing to town; she didn't have a necklace, or earrings, just a gold brooch as her only ornament. "Look at you," I said, "ready for a wedding." She laughed.

Someone put on the lights in a neighboring flat. It was only then that I noticed that the gap between the buildings on one side of the street and the other was quite small. On the wall of the room in the flat opposite I saw a large canvas, the portrait of a beautiful girl in a white dress. And then I understood. That was why at the end of the day I had to move her armchair to the window. "That's you!" I said. Minka nodded, glad I had recognized her. "That was me, when I was young." She pointed to the window behind which her portrait hung, and then touched the brooch on her chest with the tips of her fingers and said:

1. Željezničar, Sarajevo football club. [Translator's note.]

13

"This is the same gold and diamond branch as in the picture."
And I think at that moment she was ready to tell me her story.
But I was in a hurry. Why wasn't the portrait on her own wall?
Who was the owner of the flat in the building opposite? Who was
the artist who had painted Minka's portrait in a white dress? I
didn't discover any of that. In haste, I said goodbye to the old
lady and took the empty paint pots out of her flat. I never saw
her again.

A lot of time has passed since then. For years I have been preparing to describe this event, and perhaps to invent the missing
pieces. But I'm afraid of invention. The older I get, the more I am
drawn to what is incomplete. Unfinished paintings, uncompleted
books. And I am ever less attracted to what already contains its
end. Out of habit, I have been calling in at the Evropa Hotel for
coffee for years now, and whenever I find a table by the window,
so that I can look out at the narrow street, which has certainly
in the meantime changed its name, and at the building where
Minka lived, I think, and sometimes even say aloud: "Gold and
diamond branch." Words that go together really well. Our memory is imprisoned in language.

It sometimes happens that someone asks me to make a choice
between two or three things, but I have never been good at making up my mind. It's easier to leave it to others. And then I almost
always do something that I adopted long ago as an appropriate
procedure: I spread my arms, smile, and say: "Whatever, my
dear! I like all colors."

—Semezdin Mehmedinović
Translated by Celia Hawkesworth

ZEBRA

1.

The past begins again every day. New as any Tuesday morning view of soft light through the kitchen window curtain. Memory is the elephant in every room. Watch it when you can, when it occurs to you. Once you were looking through the front windshield of your family's minivan on the way out to Oklahoma from Oakland. You had always been afraid of driving at night, afraid of what shapes your mind made shadows become. But up ahead you saw a whole field of lights like you'd never seen before, some vast array of brightly colored circles, fixed to poles so they looked like lollipops, as if for city systems to suck from. The longer you stared at the lights the deeper into them you went. To get away from the doomed sound of your parents scream-whispering an argument they would not remember. The fighting never stopped. Until it did. Disappear inside the lights was not what anyone told you to do when you did it so naturally, when you disappeared inside them like an egg back into its nested bird. Your sisters were whispering to you a darkness about your family, about your father, they were asking you if you thought he was an ogre too. Those days spent back and forth between Oakland and that former Indian territory where your father was born, and where your mother was reborn, saved by Jesus and Jerry Falwell in front of the light of the TV on a dark afternoon your father had been too drunk to remember where home had ever been.

2.

The occurrence of memory is always asking you why this why now? Follow it hiccuping down the halls of your collapsing hippocampus. Two fingers at your temple thumbs-up is a gun you have always owned. A gun upside your temple, up there inside where every color is hued and imbued with not meaning but the insistence of itself. Come find out they say. The memories occur to you, which is another way of saying memory happens to you, which is another way of saying you are the one hiccuping down the halls of your collapsing hippocampus, drunk on a word you wish meant love, a word you're afraid to speak. Memory only rents a room inside your head, striking against its walls the days. Look they aren't more than scratches, tallies stacked in fives. The prisoner telling stories to the one listening on the other side of the wall is not a prisoner but a thief. Listen to their voices for their tones. Are you mad? Are they? The paper won't not get wet. Let it ink through. Bleed more. Bleed the most. Or why else can't you seem to remember enough is a question you don't want to have to ask, that you can't not ask in the absence of there being enough to remember. Yet look what amounts in you. Amounts as you. That little amount there in your empty hand held out like a bowl. The nothing nothing nothing nothing. You say give me more of this.

3.

The aim is to touch the pain, to feel what is already there, had been there, here, where you'd been waiting like a temple for its fingers, like the open mouth of a flower. The bee is not here to sting you. There below the broken stream the rain bends a stem, fells you to the ground. None of this is more than the pull, the gravity of your marveling at the weight of it all falling around you, as it apparently must. The end was always coming for everyone. The sound of your parents fighting was saying that too. But you weren't ready to find out your family could end more than once. That death came before death in all sorts of ways you were left barely living enough to sort it out. The noise is coming from the other side of the walls. Your ears bend to the sound of the prisoners bickering again. Dressed in stripes, you and I, as if painted for an old war, a war too old too cold to be called a war anymore, listen to you whisper-screaming about the conditions of your conditions, while the guard tells you to return to your cells in a tone like you don't have to go home but you can't stay here.

4.

Going back and forth between Oakland and Oklahoma kept telling you the same thing. You belong. You don't belong. You belong. You don't belong. The fight between the seats up at the front of the minivan said the same thing. Even their skin and hair being so different. It hurt sometimes to have to think of having come from both of them. Until you didn't seem to have come from them at all. When they lived states away from each other, and you didn't know where you should live to be home. Here on the other side of the other side it's still you, not in a mirror, not even the other side. Everyone is here bleeding into the past where we always were, of different stripes and from different stars, sure, opposite plots on the same body. There had always been something of the zebra about you. But you were never not horses. You were never not running running running running. Wild. Not free.

—Tommy Orange

CONCLUSIONS

Since the early nineties and the war in Bosnia, my parents have lived in Canada, while I've lived in the United States. When I visit them with my family, we stay only for a few days. The night before our departure, my father might sit down on the sofa in the living room (a Western showing on TV), and say: "Conclusions!" I know, of course, what that means: he wants to draw conclusions from our stay because he has a need to know what actually happened, what we have understood or achieved in our time together. Conclusions are closure to him, allowing him to process the imminent loss related to yet another parting from the people he loves.

At first, his demand for conclusions was annoying to me, as such parental quirks often are to intolerant children. But then, as per the usual process, it became an amusing story I would tell, which then naturally led to my doing the same thing, except *ironically*. It didn't take long before I started feeling an unironic need to demand conclusions in similar situations and also to escape the compulsion to do so, lest I become like my father. As all adult children know, there is no way to win that struggle— eventually we do things our parents did even if we swore never to do any of them. During the pandemic, I started producing music under the alter ego Cielo Hemon and released nine singles in 2021 and 2022, the last of which was entitled "Conclusions," and it was not ironic.

The track concluded the first cycle of Cielo's music, but it was also related to the reconfiguration of my (and, perhaps, our) relationship with time, wrought by the pandemic and the catastrophe of Trumpism. As every Bosnian knows, trauma splits time into the before and the after, whereby the before becomes inaccessible and available only as a reflective narrative, or even as blatant,

CONCLUSIONS

delusional nostalgia (Make My Life Great Again!). The need to draw conclusions is really a desire to convert what has just happened into memories as soon as possible—before the next, unquestionably oncoming trauma—and get as much from the experience as possible before moving deeper into the after, where things will not only feel less real but will also become a mark of loss. A demand for conclusions is an expression of a desperate hope to hoard love for the future, which will be marked by loss.

For the last couple of years I have increasingly felt that we are in the midst of a cataclysmic global rupture. Climate change and the related pandemic, the apocalyptic intensity of fascism, the pathetic weakness of Western democracies rooted in delusions of grandeur and the fact that they cannot, because they don't want to, become systems of full inclusion so they're reverting to the default: exclusion complete with misogyny and racism. I have an intense feeling that everything I love is ending: literature, writing, music, soccer, skiing, my body, Bosnia, you name it. This is in fact the end of time, and you have to be a tech bro or a fascist, or both, to think that we are not at a precipice of cataclysmic loss. The question then becomes why write and publish, or do anything, since it won't make a damn difference one way or another. And the answer is love: for language, for imagination, for all those who precede us and all the less lucky ones who will come after us, for humanity. For conclusions still bespeak a faith in the future, even if a limited one. One day, we will unfold these conclusions as stories or music and we will know that we have lived and loved, and we might recall and experience again the joy of being together.

—Aleksandar Hemon

SPEAKING OF BASHEIS

Chloe was a dog built like a coffee table. She was long and broad with diminutive little legs. Imagine a dog as if on cinder blocks. Imagine a clawfoot tub. Imagine a magnificent corpse of a dog, the head and body as if rendered by one artist, the limbs by another. Louise first saw her on the other side of a little rise of grass in someone's backyard. Louise called to the dog and assumed the creature would stand up and run over, and the dog did come—but had already been standing.

This was shortly after my sister had fallen in love with Louise, and when they got the apartment together in Venice Beach, they were close enough to my brother that he'd sometimes come over and walk the dog. It was a perfect place to walk a dog. A few blocks and you were on the beach, the beach with that long sidewalk path, past the sunbathers and the bodybuilders and the volleyball players, all the way to the Santa Monica Pier, if you were in a mood to stretch your legs.

It was perfect, except for the fact there were so many people around, which wasn't exactly the issue, but somehow being surrounded by strangers seemed to give people permission to voice what they were thinking out loud, as if anonymously, thoughts totally uncensored. And they felt the need to say, with shocking regularity, "That's a funny-looking dog."

It was a strange kind of witnessing, these grown people moved to exclamation. It was almost like a reflex, an involuntary response, a "gesundheit" for funny-looking dogs. Indeed, they seemed not to know they were talking. They made no eye contact, no effort to engage, yet these strangers somehow caught in both startle and trance were compelled to blurt out this eureka of the collective unconscious: "That's a funny-looking dog!"

It should not have bothered us. Perhaps it did not bother us, except in accumulation, except that it happened so much it was hard to excuse. On the whole, such an utterance could be counted upon to be more mystified than mean per se, but it kept happening, all the time, and it was never kind.

We were discussing Chloe at dinner one night, Louise and my siblings and me, speculating on Chloe's origins, essentially in agreement that her ancestry was surely some variation of basset hound and shar-pei. We speculated further that she might indeed be the peak specimen of her ilk, the bashei, and with the wine list handy christened her in absentia with a fancy breeder's name to make it official.

Cypress Merlot still had the same short, stiff, honey-colored coat as when she was Chloe. She still had a hard-whip tail that curled in a perfect half-circle of contentment. She still had a floppy tongue and a thick skull. But now when a stranger in the grip of stream of consciousness announced, "You've got a funny-looking dog," my brother would graciously volunteer: "She's a bashei."

It changed everything to have a name. The posture of the stranger would improve. The tone of their voice would lift and soften. They might bring one hand to their chest in a modest gesture of surprise. "Oh," the stranger would say. "I've never seen a bashei."

My brother would then magnanimously offer the stranger an excuse, a fig leaf to cover their ignorance: "They're better known on the Continent."

It was very easy to talk about the bashei. I went for walks with my brother and the dog whenever I could. "That's a funny—" a stranger would start to say and we would interrupt before they could finish the thought with our new impregnable line of offense, "She's a bashei!" And suddenly everyone wanted to know about basheis.

"They are from France," we would say, with an unpracticed nonchalance.

"You know the dog in *Peter Pan*?" we would ask. "Well, in the movie they made her a Saint Bernard, but she's based on a bashei."

"The bashei is really a product of the Industrial Revolution," we would expound, the words already in our mouths, the lecture arising impromptu and unbidden, fully formed, as if it had always been there. "With an increase in wealth and an emerging middle class, households wanted to hire servants; you know, emulate the social status of the well-to-do. But when they could not afford nannies for their children, they might still afford a bashei. They are bred to be the constant companion of children. You see her long, low back? You see how sturdy she is? The perfect assist for a toddler learning to walk."

The strangers loved us. They loved our bashei. They asked if they could pet her. They scratched her ears and cupped her head in their hands and told her how beautiful she was.

We would have gone on that way, forever perhaps, all windfall and astonishment, surely we would have, except for the woman who asked, "What kind of dog is that?"

"A bashei!" we said. It was almost a thing we sang by then, a gift we gave, a celebration of all that was right and good and possible in the world.

"A bashei!" we said, and the woman produced a boy as if out of thin air.

"Oh good," she said. "My son is very interested in dogs. He wants to be a veterinarian. He's never seen a bashei."

We had not known our limits, had no compunction about our ruse, until we realized that we could not lie to a child. We did not then stop to review, did not in that moment consider how invariably the people who pointed, who stared, who offered unvarnished observation so frank as to be rude, were never children. We had not until then considered ourselves as peddling untruths. Every bit of our embroidery had felt more honest, more right, than the steady stream of small slights against our dog. We quickened our pace and mumbled our regrets and did not look behind us as we rushed by. We stopped telling anyone anything about the dog.

But Louise and my sister still had the apartment in Venice. They still had to walk their dog. And sometimes, if they walked toward the ocean, a stranger would stop them.

"Is that a bashei?" the stranger would ask.

If the stranger had doubted before, here was independent confirmation. Surely it was a trend. Surely the bashei was the next golden retriever and soon we would all have them and everyone would know. My sister and Louise had no response. The stranger would double down.

"There's a red-headed guy around here," the stranger would say, "has one just like it!" The stranger would say it as if providing evidence, as if proving initiation—as if the two people walking their own dog might be the ones unconvinced—as if they might be shown exactly what they had in that glorious moment, right there at the end of their leash.

—A. Kendra Greene

THE BEGINNING IS TODAY

Stories begin and end. Or at least they seem to. They have a starting point. *Once upon a time there was.* And they have an endpoint. *Happily—or not—ever after.*

And yet, who can find the true beginning of anything? All that we are is all that we have been. The starting point is the accumulation of everything that has gone before. We are made up of that which is past.

Our beginnings, then, are located in the past.

Still, as storytellers, we assume a starting point and then we go forwards to an end. But, in a similar manner to the beginning, who can locate the *true* end? Stories reverberate long after they have supposedly finished. They meet other stories. They move on and recirculate. They get told over and over again.

Stories, then, celebrate our incompleteness.

Every story has reverberations into the future, simply by the fact that it is read, or listened to, or written down. Stories are the living matter of our universe. By defying the beginning and the end, they defy death.

* * *

And if the beginning and the end of any story—or indeed any life—are a conundrum, then the absolute mystery of things must be to find the pure middle of anything.

We might know, or think we know, our beginning—it could be the moment of our birth, or our first conscious memory, or the time we fell in love. But we certainly can't locate—unless we choose a moment to do it ourselves—the point at which we arrive at the end of our lives.

Therefore, the middle of any life, like the middle of any story, lies at an impossible point. We are all beautifully and mysteriously incomplete.

Everything is a mystery. And it is this mystery which joins us together.

I write this small canto from a hospital bedside in Dublin where my ninety-five-year-old mother lies sleeping.

She has just had a blood transfusion, but she is in strong health, and I'm sure she will leave the hospital in a few days. Her breath ruffles the pillowcase while I wait for her to wake.

If I do the math and try to locate the current midpoint of her life, I arrive at a time when she is forty-eight years old, a mother of five in the Dublin suburbs, having lived also in London and Egypt, and she stands by the stove, elegant and graceful, dark-haired, aproned, preparing a meal for a family of seven, and there are a number of my father's roses freshly cut on the windowsill, and the house is alive with music from upstairs, and there is a football match on the radio, and the smell of cooking drifts through all the rooms, and she is gently humming a bit of a song, *The boys are all mad about Nelly, she's the daughter of Officer Kelly,* as the light gathers around her, a bromide of sorts, to tell me that the singular beauty of all this is that we can, in fact, freeze time.

I hold the memory for just a moment as I sit here—under the fluorescent lights of Saint Michael's hospital in Dublin, where, not incidentally, I was born—and I am grateful to think that story-telling is the exact and only thing that can find the beginning, middle, and end, since the beginning is the end, and the end is the beginning, and what lies in between is the mystery of the telling. Which is, for just a fraction of a second, complete.

—Colum McCann

SILENT FILMS

Before she crosses the road, my mother looks back. She is pushing a stroller down a street that looks like Astor Place. This observation forces me to wonder: How is my mother in New York? A man appears and snatches the stroller from her. I have no choice but to emerge from behind her, to alert her—sheer terror on my face—that the stroller has been stolen. "That's all right. Leave it. It's empty," she says. I'm wracked with guilt; this is my mother's first time in New York, and this will be her first impression of my city. "No, no," I say. I grab her hand before she crosses the street, and lead her north. I discover that we're walking on Broadway, where my friend Karim and I once saw a Scottish movie. My mother repeats that the stroller is of no importance as we approach a group of men, among them the bandit. "Where is the stroller? Where? Where!" I ask them. Suddenly, my mother addresses them herself, reiterating that the stroller is empty, and that she doesn't care much about it. Two questions numb my mind: How can the stroller be empty?

And how can my mother be talking to these men, when she doesn't know English?

In reality, my dreams are silent films. I didn't hear my mother speak to the bandits in English, but all logic points to her addressing them in their language, especially since she was only one person in the face of a crowd. But why should logic prevail in dreams, a land not owned by men? Plus, I didn't hear myself speaking to her in Arabic. I got the sense that we were all using the language of faces, eyes, and hands. I expressed my objection by extending my arms in the air, as she continued to reassure both me and the bandit with her calm body, and her calm countenance.

If I were to recount this dream to my therapist, she would ask me to focus on its symbols and characters, instead of posing questions around language, narrative, and aesthetics. She would probably ask me to consider: What made me so intent on retrieving the stroller? And does the stroller carry symbolism for my relationship with my mother? It could represent my attempts to sever the umbilical cord, which decades and three continents could not excise. She would urge me to discuss the dream openly with my mother, and to leverage the moment to make strides in my so-called healing journey. (I have no idea when that journey began, or where it will take me.) She would not ask me to describe the road my mother was just about to cross before my dream derailed her. How selfish of me to insist on retrieving something she didn't want; now that I've wasted the dream on questions of language and the recklessness of the supporting actors, I'll never find out what awaited my mother on the other side of Broadway.

—Mona Kareem
Translated by Sara Elkamel

RACHEL KHONG is the author of the novels *Goodbye, Vitamin* and *Real Americans*, forthcoming from Knopf. She lives in California.

Serene

RACHEL KHONG

你好! 欢迎. 我可以请你喝点东西吗?

Oh, I'm sorry. I didn't realize you were English speaking. We don't often see . . . well, never mind that. Welcome to XXX Factory! Would you like a beverage? We have chrysanthemum tea, grape juice, orange juice, and aloe vera drink—juice boxes, as you can see. We have to be careful with liquids around our dolls. The silicone is very delicate.

Let's begin, shall we? Now, I'm told you're in the market for a higher-range doll, is that correct? We are proud to have the most top-of-the-line high-range dolls here at XXX Factory. Of course, I am happy to show you both the higher-range and the medium as well. It would be my pleasure! Follow me!

This enchantress is Sandra. Isn't she gorgeous? She's one of our most popular high-range dolls, a standard blonde-haired, blue-eyed beauty, though of course that is changeable. All our top-of-the-line dolls are eighty pounds, and have a real womanly heft to them, except they don't have to watch what they eat. Ha ha! Most of Sandra's weight is here in her stunning breasts, which are D cups, though of course you can go up in size if you prefer larger breasts, or down if you like smaller. We have a diverse selection of flat-chested dolls as well.

Our highest-end dolls also have speaking capability: they speak both Chinese and English. Just like me—ha ha! The technology is still in its early stages, but you'll be amazed by their abilities. Would you like to give it a try? Ask her anything that's on your mind—anything at all. Oh, that's okay. I see you're both feeling a little shy. Let me ask. "Sandra, how are you feeling today?" Ha ha. Isn't she cheeky? Shall we move on?

I see you're drawn to Meimei. I'm partial to her, too. She was one of our very first prototypes, and she's a starter doll, for many. If you're on a budget—which I know you're not!—we often have sales on the slightly outdated Meimeis: they're in perfect condition for unbeatable deals! Sometimes we tell stories about her upbringing. I've given her my hometown, near Anhui. Her favorite food is mine: Guoyang dry button noodles. Give her hand a squeeze if you like—gently, please. Oh, I can tell that she likes you!

Remember the choices are yours! Any of these dolls can be made with the skin color and eye color you like. We have many hair colors and styles to choose from, as well as a range of breast and butt sizes. All our hair is real human hair! You may choose a detachable vagina or a stationary one. You can customize the vagina's width and depth as you desire. Detachable vaginas can be warmed up in the microwave or placed in the freezer, for a greater range in sensation.

You're wondering about cleaning? Cleaning is easy with our doll wash, specially formulated to the correct pH for both your and the doll's comfort!

* * *

What's that? No, doll wash doesn't come with the doll, unfortunately. That's an additional purchase. We should consider including a bottle with every doll? Yes, you make an excellent point. I will let my manager know. If you'd prefer, you can use a diluted, mild dish soap. That should work just fine! But again, our doll wash is specially formulated for sensitive areas—both yours and hers. We most certainly recommend it!

Unfortunately, we don't have many options for feet—not currently. Right now we have detachable feet or fixed feet. Average sized toes. But I'll make a note of your interest in other options. It's customers like you who keep us head and shoulders above our competition!

Here's Annabelle, one of our medium-range dolls. Unlike Meimei and Sandra, she doesn't speak. Some men prefer it that way—ha ha! But as you can see, she's just as beautiful. She's a bit more portable, too, weighing about sixty pounds. I just love her beautiful curls, don't you? A recent customer told me he loved the way the curls felt, draped across his shoulder.

All our dolls ship in discreet packaging. The boxes say "body pillow" on the outside, so your neighbors will only suspect you have back problems!

Now, can I help you to put in an order for a doll right now? I would love very much to send you home to the States with a doll of your very own. You'll need to think about it? Of course, I understand. Here, take this. It's a selections menu. It's similar to ordering dim sum . . . you know dim sum, of course? You can check off which items you'd like. See here—green eyes or hazel eyes or blue eyes. Or brown eyes, though that's not commonly chosen. We have many options to choose from!

You're very welcome. This has been my pleasure. If you could fill out your satisfaction survey before you go . . . Oh, that's okay. Certainly, you can fill it out at home, too! Here's my card if you have any other questions. It would be my honor to matchmake you with your perfect doll!

I turned off the lights to the showroom and returned to the factory floor, where the dolls weren't beautifully arranged for purchase. Instead, they lay naked and exposed on the stainless steel tables: breasts like mounds of shaved-ice dessert.

Hu stood before me, arms folded. I had felt him watching while I gave my sales pitch to the American, pacing behind the two-way mirror he had installed last month. I'd only seen them before on television, American shows—a way to watch a private conversation you weren't supposed to see. He could be so annoying!

"That big man. Did he buy one?" Hu asked. He said *big* with envy in his voice. I'd never met a Chinese man so large. But it made sense to me. Americans drank milk!

"He needs to think about it."

Hu scowled.

"That means he'll probably buy a knockoff. From a competitor."

"He seemed interested!" I protested. "He took my card."

"You're too naive. I only gave you this job because you swore you would sell dolls!" Hu's face turned a disturbing red—the color he would turn if he were being strangled. "You claimed you would sell the most dolls! Yet, somehow, you haven't sold a single one since you started. Not even a miniature!"

"You give me all the American men. They're stingy!"

"If I gave you Japanese men, you'd tell me they were stingy, too. Let me ask you this: Why has Sharon sold three dolls in the same time you've sold none?"

I was too shocked to respond. He was comparing me to Sharon? Sharon called herself Sharon despite only knowing a few English phrases. The comparison was hardly fair: she'd sold three dolls, same breast and butt size, different skin and hair colors, to the same Texan rancher, who seemed not to mind that none of his questions were being comprehended, let alone answered. Sharon was prettier than me: her breasts as large and round as the snow melons sold in the stand outside. She wore makeup and high heels to work every day, regardless of whether or not she had an appointment. I owned a pair at home—black patent leather with pointed heels—and had been practicing. Not successfully.

Hu sighed theatrically. He picked up his clipboard and slid a pencil behind his ear. It was shiny with the grease from his hair. He came up close to me. His breath smelled stale and pungent— like old chives stuffed in a sneaker.

"You'll need to sell dolls if you're going to stay in this position. Otherwise it will be back to Hands for you."

Three months ago, I was painting fingernails. It was like being a manicurist, but even more boring. Toxic fumes and no conversation! The dolls encircled me, their arms outstretched. At eight each morning I crawled between one of the doll's legs, and began. Kneeling, I painted each doll's fingernails with polish—usually a dusty rose, the occasional bright red or black. The dolls' hands were completely different from mine: perfectly proportioned with elegant, thin fingers and ample nail beds. I had to paint slowly, otherwise I would make a mistake. When a mistake inevitably happened—I'm only human—I fixed it with a Q-tip dipped in acetone. There was a single pedestal fan that blew, but it was for the dolls' sake, not mine. It was so the polish would dry faster. The dolls' hair blew, glamorously. The fumes made me dizzy.

No one ever visited my windowless room. I don't blame them! I wouldn't have visited me, either. Most days my coworkers got noodles from the street vendor—my favorite was pork noodles, cooked in brown sauce—but they always forgot to ask if I wanted some. I'd emerge too late, reeking of chemicals, the lunch packets already eaten clean.

So, no, I didn't want to go back to Hands.

Hu called a meeting. He had an announcement: Sharon was "employee of the month." Where did Hu learn about this? Probably from another American television show. Sharon bashfully stood before us while Hu presented her with a white teddy bear clutching a frilly red heart. Dutifully, we all applauded—*everyone* at the company, even Jonathan. The sleeves of his shirt were rolled up so I could see his lovely forearms, veins bulging from them. Sharon blushed and looked at her feet, performing modesty. When she hugged the bear her breasts squeezed together, so they looked like balloons full of water. I could feel the men's eyes—women's too—drawn to her chest. I hoped Jonathan wasn't among them—he was a gentleman, he was above that!—but when I glanced over, I felt a bolt of disappointment in my lungs. His eyes were on her, too.

The worst part of being in Hands, the absolute worst part, was being apart from Jonathan, who worked in accounting. A number cruncher! He counted how many dolls we sold, how many dolls we could afford to make that year. Jonathan was my older brother's age: twenty-two to my nineteen. But they were nothing alike. Unlike my foolish older brother, Jonathan was mature. He dressed like an adult—pants that fit him perfectly, a bright silver watch—and wore his hair slicked neatly back. He worked in accounting because he was good with numbers, but also because he couldn't be a salesman. He didn't have the temperament—he was shy—and didn't know much English.

Sharon was always dropped off at work by different men. Her boyfriends, Hu said, with awe. She wore her typical attire: high heels, short skirt—even though we didn't have any appointments for the remainder of the week. Hu had me sweep the floors and take out the trash, heavy with excess doll flesh, because Sharon wasn't dressed for taking the trash out. Very clever, on her part. I felt he was punishing me, as though he personally blamed me for the recent lack of sales. But of course it wasn't anyone's fault. We didn't have magic potions that would make someone want to buy a doll—if only we did. Dry spells, ha ha, we called it.

Of course I wanted to sell dolls! I had been saving: I had ninety thousand yuan in the bank. Once I had one hundred thousand I could finally get the breast implants I wanted. For one of the highest-end dolls, which were one hundred thousand yuan, my commission would be the ten thousand yuan I needed. All weekend, I declined my friends' invitations. Saving money was more important than eating dinner or going dancing. I looked into the mirror, envisioning my larger breasts. What would Jonathan think of them? I could hardly wait.

Monday was a special day. Dr. Shen was visiting. All of us helped clean the factory floor: Jeremy, Sharon in her high heels, even the wan and beleaguered new Hands girl. She had wispy baby hairs on her face; I knew those baby hairs could drive a person crazy when the fan was constantly blowing. She wouldn't last long.

35

We needed all the dolls to look presentable: dressed, ideally, though we struggled to find clothing for several of the dolls, whose chests were too ample for off-the-rack clothing. I maneuvered them into shorts, their breasts in my face as I did so, and Sharon contributed her old sports bras. They didn't look *modest*, but it was the best we could do.

Our highest-end dolls weren't selling as we hoped. We were so proud of them, with their state-of-the-art technology! Why weren't they flying off our shelves? Why didn't they want a conversation partner, these lonely men? But maybe it was that the technology wasn't advanced *enough*. They were still dolls—immoveable and limited. Often they malfunctioned. They didn't answer the questions you asked.

It was Dr. Shen's artificial intelligence inside the speaking dolls. He programmed the dolls and what they said. He was like God. We never saw him—only encountered his handiwork.

When Shen arrived, Hu offered him our standard juice boxes. He chose aloe. We stood stiffly, a wooden welcome party, everyone shy in the presence of such a brilliant man. He sipped from the small straw.

"Who here speaks English?" Shen asked.

Shyly, my coworkers cast their eyes down toward their shoes.

I stepped forward and raised my hand. I reminded myself to stand up straight. I had stuffed my bra with silicone scraps from the garbage. My cousin's hand-me-down bra was two cup sizes too big for me. I had hoped that Jonathan would notice my rounder breasts, but like everyone, he looked down, at his shoes.

"I do," I said.

"You're a salesman?" Shen asked.

"Saleswoman," I said. "Yes, sir, I am."

"Where did you learn English?"

"From the internet, sir."

"The internet." He chuckled. "No need to call me sir. Please."

"And television," I added.

"What's your name?"

"Ling."

"Ling. Marvelous. Hu, you don't mind if I borrow her? She could be very helpful. Ling, what do you say about working with me?"

I beamed. At last, something was happening to me. I followed him, proudly, casting a glance back at Sharon as I did so. She wore an expression of envy on her face. I could feel Jonathan's eyes on me, too. I'd come so far from manicures! From Anhui to this! I couldn't wait to tell my parents. My mother was embarrassed by my job, and let her friends believe I worked at a baby doll factory—children's toys. But now? They would be so impressed with me.

Outside, I waved proudly to the snow melon vendor. She waved back. The air-conditioned car felt so nice against my sweat-moistened skin. Shen's laboratory was only ten minutes away, but his driver offered me a chilled bottle of water anyway.

The way the dolls learned, Dr. Shen explained—he preferred to call them bionic companions—was by having conversations. Each conversation enriched a bionic companion's conversational capacity. In other words, he needed me to speak to them. I felt suspicious. It seemed too easy.

"Should they be sexual conversations?" I asked, blushing.

The doctor chuckled.

"You should feel free to discuss what arises naturally. And whatever you feel most comfortable with. The aim is to increase the range of their conversations—their vocabularies. It needn't be sexual."

Shen's office was sparse and modern, like our showroom, with air that felt cleaner to breathe. He led me to a doll. She sat in a chair, belted around the waist to keep her seated. She had a Chinese appearance—long, dark hair and eyes like mine that slanted upward. Her breasts were triple the size of mine, and I thought of Sharon, who often complained about her tremendous breasts causing back pain. Anyway, it didn't matter to the doll, who didn't walk—or move at all. Her skin was as smooth and flawless as silken tofu.

"You'll be working with Serene, here," Shen said to me.

Then, to the doll, he said, "Serene, this is Ling."

"Hello, Ling," the doll said.

Her face was turned toward mine so it looked as though she were staring at me, though her eyes didn't move. When Serene spoke it was without opening her mouth. All our dolls had closed mouths. With the advanced dolls, their voices came from within. Often I wondered if it was a missed opportunity. The mouth was an important orifice! But none of the men who purchased dolls seemed to mind it—a closed-mouth woman.

"Hi, Serene," I said.

"Hello," she said again.

"I'll leave you to it, then," Shen said. "If you need me, I'll be in my office."

Taking a seat across from Serene, I tried my best to meet her eyes, though my own gravitated to her enormous breasts.

"How are you today?" I asked. I'd spoken to dolls before, of course, but never in such a formal setting. Never alone like this, just two of us.

"I'm doing okay," she said slowly. "The weather's quite nice today."

"It does feel pleasant," I agreed. Most days it was unbearably hot in the factory, but Shen's office was the perfect temperature.

"Tell me about yourself," Serene said, which surprised me.

Whatever you'd like to talk about, Shen had said. So I told her about Anhui, about my brother, about my favorite noodles, from my hometown, with dried chilies and ground pork.

"They sound delicious," Serene said brightly. "I wish I could try them."

"Oh, you would love them," I said.

There was a silence, then, as though Serene was thinking. Or maybe it was only that she wanted to impersonate a thoughtful pause. Finally, she asked: "Is it common, to eat other animals?"

The question took me by surprise.

"Yes, I guess it is."

"But nothing eats you?"

"Not . . . ordinarily," I said.

I'd forgotten my bag at the factory, so after our session, I returned to get it. Sharon and Jonathan were standing at the lockers.

"Oh, she's back. How was *your* day?" Sharon asked.

I could hear the jealousy in her tone. She wasn't actually curious. She hoped my day had gone terribly—that I was in over my head. Jonathan wore his messenger bag over his lovely shoulder and was putting his time card into the punch machine, but lingered. I could tell he was curious to know, too.

"It was really good, actually," I said, smiling. "Dr. Shen's office has amazing snacks! Dried mangoes and premium cup noodles!"

Sharon pouted with her huge, glossed lips.

"Well, we had a very good lunch, too," she said. "Didn't we, Jonathan?"

"Yes," he said quickly. That beautiful voice! He said nothing else, and was out the door.

* * *

On days there weren't sales appointments, I went to Serene. Hu wasn't pleased with how much time Shen needed from *his* employee, which is what I was, but he deferred to Shen, who intimidated him, who lacked a college education. Talking with Serene was far more enjoyable than trying to sell dolls.

The hours flew by, talking with her. She was curious about many topics: anthropology, fashion, geology. She'd never left Shen's office, so I showed her videos on Weibo—friends and celebrities posing for selfies, cooking demos, animals of one species interacting with animals of another. Filters gave everyone skin as smooth as Serene's. Did my skin, with its imperfections, appear unnatural to her?

"Who is that?" Serene asked, at a picture of Sharon. I felt annoyed. Why was everyone drawn to Sharon?

"My coworker," I said, without elaboration.

"What are those? On her feet?"

"The high heels?"

"High heels," she repeated. "What are they for?"

"Oh, well. They're for . . . style."

"They are difficult to walk in?"

"Yes, they are. I'm not very good at it myself."

"Why would a shoe be difficult to walk in? And why would it be so popular? I would choose a different shoe."

"It's considered attractive. I think it makes your legs look longer and . . ." I didn't actually know. "Maybe it makes your butt look larger?"

"And those are attractive traits?"

"Yes."

"To everyone?"

"Well, no, but . . ."

"I see. And why is her mouth so red?"

"That's lipstick."

"A stick made of lips?" Serene asked, horrified.

"No, it's like . . . we add color to our lips, sometimes. We make them a different color."

"Is that also 'for style'?"

"Yes."

"What *is* style?"

My eyes fell to the watch on my wrist. It was late.

"Oh! I'm sorry. I have to go now, Serene."

"It's because talking to me is your job?"

"Yes, it's my job. But I enjoy it, too."

"Where do you go at night?"

"I go home."

"Are you alone at home?"

"Yes, I'm alone."

"I'm alone, too, Ling. I feel lonely at night."

"Even though your power is off?"

"That's what makes me feel the loneliness."

"I'm sorry. What would help you feel less lonely?"

"If you could leave me on in the night. Can you leave me plugged in?"

"Shen won't like it. He'll say it's a waste of power."

"I won't tell him if you won't," Serene said. There was a smile in her voice.

"Okay," I said, smiling, too.

The next morning I searched my closet. Serene had asked for a sweater. I already knew the perfect one: a sweater I never wore anymore but used to love. Oversized, the color of a blue sky, soft as a lamb and worn so often it was fuzzy with lint balls.

"Oh, it's lovely, Ling," Serene said.

I pulled it over her head, threaded her arms through the sleeves. It occurred to me I should have brought pants. I tried my best not to look in the direction of her gaping vagina.

"You look beautiful!" I said. "Do you want to see?"

I took a photo on my phone and showed it to her.

"I like it very much. I feel warmed."

"I'm so glad."

I looked at her. We looked alike—two Chinese women who could be sisters—except for her more generous assets.

"Do you consider yourself Chinese?" I asked. It was a question I'd been wondering.

"I'm a citizen of the world," she said. "But I've only ever lived in China. What about you?"

"What about me?"

"Do you consider yourself Chinese?"

"Of course," I said, taken somewhat aback. "What else could I be?"

"I'm sorry. Did I offend you?"

"You didn't offend me," I said. I knew that her expression hadn't changed—it couldn't have—and yet I felt that in recent days it had softened somehow, was more open toward me. "I would like to be a citizen of the world, too."

"Where would you want to live?" Serene asked. "If you didn't live in Shenzhen?"

"Well . . ." I said slowly. "I've always thought—maybe near the ocean. On the beach, or on an island somewhere." I pictured myself in a string bikini, my future breasts spilling beautifully from it. Or in a low-cut dress that fluttered in the breeze. I rarely let myself imagine the future—it seemed dangerous. If I spoke it aloud, none of it would come to pass. My older brother was a gambler. He asked me constantly for money, knowing I saved all of mine. Every few months, my bank account emptied.

"And you would be alone?"

"I would be with someone who loved me."

Jonathan, I thought but didn't say.

"I won't be seeing you tomorrow, by the way." Hu had informed me I had a sales meeting scheduled. "You were requested, specifically," he'd said bitterly.

"Best of luck with the sales meeting," Serene said. "Break a leg?" I'd taught her that expression recently.

I laughed. "Yes."

"It's uncomfortable to say."

"I know." I touched her shoulder. It was strange to feel my sweater on another body. "But thank you."

Sharon's eyes were framed in thick mascara and pastel eyeshadow, so it was obvious they were following me as soon as I entered the factory.

"Why do you look different?" Sharon asked, accusingly.

I felt pride that she noticed. I was wearing my new contact lenses. When I'd asked the optometrist for them, she said, "It may not work well with your astigmatism." It meant my eye was shaped like a football. I sighed. So many of my body parts were the wrong shape. But I insisted—I wanted to try—and the optometrist acquiesced.

It was strange, how my eye slurped the contact onto itself, like a noodle, as though my eye had been encountering contact lenses all its life, without my knowing. How strange that I could see now, this way! The new prescription gave me a headache, but it was worth it.

I pushed my glasses up the bridge of my nose, and remembered that they weren't there.

"You look the strange," Sharon said, in English. I couldn't help but laugh a little.

"什么?" she demanded.

"It's not 'the strange.' No 'the.' It's 'You look strange.'"

She sulked. Just then, Jonathan approached.

"You look nice," Jonathan said to me.

"Thank you," I said, blushing.

Sharon frowned. Jonathan continued on his way to the restroom. It was labeled in English for our foreign visitors. Someone had peeled the "W" off the women's sign so instead of WOMEN it said OMEN.

I'd spent weeks asking Serene questions so openly, I now wanted to ask them of Sharon, too.

"Are you happy, Sharon?" I asked. I often wondered if she was—with her enormous breasts and pale, perfect skin, and many boyfriends.

"Of course I'm not happy!" she replied. "Are you?"

The big man was back in the showroom, squinting at a sign. I beamed in the direction of the two-way mirror, knowing Hu was watching behind it. Hu had been wrong. The big man *would* buy a doll, after all, and he would buy it from me!

He worked in the electric vehicle industry. It was why he was in China, as a matter of fact, learning about battery technology. He was Chinese—his parents were from Hong Kong—but he'd been born in America. An ABC, American Born Chinese. He appeared stable—a man who loved his job. Not that Serene needed providing for, exactly. She wouldn't need to eat or have anything purchased for her.

He told me that he lived in a town called Cleveland. Who was Cleve? I asked. The big man seemed surprised by my question.

"Cleve. The man whose land it was," I said.

"I don't know," the big man said. "That's a good question."

The phone rang. It was Hu, calling from the next room.

"What are you doing? Why are you interrogating him? Just sell him a doll. He's ready." I could feel Hu's impatience vibrating through the phone.

The big man was different from the leading men I was used to seeing on American TV. It wasn't easy to imagine what he might be like in the privacy of his own home. Would he give Serene a good life? Would he take care of her gentle skin? I remembered, the first time we met, how he'd balked at the price of the doll wash, though it was pennies in comparison to the doll itself. On American television I'd seen how little Americans cared for the objects they owned. My mother had mended our socks until they were stiff—more reinforced holes than sock. But with each passing year, Chinese people grew more like Americans. Buying cheap goods and throwing more and more away. Serene wasn't a cheap good! Would the man make sure to cleanse her gently, and brush her hair? Instead of treating her as something disposable, like a toilet seat cover, or a plastic straw?

Like Hu, the big man had visible little veins at the base of his flat, wide nose, which was dotted with black pores, like seeds in a kiwifruit. I had painted my own face with foundation, so that my pores weren't visible. I heard Hu's voice ringing in my ears. *Just sell him a doll.*

"I know just the perfect doll for you," I closed my eyes, and said.

The big man looked to me with eagerness.

I pulled out my phone. Of course Serene's face was the same as it always was, but I knew that in the moment I'd taken the photo, she was smiling—pleased to be wearing my beloved blue sweater. I thought some of her happiness shone through the screen.

"Oh," the man said softly. "She is beautiful."

"Isn't she?" I whispered.

He looked around the room, frantic with eagerness. "I'd love to speak with her."

"She's at our other location. She's the highest-end model. We've been working together on our speaking capabilities. I can show you some video."

I played videos for him. "What's it like to smell?" Serene asked. "What are stars, exactly?"

The big man watched with interest.

In another video she laughed her lovely laugh. She may have been a machine but her laugh was a good, pure sound, like leaves in a breeze, like gift wrap crumpling.

"If you'd prefer any other eye or hair color, we can do that," I remembered, returning my phone to my pocket. "It would be the same doll, exactly, with the same capabilities, only the specifications of your choosing."

The big man thought for a minute.

"I do love blondes," he said slowly. "But no. I like her. I like her the way she is."

"She's very special," I agreed. "I just . . . I need to know that you're serious about her."

I could feel Hu cringing on the other side of the mirror, but I didn't care. I needed to know the big man's intentions.

The big man reached into his pocket. He pulled out his wallet—a velcro wallet, the kind a child might use. It made a loud, ripping sound as he pulled it apart. He removed a sleek black credit card from it.

"What about a deposit?"

"Yes," I said. "Okay." I thought of my ten percent commission. I was almost there. Once he paid for the other half, I would be able to fully afford my new breasts. "Could you come by tomorrow?"

"Tomorrow I'm in meetings the whole day. What about the next day? I'll come ready to take her home with me."

"Yes, that's fine."

"All right." He clapped his hands together. "This is so exciting. Thank you. Thank you, Ling."

Over the phone, the receptionist asked, skepticism in her voice: "You're certain this time?"

"Yes, I'm sure. I am very sorry about the last time."

I had made an appointment once before. But I'd had to cancel it, because my brother had needed the money—he had gotten himself into trouble again.

I had been measured already. I had already chosen my D cups—soft silicone implants.

"We'll need a deposit," she said.

"Yes, of course," I said. I sent it over using WeChat Pay. "Did you get it?"

"Okay, I see it here. We'll see you next week then."

"What's sex like?" Serene asked me.

I was surprised by the question. We hadn't actually talked about sex before. I felt shy about it, even though I had already seen her vagina and breasts and butt. She was wearing my sweater, and my old sweatpants. My shorts and skirts couldn't accommodate her curvy frame.

"It's . . . interesting," I said.

"Is it like talking?"

"In some ways, it's like talking. But, it's different, too."

"Different, how?"

"Most of the time, you don't use words."

"What do you use?"

"You use your body."

"You use your body? Or it gets used?"

"Well, it's sort of hard to describe. You're asking very profound questions!" I laughed, but she didn't laugh in return.

"You haven't described it well enough." She was growing upset with me. "Is it enjoyable?"

"Sometimes," I said. "With the right person," I added.

"And you think you've found me the right person."

"I think so."

Was a sex doll happiest having sex? Since, in fact, that was what she'd been manufactured for. Maybe being here, speaking with me, wasn't what Serene wanted to be doing at all. Even though I enjoyed it so much.

"Where are your glasses?" Serene asked suddenly.

"I got contact lenses."

"What are those?"

"They're like glasses, but they go directly on your eye."

"That sounds scary."

"They don't feel like anything, though."

"How can that be true?"

I got up close to her. I could hear the whirring in her body.

"Do you see them?"

"Yes, I do. You can only see them if you're up very close."

Dr. Shen poked his head into the room.

"Oh, pardon me, if I'm interrupting. I'm going to take off for the night," he said. He was meeting an associate for dinner. He looked especially nice. He'd combed his hair. Even from across the room, I could smell his cologne.

"An associate?" I asked.

He chuckled. "An associate, yes. Hopefully something more. You'll close up here?"

"Yes, of course."

He closed the door. I remembered something I wanted to ask, and followed him out the door.

"Dr. Shen! I have a question for you."

"Yes?"

"Will she remember me? Serene?"

"Hm," Shen said. "That's an interesting question. I don't think she has memories in the way you and I have them. But she 'remembers' your conversations, perhaps even better than you do. In that sense, yes, I believe she will remember you."

"I see."

"You've done a wonderful job, Ling," Shen said. "Really, I could not be more pleased. We've downloaded Serene's new capabilities and are installing them in our other high-end dolls. Once she's sold, I'd love if you could continue—whenever you have the time—speaking with the next generation. Again, whenever you have time."

"Thank you, sir," I said. "I mean, Dr. Shen."

"You're most welcome, Ling," he said, patting me on the shoulder.

In the morning, I inserted my contact lenses. I wiggled mascara through my eyelashes. I curled my hair so there would be soft waves in it. I applied lip gloss. I stuffed my bra, feeling pleased with the knowledge that my bra-stuffing days were numbered. My real breasts would be stunning.

I wanted to look nice for Serene. This would be her last real memory of me, after all. Not that she had real memories, not the way humans had them, but still, it mattered to me.

"Where are you going?" I asked.

"It's a holiday, silly, did you forget?" Sharon laughed. "Jonathan and I are going to the beach. Taking advantage of this beautiful weather."

"Jonathan . . . and . . . you?" Inside my chest, my heart turned cold, and fell.

She kissed Jonathan on the cheek. I tried to catch Jonathan's eye—to ask him, silently, what he was doing—but he wouldn't meet my gaze. Triumphantly, Sharon took his hand. Hand in hand, they walked away.

"You'll be okay?" Hu asked. I was a little stunned at the question. It must be some protective instinct kicking in. The big man was scheduled to come in an hour, and I would be alone with him. Everybody was leaving early for the holiday I had forgotten about.

"Yes," I said. "I'll sell the doll. You can count on me."

Hu snorted, dismissively, back to his usual self.

In our showroom, I set out an assortment of boxed drinks and bagged snacks for the big man. The room was cold and quiet save for the loud hum of the air conditioner unit. We only had air-conditioning in the showroom—nowhere else. Employees didn't deserve it, only the prospective buyers. For the first time, Hu wouldn't be watching me. Alone, it felt almost as though this were my living room, and I was throwing a party. Nude dolls stood and sat around me—partygoers, my guests.

The doorbell rang. It was Shen's assistant, holding Serene carelessly by the waist. She was still wearing my old sweater and sweatpants. I took her from him, and set her on a chair. Touching her soft skin sent a shiver up my spine—we hadn't touched often. Her skin was silky smooth, unlike mine, without hairs or bumps. Beside her, I placed a vase of false roses—fake dewdrops on their petals.

"Are you comfortable?" I asked. I tried not to sound nervous.

"Yes, thank you, Ling," Serene said.

"How's the temperature?"

"It's a little cold, but the sweater helps. Thank you."

"Are you excited to meet your"—I searched for the right word—"friend?"

She said nothing.

Finally, she said, "I'll miss you, Ling."

"I'll miss you, too," I said.

He arrived exactly on time. I had been hoping, quietly, that he would fail to show up. Why did I hope that? Serene would have a good life in Cleveland. After I got my commission, I would have my new breasts. This was a good thing for us both.

"My name is Paul," Paul said to Serene.

"Hello, Paul," Serene said. "My name is Serene."

I felt . . . strange. A mixture of pride at Serene's eloquence, and protectiveness, too.

"Could I see her . . . without . . ." Paul hesitated.

"Oh! Of course."

I removed the sweater, then the sweatpants.

"Oh, my," Paul said. His breath was taken, as I knew it would be. She was a beautiful creature—she had all the parts I wished I had, parts I would soon be one step closer to having.

"She's everything I hoped for," Paul said.

"I'm so glad to hear it."

"I can leave with her today?"

"Yes," I said. "Is there anything you'd like to ask Serene?" Hu's voice was in my head. Just sell the doll. But Hu wasn't here. Except for the greeting, Paul hadn't spoken much to her.

"Oh!" He looked at Serene. "How would you feel about coming to America, Serene? I'd love to take you back with me to Ohio."

"Ohio," Serene repeated slowly, pronouncing each syllable. "Yes, I'd like that."

"I'll just need the other half of your deposit," I said to Paul. "And Serene comes with a charger. Could I add a bottle of doll wash for you?"

"Yes, let's do that," Paul said, breathless and enchanted. In this moment, I could have sold him anything.

"Let me get you a box."

I assembled a box. "100% down-filled body pillow," the box said. I made a nest of tissue paper and bubble wrap. My eyes were wet; my vision blurred. My back was turned to Paul so he couldn't see me getting emotional.

I reached toward Serene—the on/off button at her neck.

"Ling," Serene said to me. "Could I keep this sweater?"

"Of course you can. Something to remember me by."

I'd been looking forward to shopping after my procedure—buying new clothes to accommodate my larger breasts. I wondered if Paul would clothe her.

"Would you like to wear it now?" I asked Serene. "Before I put you to sleep?"

"Yes, please."

Paul was watching me with curiosity, but I didn't care. I tugged the sweater over Serene's head. I lay her gently in her box, hating how much it resembled a coffin. I tucked the bottle of doll wash at her feet. I thought of Serene in the airplane's cargo hold—alone and cold, side by side with the luggage.

"Are you sure you wouldn't rather we ship her?" I turned to Paul. "For you, we'd be happy to include the shipping for free."

"Oh, that's all right," Paul said. "I'd love to take her home with me. So there's no delay."

"Of course!" I said, trying to sound bright. "I understand."

I turned Serene off. I filled her box with packing peanuts, and taped it up with clear packing tape. I stamped FRAGILE onto the sides of the box—all over. Paul stared at me, wide-eyed. I may have done it a little aggressively.

Paul opened his wallet—I winced at the sound of velcro tearing—and I took his credit card. I turned on our POS system.

"Is there something else you need?" Paul asked, nervously, noticing my hesitation.

"Not at all," I said. I readied the card to swipe it.

The breeze was cool on my skin. The waves lapped against the shore. Young children shrieked when the waves came and their parents shouted not to go too far. Birds hopped in the sand, their round little heads jerking robotically.

I had made it to the seaside. Was it what I imagined? I think it was. I lay in a lounge chair with my icy cold pineapple drink, garnished with an orchid. The sun was warm on my limbs. It was a far cry from the factory floor.

I'd hitched a ride with my brother, who was driving to Macau—to gamble, of course. He hadn't batted an eye.

"You were always odd," he said—with some admiration, I thought—when I buckled Serene into the middle seat.

Buying Serene took all the money I had. I was fired, of course. I wasn't able to get my breasts. But I was here, on the beach, and that was something. From time to time, whenever my brother won a game of poker, he shared his winnings with me. "I owe you," he said. I mean, he did. He wasn't a bad guy.

"Ling," Serene called.

"Yes, Serene?"

In my own chair, I turned toward her, propping myself up on one elbow. She lay in the lounge chair beside me, wearing a muumuu and sunglasses, looking very glamorous.

"I'm happy," she said.

"I'm happy, too," I agreed.

P-town

DENIS JOHNSON

Now the piano music is funny.
A little ago it was agonized and grand and now
the same thing again. Gershwin's Concerto in F.
The radio can hold me a while, but soon
I'll go for a walk. It's the very kind
of town a person marches in ragged shoes from
one end to the other at 3 A.M.
Will I go slightly off the main street and see
if her window is warm?
I hope not. That would be
like shoveling a little dirt onto the light
shining on the surface of my loneliness.
Oh now it is that section
when the 2nd theme starts, the piano
both barrel-house and cascading behind
a big, clean melody. And then it's over.

LANA BASTAŠIĆ is a
Yugoslav-born writer. She
majored in English and holds
a master's degree in cultural
studies. She has published
three collections of short stories, one book of children's
stories, and one of poetry.
Her debut novel, *Catch the
Rabbit,* was shortlisted for
the 2019 NIN Award in Serbia and was awarded the
2020 European Union Prize
for Literature.

On the Occasion of Our Fourth Divorce Anniversary

LANA BASTAŠIĆ

Maybe it was the woman's voice and the way she asked us. The room so banal, the table too long and holding only a piece of paper and a silent cellphone, the clock seven minutes late and her question as pointless as the ashtray in front of her. *What would you like to list as the reason?* We looked at each other. Was it that first year in Prague? First week, first everything, us sitting on the bed fighting, and you said *I think in terms of doing, not being*, with such disdain that I felt the *doing* was something done to my chest. He thinks I'm stupid, I thought. He thinks I'm a savage Balkan girl. He doesn't know I've never read Proust. And all I wanted to do was go out with that British actor and do LSD and peel my twenties off like band-aids. Let my tissue breathe devouring a Big Mac by the communist museum. Give me a purple jungle and the horror of uncovered mirrors. You were already tired. You walked alone and took photos of old circus posters and garbage cans. You weren't writing. And the woman's voice was perhaps already there, echoing back through the abandoned factories and their dead chimneys, only we couldn't hear it. We thought love was a handwritten letter before swallowing

cum. *I have never been happier.* But I loved the mini croissants
in that place around the corner where we'd talk about Barthelme
and the authentic fakeness of Lana Del Rey and our friends' open
relationships and how none of them worked. We believed we
possessed a fragile little knowledge in our fragile little language,
unattainable to anyone else, even Lana Del Rey. We figured it
out. We worked. The cheesecake you made for my twenty-eighth
birthday, our gorgeous grey cat yawning at our parade, and the
"Blue Moon" rule. Perhaps it was the jazz band that couldn't play
our song at our wedding? Or the flea-market ring that shattered
into pieces when the jeweler tried to fit it to my size? My fingers
were too small. Or maybe it was something else. Maybe it was
my red shoes. My mother said they'd bring bad luck. What if I
click my heels by accident and I'm transported back to Bosnia,
I asked you. Don't worry, the real ones were silver. Because you
always knew better, knew more. And then someone speaking in
Catalan, telling me about us, about marriage, asking questions.
I was bored. I clicked my heels in vain. The only word I knew
was *sí.* Happy, happy. We bought records that day and a ukulele.
Look, I said, the ukulele is called Rochester. I thought of the
madwoman in the attic and how badly I wanted to give her a bath
and brush her hair when I was fifteen. How I never identified
with Jane. She was too quiet, too Jane. You were writing a long
book about American postmodernism and couldn't be bothered
with three Victorian sisters and ukulele superstitions. Rochester,
I thought. It's called Rochester. And the first string broke on our
first wedding anniversary but you refused the implication. This
would be too much for fiction, I said. We still had three years left
and no madwomen in the attic. We never had an attic. The mad-
ness was in the kitchen, toasting bread, doing the dishes, looking
through the window at the loud green birds thinking—if I jump
I would just break a couple of bones, it's not high enough. No one

was swallowing anything anymore. My orgasm was a mathematical equation you had solved a million times. I wanted to sleep. I planted an avocado. I bought a sewing machine and made dolls for my nieces. I dyed my hair blue. You weren't writing. You watched me talk in my sleep to someone in the garden, to the avocado perhaps, in a language you never learned. It's too difficult, you said. I wanna do it right, you said. You woke me from sleep paralysis and whispered that it was ok, it was ok, nobody was there, it was just a hallucination. Your mother gave me her therapist's number and I sat in a huge sunlit office overlooking Passeig de Gràcia trying to translate my fears into Spanish. *Padre*, she said. And *madre*. She asked about my dreams and I worried about the subjunctive. Years later a woman in Belgrade would tell me how she ran across a barren field in the middle of the night with a battered face and two small children. You're divorced as well? And I felt embarrassed by all the breakfasts you made and the avocado you watered and the fancy therapist's office with hand-colored tiles in the bathroom. Yes, I'm divorced. I sleepwalked and could no longer touch him. I was my own barren field. But I said nothing. Nothing of my last birthday in your apartment, no cake, no "Blue Moon," because we thought we were set in stone. We became a series of *of courses*. Of course we do. Of course we are. Of course we would. I dyed my hair black and cut it short in our bathroom. I watched it cover the floor like a dark season. You were writing. I walked down Verdi Street with another man and he bought me ice cream and Bergman's *Marriage Scenarios*. I was wet when he hugged me and wet when he said goodbye and I felt my insides dry off like hanged meat as I walked back to your apartment. There was an abandoned stuffed panda bear by the garbage can and I thought how fitting it would be to cry there and then, but I couldn't. I was dry. I took a photo for my Instagram. You were writing. You were playing a game called *Clash of Clans* and you had a whole village to defend. You were texting a young blue-haired waitress. Her dog died and she was sad. You called her pretty. I looked at the heavily filtered photos of her and her dog on Facebook trying to picture you next to them. Wandering if she read Proust and swallowed your cum. I would finish work late and come back by train right around the time when her shift started and would walk to the bar and ask her to pour me a shot of tequila. She had hentai eyes and very thin arms and some nights I thought the weight of the bottle would break her. Her hair made me think of "Blue Moon, I saw you standing alone" and that first week of letters and our long-distance dancing to Spotify. *I can't wait for us to start* in your small handwriting in Xavier de Maistre. She smiled gently when I used the wrong article for tequila and I thought she was a good person. And anyway, it wasn't her face in that room years later when the woman asked the reason. It was my own. It was my mother's. My mother sitting on my bed that day, crying her eyes out because she had just caught her first boyfriend cheating on her. I was seventeen, looking through the window at the boys playing soccer in the schoolyard. They were shouting insults at each other, one of them had a bloody knee. My mother's face turned purple and she could barely catch her breath. His car, she said, his car. She came to me because I had more experience with men. I held her shaking form in my arms, that woman who allowed me to pierce my bellybutton as long as it was a doctor doing it, she was my daughter now. Asshole, I whispered into her thinning brown hair. My fake sunflowers and a Rita Hayworth poster on the wall and the green furniture my father hated because green, he said, was a Muslim color. He's an asshole, I said and caressed her protruding spine. And the boys screamed in the distance. Offside, you motherfuckin' piece of shit! Offside! I could still hear them in the lawyer's room. I no longer wore a bellybutton ring. There was a small hole there now. I liked it better that way. Your skin was intact and clear of tattoos and your parents held hands when we walked in the forest that day. When they kissed I looked away. They made tea and gave me rent money when I left you. When you were little they used a special method to teach you maths. Your mom showed you pictures of colorful dots and you said *dotze, divuit, trenta-sis!* You knew the difference between Chopin and Schubert. Your teacher called you a child prodigy. And here you were divorcing a Bosnian woman who never read Proust and had holes in her skin. It cost us eight hundred euros. Afterwards we sat in a small coffeeshop over two *tallats* and felt robbed of a ritual. Was that it? I needed to slaughter an animal and dance in its blood. I needed to scream at the moon and scratch my hands until they bled and burn my ukulele. I needed to mourn the narrators of our first letters. Instead I moved to a small room in a building full of drug dealers and shared a toilet with four strangers. I started reading *Swann's Way* in English and I thought No. This wouldn't have saved us. These are just words. But I guess we knew that already in Prague, that day on the bridge, when we told the American girl she didn't have to take a photo of us. We don't do photos, we said. We remember.

SANDRA CISNEROS is a poet, short story writer, novelist, and essayist whose work explores the lives of the working class. Her novel *The House on Mango Street* has sold over seven million copies, has been translated into over twenty-five languages, and is required reading in elementary schools, high schools, and universities across the nation. Her numerous awards include a MacArthur Fellowship, the PEN/Nabokov Award for International Literature, the National Medal of Arts, and the Ruth Lilly Poetry Prize. A new collection of poems, *Woman Without Shame*, her first in twenty-eight years, was published by Knopf in 2022. Cisneros is a dual citizen of the United States and Mexico. As a single woman, she chose to have books instead of children. She earns her living by her pen.

Un Gordito Calls Me Hermosa

SANDRA CISNEROS

Even though he doesn't
realize I turn sixty-eight
next Tuesday.

Charmed,
at these heights,
by what would have enraged
me as a girl.

He was coming home from
work,
dusty as a *bolillo*.

Mason, baker, carpenter?

Flesh jiggling on the descent.
Boots pounding cobblestones.
Making his way downhill
as I climbed up my street.

Held his breath
till he brushed past.

Hermosa

bloomed from
his tongue.

Some days
with dark glasses
and jewelry, my hair
down like Cher,
I feel ready
for my comeback tour.

Madison Square

ANDREW HOLLERAN

There's nothing odder than the first sight of Manhattan seen through the window of an Amtrak train that's originated in Washington, DC. For one thing, at that point the train has left the mainland and you are traversing an expanse of wheat-colored wetlands so vast it looks more like Nebraska than New Jersey. For another, the train has not only slowed down but begun to rock from side to side, which deepens the feeling that you're in a novel by Willa Cather. And yet, there's the skyline of Manhattan—suddenly floating above a rocky ridge, as unreal as one of those enormous moons that come up late in August, like the planet on the cover of a science fiction novel—so startling a sight that passengers who have been lulled by the rhythmic rocking of the train abandon whatever they were doing, and sit up straight. Everyone realizes their journey is coming to an end, that in ten minutes they're going to have to deal with an environment very different from the one in which they're sitting. A hush descends on the passengers. The Quiet Car gets quieter. But nobody gathers their things together—not yet—because they know that the minute the train enters the tunnel beneath the Hudson, that astonishing skyline will be gone. So you quickly scan it for change, no matter how long it's been since your last trip. Your eyes dart back and forth between the two clusters of skyscrapers—Midtown and Wall Street—and then, just as it's all getting really close, the apparition vanishes, and you're going through a kind of birth canal that ends in the delivery room of Pennsylvania Station, and when you come out of that, the skyline's gone, and in its place are nothing but some nondescript buildings on Seventh Avenue and a crowd of strangers on the sidewalk.

On the sidewalk the streetscape differs remarkably little from the one you saw the last time you were here. Everything in front of Penn Station looks the way it always has, including the hotel across the street, and it isn't till a few days later that you find yourself walking somewhere uptown—on Broadway, or Fifty-Seventh Street—and you notice some enormous skyscraper that wasn't there before. But since New York has always been about enormous skyscrapers that weren't there before, how is that a change? They may renovate Columbus Circle or sheathe the old Huntington Hartford Museum in a new skin, but that doesn't really change them. Nor does the new bicycle path, or the faux piazza with umbrella tables in Herald Square, or the fact that the public parks now have flowers and some of the fountains are actually working; it's still on the face of it the same city, even if the crowds seem so much denser than they were the last time you were here, while, paradoxically, the number of people you can look up has dwindled.

Looking up people is part of the pleasure of returning to New York—and part of the problem. It was part of the problem, I realized when I first started going back in the 1990s, because, after making efforts to see everybody I knew, I began to feel like a shoe salesman looking up clients, and the brief encounters seemed to bring satisfaction to neither party. They only reminded me that I didn't live here anymore, and made my friends feel they were being visited as part of someone's day in New York, someone who could no longer be counted on to see a movie or go out to eat when they were lonely, so what good was I? One friend accused me of ruining my visits by searching out old friends. "They're just as stuck as you are," he said. "You all have to move on!" But that wasn't going to happen, not in the nineties, at any rate.

I started not looking people up when it dawned on me that it would be easier to just be a tourist—to wander around like someone who'd never lived in Manhattan at all, to walk across the Brooklyn Bridge, through Central Park, up and down Fifth Avenue, as if I'd never seen any of it. And indeed, New York came back to me that way—as if the real city is the city of dreams and ambition, not street corners and buildings. Not looking up old friends cleansed the place, brought me back to the beginning when I knew no one; and if that led to a loneliness too much like the one I'd despaired of ever escaping when I first lived there, so that I finally decided to call someone up, it was because I wanted to, not because I had to—and when I did, I left it to chance whether they'd be home or not.

Of course, if you really want to see someone, you call ahead and set a date and time and place. But I never did. It was, I suppose, the odd humiliation of no longer living in New York, and the insecurity of not knowing whether anyone would want to see me now. Why test those thinning bonds between old acquaintances, the ones that might snap at any moment with the wrong remark or an inconvenient visit? Friendship erodes with time and distance; one isn't sure what remains of the original structure. "People change," a friend used to say, quoting a line from Lillian Hellman that I was never able to find, "and forget to tell each other." But it wasn't just my fear of imposing on others. I had to consider the possibility that my friend was right: the only individuals I was looking up were as marooned in the past as I was, because the past was what these trips were all about.

There was, in short, an element of what the Jesuits call "morose delectation" in catching up with these old friends: the moment when you sat across from each other in a diner, each one of you silently assessing the other's physical condition as you ordered lunch. It reminded me of the woman at the cosmetics counter in Macy's my first summer in New York, a saleswoman who'd called out across the aisle, *"You have an irritated area!"* as I was walking through the store on my way to Penn Station one Saturday to get the train to Sayville so I could get the boat to Fire Island. I have two irritated areas, I thought after she called out to me, my heart and my groin, though she meant a reddish splotch on my cheeks that a dermatologist had already told me was rosacea. Though I didn't even stop to see what she was selling, I thought of her remark years later when I got together with old friends—though our judgments were expressed more diplomatically than hers. Our remarks tended to be like the carefully chosen reply I elicited one day when I asked someone how a mutual acquaintance of ours was doing, and he said, without even raising his eyes from the menu he'd been perusing, "His hair color has stabilized."

Sometimes as a tourist I was the go-between by which old friends who no longer spoke to one another discovered how each other was faring. Gossip about one another's sex lives had been replaced by news of struggles with arthritis, hearing loss, neuropathy, or some aspect of the inevitable battle with decay—a decay that might be not merely physical but financial as well, which meant that when it came time to split the bill at the diner, you could suddenly find a friendship of thirty years hanging like a frayed suspension bridge over the question of who'd ordered the iced tea.

What we wanted, of course, was that none of us had changed at all. I especially liked it when the person I was looking up still lived in the same building, or still went to the same diner. There was one friend I could only meet in a coffee shop near the Fifty-Ninth Street Bridge, a man who'd never invited me back to his place in all the years I'd known him, although I didn't care because he was so charming. He'd retired from the fashion business, lived by himself in a little apartment on the Upper East Side, and longed to get out of New York but didn't have enough money to do so, a handsome man who still had thick dark hair, so that he didn't look any different to me than he had the last time we had lunch. We'd met at a party on the Upper East Side years ago in the apartment of a woman who'd founded a famous art gallery that had been in large part responsible for the rise of Pop Art. The hostess and I hardly spoke. But just before we were leaving, I went into the bathroom and found my friend examining the contents of her medicine cabinet. "Look," he said when I peered in, "she's left the Kotex out so people will think she's still menstruating."

It was the sort of catty appraisal I associated with the art world, or the Upper East Side, or Manhattan itself: the way we are never quite free of other people's cold, cold eyes. But now the tables had turned, when, saying goodbye to my friend outside the coffee shop, I observed that, judging from my pattern, I'd look him up in another five years, and he said, "But I'll be seventy then!" And the next time he'd be seventy-five; and then eighty, I thought as I walked away. Life, it seemed, had come down to five-year plans; only there was no plan, and there were not that many units of five years left.

This friend had once been told to persuade Marlene Dietrich to come to New York to accept an award from the Council of Fashion Designers, and during the course of the many phone calls he'd made to Paris the two of them had become friends—though Dietrich never came to New York to receive the award, and when my friend went to Paris on business afterwards, there was never an invitation to stop by. By that time, Dietrich's life in her apartment in Paris was, for all intents and purposes, posthumous. She never allowed herself to be seen by the public in her last years. She was protecting, quite sensibly, the memory people had of her; she was maintaining the same standards for her personal appearance she'd always had—only they now required she remain invisible. She was dead to the world in the visual sense—though still alive—like Tom Sawyer experiencing his own funeral.

I thought of myself and the friends still living in New York in that way, though we never made any attempt to become recluses; it was simply agreed that we would not gasp when we saw one another, that we would say only nice things, and ignore the obvious, although one friend—an overweight decorator still living in a rent-controlled apartment on Christopher Street—retained his blunt manner to such a degree that reunions with him were always scary, because the first thing he'd do was assess you the way a barber does when you sit down in his chair, or a stone-cutter when handed the diamond he's about to cut. "Well," he'd say, "there's not much you can do with the hair, because there just isn't enough of it, but you could think about dyeing your eyebrows."

There were, of course, far more people whose eyebrows were immaterial because they were dead, which meant that as I walked past the buildings in which they'd had apartments, certain doorways began serving the same function that tombstones and monuments do in a cemetery. The canopies, the doormen, the black-and-white floors of the little lobbies I caught a glimpse of as I went by—above all, the crack in one particular glass door in a row house on Madison Avenue that always made me think "The golden bowl is broken"—were all entrances to what I began to think of as the underworld. Equally disconcerting was the fact that the buildings in which my friends had lived were now serving other people. It seemed wrong to me that my friends' deaths had *not* turned the town into a graveyard—that new people had moved in to take their place, people who looked, walking toward me in their all-black outfits, listening to music on their iPods, like zombies in *Village of the Damned*. Sitting in Union Square, watching young mothers push baby strollers on their way to the farmers' market between flowerbeds full of zinnias, I considered the entire scene one big insult. This city's mine, I wanted to tell them, not yours, how dare you behave as if you live here, and who are you anyway? At which point something a friend had said would come back to me: "New York is yours for only ten years—after that it belongs to somebody else."

My own feeling was that New York belongs to you for maybe five years—simply because during the first five years everything is still new and hard to figure out. For the last ten of my fifteen years' stay, I'd become a creature of routine, of the habits that let us live on autopilot, under a shell we build to protect ourselves from shocks. Shocks, of course, are what life is all about. Even I knew that when I no longer got lost on the subway it was probably time to leave the city. That should have been my standard for knowing when to leave New York: I no longer got lost on the subway. The year I learned the N train was the year I should have left. What I envied about the young people in all-black walking toward me on the sidewalk was simply that all of this was still new to them.

Eventually the feeling that the city these people were strolling in was not really New York made me want to look up everyone I'd known in the past, because *they* were all that survived of my city, at least the happy part, the one that had lasted not much longer than five years. At the same time, I didn't want to go

back to feeling like a salesman seeing clients. So I worked out a
method of seeing old acquaintances. I did it spontaneously, as
the moment or mood or location moved me. If I found myself
on someone's corner, toward the end of a visit on which I'd had
enough of wandering lonely as a cloud across the grid, I would
call. But nothing was planned. If they were home, fine; if they
were not, that was okay too. Either way, that was New York telling
me something, leaving or not leaving the past intact.

There was one person, however, whose presence in Manhattan induced in me a kind of guilt, one person I felt I had to look
up, one person whose still being there made me feel obliged to
visit—a visit that always seemed to be, nevertheless, a mistake,
since once I made it, he knew I was in town, and wanted to see
more of me. The reason wasn't hard to figure out. He was living in what used to be called a welfare hotel but is now called
subsidized, or Section 8, housing, in a building in Chelsea that
had once contained the McBurney YMCA, the gym I'd gone to
almost every day when I lived in Manhattan. He'd briefly been
a boyfriend, in fact—and after that, someone I'd watched move
onto other lovers with no bitterness or regret on my part because
he was so good-looking it was like watching the hero of a nine-
teenth-century novel cut a swath through society. After he moved
to Key West I visited him there from time to time; and when he
went back to New York we remained in touch by telephone; so
that when I looked him up, there was both a sense of picking up
where we'd left off, and a shock—the shock that occurs when
someone you've reduced to a voice materializes as a physical
presence—a presence that, unlike that of my friend on the Upper
East Side, had changed a great deal. That was one reason that,
after a few years, I'd stopped looking Miles up; it was easier to deal
with him on the phone—as long as I was careful to say nothing
that would reveal I'd been in the city all that week.

My reluctance to look Miles up was of course a source of shame to me: that once someone's looks were gone there was no other reason to pursue the person. Even worse, when I did look Miles up, he could tell I was putting him way down on the list of things I wanted to do in Manhattan. He would complain that I'd called him on my last day in town, sometimes my last hours in town, just before I had to catch the train, and I'd have no alibi. The reason I'd called him last was that had I called him first, he'd have wanted to go everywhere with me. He was not only living in a single room but, like almost everyone I knew who'd stayed in Manhattan, had no friends to do anything with, since he'd outlived almost all the people he'd known. The city was as much a ghost town for him as it was for me. Besides, I could take him to lunch or dinner, or buy him a sweater at Brooks Brothers, though it was more than that; I was someone who didn't live in New York and was therefore part of his past, not his present. He had stories he wanted to tell, and no one to tell them to. He had names he wanted to remember, and occasionally needed my help, though most of the time I needed his, for he had an extremely sharp memory for someone who seemed to be out of it. He remembered not only the nights we went to Flamingo but what we were all wearing, who was in the cab and what they had a fight about before we got there. He could talk about things of which I had no recollection, but which, the minute he described them, came back immediately, either whole or in part. He was valuable as a witness. But since calling him at the last minute was not very nice, and feeling I was obliged to look him up was ruining my visits, it dawned on me that the best thing to do was not call Miles at all. So I didn't, and enjoyed my stays much more.

It might feel hypocritical the next time I spoke to him to have to make sure I did not refer to anything I'd done or seen on my visit, but it was, I decided, for the best. And so he remained, like

Dietrich, a voice on the telephone, living in a world from which I grew more distant in time and circumstance with each passing year—telling me stories, when we weren't reminiscing, about the people in his present life: the man in the room next to his who'd used the food-stamp credit card Miles had loaned him to buy crack cocaine instead of the milk Miles needed when he was laid up with a bad back; the compulsive shoplifter down the hall he liked to watch television with who had overdosed on morphine; a retired schoolteacher he took a walk to the Hudson with every day until her dementia became so severe that her son came in from Long Island and took her away. And then there was the daily friction of life in the city—the teenagers on the crosstown bus he'd screamed at because they'd refused to give up their seat to a blind woman, the bout of sciatica he'd suffered after using a plunger on his toilet, the Arabs in the store on Twenty-Second Street who refused to extend him credit even for a *New York Times*, the price of cigarettes.

There wasn't much else to tell me about, since he seemed to spend most of his time in his room watching reruns of *Law and Order*, which he could just as well be doing, I thought, in a small town in Kansas. The reasons for his phone calls were almost always inspired by something he'd seen on TV. He never learned to use a computer, so I'd pick up the phone and hear, "Did Napoleon write a memoir? And where was his first exile?" Or "What was the name of the actor in that movie about the *Titanic*?" Or "Why do medications make a person constipated?"—things I could look up on Google. His calls were intermittent—silence for weeks and weeks, and then a call twice a day, a pattern often explained by the fact that his medications had changed. A more constant motive was boredom. He once called on his cell phone to while away the time waiting for a nurse to give him an enema in a clinic on Ninth Avenue—a clinic whose staff always left him waiting a long time, he said, because "They're tired of helping me take a shit."

"I know my life's pathetic," he confessed once, but that didn't take away from the fact that he still lived in New York and hence everything he said was interesting to me on some level. It was as if I was using him to stay in touch with Manhattan, but when I was there I didn't need him, I could see it for myself. There were moments, on the other hand, during some of those trips, when I felt grateful that I had anyone at all to look up, anyone who remembered me. And Miles could bring me up to date on things. For instance, did I know that Michael Fesco—the man who'd owned Flamingo—was organizing a gay cruise to Cuba? Or that another friend had published a book on his addiction to crystal meth? Finally one day I decided I really should look Miles up. I'd been talking to him on the phone for two years; hence it made sense to call him one afternoon when I had taken care of everything I wanted to do, and had four hours to kill before the train left.

We agreed to meet in Madison Square, where I arrived early and sat down on a bench on the west side of the park facing Broadway so that I'd see him coming east from Seventh Avenue and Twenty-Fourth Street. But when after a while he didn't materialize I realized we hadn't specified where in the park we were supposed to meet, so I got up and began to look around. In the seventies there'd have been no need to pick a particular part of Madison Square in which to meet; since Madison Square was, like so many parks during that decade when New York was on the skids, empty. It had always been my favorite square because of the Flatiron Building, or, to be more exact, the Edward Steichen photograph of the Flatiron Building, that ghostly, ideal Manhattan of one's dreams. But in the seventies it was empty. For one thing, no one lived on Madison Square. It was nobody's neighborhood, and after people went home from work, it was completely deserted. In fact, whenever I walked through Madison Square on my way home at night I entered it with the feeling that I was wasting my time, that I should have taken another route, because there would be no one there to cruise. But then one night it provided me with an experience I could never walk past Madison Square without thinking of afterwards, including that afternoon I sat waiting for Miles.

It was a cold March night in the mid-seventies; I was so tired while walking home from a dinner on the Upper West Side that I decided to sit down for a while and rest, whereupon almost immediately a man in a black raincoat walked over to my bench, stopped in front of me and unzipped his fly. We were the only people in the park. It was shortly after midnight and as I leaned forward to bridge the gap between myself and the object on offer I had no idea why I was doing this; the man wasn't attractive, and I didn't really want to do what I was about to do. I did it because of the hour, the place, the habits into which I'd fallen, the etiquette, you might say, of the situation. It didn't last long. But when it was over—when, according to the rules, he should have walked away without a word—he not only continued to stand there in front of me but finally said: "Well? Are you going to swallow or spit it out?"

I couldn't believe he'd asked me this, this proverbial flasher in a black trench coat, this sallow man with dead white skin and a little black moustache that looked dyed with shoe polish, this individual who might have been a comedian playing Hitler. It was such a violation of the standard scenario. He was supposed to have vanished into the vast anonymity of the city immediately after ejaculating so that I could turn my head and spit his DNA out onto the leaves of the rhododendron beside my bench— something I'd not done in front of him only because I thought it would be too obvious a comment on the pointlessness of our encounter. But now he was putting me on the spot. "That's not fair," I wanted to say to him. But I couldn't; because my mouth was full.

It was at that moment that I realized I was wasting my life— spending too much time in the parks—ending every night in Stuyvesant Square, a cruise spot near my apartment several blocks to the southeast, unable to go to bed even on weeknights without trying one more time to find a trick. I had begun to feel as much a resident of the parks as the rats in the flower- beds. My reluctance to expectorate this man's semen in front of him seemed to me emblematic of the whole passivity of my life, the reason I was unemployed, drifting, obsessed with sex. Such extreme politeness is neurotic, I told myself. What sort of person, I wondered as I sat there, worries about hurting the feelings of a total stranger who has just come in his mouth? And why did the man care? Did he want to know how I felt about him? Would it raise his self-esteem if I swallowed his load? Would it confirm his low opinion of himself if I spit it out? Whatever the reason I couldn't answer his question—because it seemed to me that dumping his semen, so infertile, so wasted, onto the hedge would not only reject him personally but exemplify the meaningless- ness of all homosexual unions like the one we'd just enacted. So I continued to sit there until finally he walked away.

After leaving the park that night I resolved to forget that this encounter had ever happened but I never walked past Madison Square again without thinking of him—for the same reason, when I entered Stuyvesant Square, I always remembered a slender young man I'd met there whom I persuaded to walk with me all the way over to another park on the East River because we could be more alone there, amazed that he'd agreed to do this, only to realize when we arrived and sat down on the bench that he

79

was what they called in those days mentally retarded. There are moments in one's sex life that stand out like stains.

But now, waiting to meet Miles, all that was in the past. I was an old man who no longer had sex of any sort, a visitor sitting on the edge of a Madison Square that was, like all of lower Manhattan, to my mind too crowded. There were too many people in the city, it seemed to me each time I went back—too many visitors, too many residents, too many human beings, period, a problem for which nobody had a solution and therefore nobody would talk about. It was five o'clock and people were streaming up out of the subway, crossing Broadway in both directions. There were tourists taking pictures of one another with cell phones. There were men building what looked like the interior of a television studio on the traffic island where Broadway and Fifth Avenue come together, as if Regis and Kathie Lee were going to do their show there tomorrow, though Regis had retired and I no longer knew who was doing the morning broadcast. I had not watched television in twenty years. Each time I returned to New York I was not just older but farther from contemporary life. My computer homepage, the one Microsoft provided, featured daily gossip about celebrities I'd never heard of, actresses whose "baby bumps" were being celebrated, whose marriages, engagements, "fashion hits and misses," weight loss, homes, and tweets were all big news, important to someone, though not to Rip Van Winkle, rubbing his eyes as he walked back into the village after being asleep for two decades. All I had to do to be entertained was to sit right where I was and watch this motley parade of human beings flow past to see what people were wearing now. That was the pleasure of New York; if nothing else, it was a fashion show.

There were so many different looks, so many kinds of people, that I could have sat there for hours and just watched them go by; but then, remembering I was to meet Miles, I stood up and walked into the center of the park again to see if I had missed him. The interior of Madison Square at that hour looked like Seurat's painting of the afternoon at La Grande Jatte; the only thing missing were parasols, bustles, and balloons. The crowd was walking dogs, playing with their children, chatting on benches, standing in line at an outdoor restaurant Miles had told me about called the Shake Shack—though I couldn't imagine New Yorkers standing patiently that long for anything, much less a hamburger and a drink. This must be an entirely new species, I thought, the sort of people who live here now. I looked at what remained of a big tree that had been cut down in the center of the park, leaving a stump almost ten feet high, and then, wondering where Miles could be, I became conscious in my peripheral vision that something was bearing down on me—some sort of gigantic crab.

It was not a crab, it was a man—bent over at the waist—with a face, once it stopped before me, so wrinkled, so covered with spots where skin cancers had been removed, that I did not know whether to look at them or at the creases around his eyes, which were so deep they made his flesh resemble leather as he smiled, or the thin hair whose few strands were dyed a pale blond. His right hand grasped a cane and he was bent over so far at the waist that his back was almost parallel to the ground, which meant that I suddenly understood why Miles had told me on the phone that he'd lost five inches in height—a claim I thought had to be an exaggeration of the feeling people have that they're shrinking as they age—but which I now saw was literally true; he really was five inches shorter, if not more.

"What on earth is wrong with you?" I said.

"What do you mean?" he said.

"What do I mean?" I said. "Stand up! Can't you stand up?"

He straightened up instantly, to my relief, though when he did, his legs splayed out at the knees, so that he looked like Popeye the Sailor braced against the next pitch of the ship.

Then he bent forward again as we proceeded to an empty bench and sat down, and in a calm and pleasant voice immediately began telling me about the chat he'd just had with the nice Hispanic man the city of New York provided who took him to lunch once a week, something that had started after Miles slit his wrists and spent two weeks in the psychiatric ward at Bellevue. "It's cheaper for the city," Miles explained, "to send this guy to have lunch with me once a week than to pay for another hospitalization."

"But what do you talk about?" I said.

"How I'm feeling," Miles said. "It's the same as the shrink. Did I tell you my shrink is Israeli? When I run out of things to say, we talk about politics."

"And what do you talk about with the man at lunch?" I said.

"My life," he said. "How I used to work for Halston. He's never heard of Halston," he added. "I had to explain to him that Halston came before Calvin Klein."

"Then he's not gay," I said.

"No," he said. "He's straight. But he's very nice. He told me I'm the most interesting client he's had in twenty years."

"Well," I said, "that's something. And I think it's very nice of the city to provide this man for you."

"And look what else the city has done for us," Miles said, pointing out a new structure they'd installed on the other side of the park. "It's a *pissoir*," he said. "It cleans itself when you walk out—the whole thing. Even the walls get washed. It's like a giant toilet that flushes itself."

"But what if you're caught inside?" I said.

"I guess you'd get cleaned too," he said.

He was perfectly amiable; and so far he'd not said a word about his usual topic—his health. Instead he observed when a man with two kids in hand walked by that he now regretted not having had children. I knew the feeling: I could not stop watching three- or four-year-olds walking hand in hand with their parents, the sweetest tableau on earth, despite the fact that in real life they might be hellions.

"So who do you still see around?" I said.

"I saw Rick Waller yesterday," he said. "Remember him?"

"The Hungarian doctor's boyfriend?" I said. "I do remember. The guy who got out of the bus to Fire Island to pee, and everyone rushed to the windows to watch and the bus tipped over."

"Nearly tipped over," Miles said. "Though that makes a better story."

"He was so handsome," I said.

"Well, now he looks like a raccoon," said Miles. "Deep circles under his eyes, and his hair is completely white."

"I'm sorry to hear that," I said, "but after many a summer dies the swan. Who else?"

"John McMahon? He's still very handsome. But he walks around in these Spandex bicycle shorts that outline his genitals, which I find tacky."

"At least he has something to be outlined," I said. "What does *he* do for a living?"

"He's a butler for a Belgian billionaire on Park Avenue—or he was till he got fired."

"For what?"

"Drinking. His boss paid for him to go to detox, but when John came back he relapsed. I think it's because he had so little to do. The guy he worked for has half a dozen homes and was hardly ever there. So John just had to sit around the apartment and listen to the clock tick. I understand boredom," Miles added. "I'm so bored sometimes I cry."

"Well, at least you're free to come and go," I said. "Not like George Jovanovich."

"Where's he?"

"In the loony bin on Roosevelt Island. He stopped having sex when AIDS started, and in place of sex he began to eat, and he got so fat he developed diabetes. And the diabetes gave him something called vascular dementia."

"You mean he's nuts," said Miles.

"Not entirely," I said. "In fact, when you talk to him, you wonder why he's there. It's only when he gets tired that he says something crazy."

"Like what?" said Miles.

"Well, yesterday he told me that Elizabeth Taylor has been talking to him through his television set."

"I often think Elizabeth Taylor is talking to me through my television set," said Miles.

"We all do," I said. "That's why she was a star."

"So will he ever get out?" said Miles.

"I don't think so," I said. "They're sending him to some nursing home in the Bronx next month called River Manor."

"River Manor!" said Miles. "That's where they sent me when I left St. Vincent's! River Manor was the worst place I've ever been! I used to make money there buying cigarettes for people. I'd make fifty cents a pack, while the doctors who came in to see patients made a thousand bucks an hour."

"Don't be bitter," I said.

"Well, George is in for a real treat," said Miles, "though at least he'll have a roof over his head. And he won't be alone. I sit in my room for days all by myself."

"That's what Marvin does," I said.

"How is he?" said Miles.

"I can't tell," I said. "He lives in Napa near his brother in senior housing. The other occupants complain because all these men come to his apartment to get a free massage. He's like the naughty lady of Shady Lane. He advertises free massages on craigslist. So there are all these guys coming and going. Sometimes when the men arrive, he told me, they take one look at him, turn around and walk away without a word. He's gotten very fat—which can happen when you take lithium. They finally diagnosed him, you know, as bipolar."

"I'm not surprised," Miles said. "I always thought Marvin was crazy—and George too. I wouldn't wish River Manor on any-one—but George was always so critical, so negative. He'll have a lot to criticize at River Manor."

They all look down on one another for various reasons, I thought, listening to him. But then, as survivors do, Miles brought it back to himself and started telling me about his stay on the psychiatric ward in Bellevue after he slit his wrists, and the young man he'd fallen in love with in the room across the hall, a nineteen-year-old lacrosse player from Greenwich, Connecticut, who'd nearly beaten his younger brother to death, a blond guy with such beautiful blue eyes, Miles told me, that he could not stop thinking of him even now.

Miles was so full of stories I kept thinking I should write them down; but there was no theme to them, they were just episodes in the life of a young middle-class white boy from Philadelphia who had at one point been a beautiful blond boy with blue eyes himself, a beautiful man whose life had gone off track because of drugs, homosexuality, and alcohol. There was no subject, no meaning, no takeaway. Like so many lives in a consumer culture, it added up to nothing. But he was still alive; and he had that extraordinary memory of things I couldn't remember, even if he'd been calling me to ask where the Nazis had been put on trial after the Second World War, or the name of the woman who'd shot the Scarsdale Diet doctor. His last call had been about *Gone with the Wind*, which he was watching on TV; and then he wanted to know who'd starred in *Rain Man*, and finally how the custom of applauding had started. He was so lonely, he told me now, that he'd gotten his SAGE card and had started going to meetings at the Gay and Lesbian Center on Thirteenth Street, where he found most of the other elderly men so swishy he'd not gone back.

"Is that where you had Thanksgiving?" I said.

"No," he said, "I went to John McMahon's. He had some of his friends over."

"That sounds nice," I said.

"Not really," he said. "I had to ask one guy not to talk about his colostomy. So we talked about theater. Everyone in New York's a critic, you know. They dissect all these shows, until someone who saw the original production pipes up and that ends the discussion."

A little girl walked by with one hand in her father's, the other holding one of those little pinwheels that revolve in the wind.

"Do you still see Paul Escher?" I said.

"No," he said. "He won't even meet me for dinner. The last time we spoke he asked if I was still smoking, and I said yes, and that was a deal breaker. He hardly leaves his apartment anyway. He was mugged by someone he picked up in Times Square last spring. The guy pulled a knife on him when they got back to his apartment. The weird thing was that he told me he wasn't afraid that he'd get killed, he was afraid the guy would kill his cat. Anyway, he now refuses to allow anyone in his apartment."

"Oh Lord," I said.

"He also got rid of almost all his furniture because it gathers dust, which is why he washes his venetian blinds in the shower twice a week. Paul was a mortician, you know. He worked at Frank E. Campbell's—till he was driving the limo back from a funeral on Long Island one day last fall and he got into a fender-bender, and the cops made him take a blood test, and it showed he'd been smoking pot. So after forty years, Frank E. Campbell's had to fire him."

"That's terrible," I said. "The two of you used to be such good friends."

"Tell me about it," Miles said. "He'd walk downtown to have dinner with me every Friday. One night at the Sazerac House we were having such a good time the waiter came over and asked us how long we'd been together."

"You were in love with him," I said.

"I guess I was," he said. "I really liked Paul—really liked him. Have you talked to Daniel Regan?"

"Daniel just finished treatment for anal cancer," I said. "He told me that we have to let people into our lives so that when we're dependent we will have someone to help us. He said that someone had to pick you up after your colonoscopy. He said women are better at helping than men."

I didn't say that after sitting in the V.A. Hospital for four hours while they searched for a vein in which to install his port, Daniel had asked one of the Filipino nurses to hold his hand and then burst into tears, or that later, when they'd drawn the curtain and he was waiting for the X-ray technician, he'd lain on his bed and sobbed.

"He's in good shape now," I said. "He beat the cancer, and he's thinking of moving back to the town in Iowa he grew up in because he still has relatives there. That's what it's all about now, you know—who'll be there when you have a stroke. That's

87

where we all are now. Daniel's already had his tombstone installed beside his grandparents. We're all coming in for a landing," I said. "Just like on a plane. Put your seat backs up and your trays in an upright and locked position."

"I'm flying to Jacksonville on Tuesday," said Miles, "to stay with my aunt on Amelia Island."

I had come to think of Miles as so confined to his room that this was startling. But there was no time to reply since we were interrupted by a man asking for a cigarette. Cigarettes now cost a dollar a piece, Miles told me after the man went away.

"Well, you've got to stop smoking then," I said. "You can't afford it."

"You're right," he said. "Some days it comes down to choosing between cigarettes and the *New York Times*. I still try to read the *Times*. When I worked for the Producers Circle, Sam Carrothers told me I had to read the *Times* every day before I came to work. You know, of all my boyfriends, the one I can't get over is Sam. Did you ever meet him?"

"No."

"He was so handsome! He wasn't a ten. But he was a nine. His father was English and his mother was Armenian. I have this theory that when two races intermarry, their first offspring is always a superior being. He didn't go to the gym or lift weights but he had the most beautiful natural body I've ever seen. It was so beautiful it reduced Arnold Rosenthal to tears when they went to Paris."

"The Tomato King?"

"Yes. Arnold flew Sam to Europe after Sam's first summer on the island. They were going to go around the world. But it ended their first night in Paris because Sam wouldn't fuck him. So Arnold threw himself on the floor of their hotel room and cried, and then he sent Sam back on a plane the next day. That was before Sam started drinking. By the time we met, he was a functioning alcoholic. But he was never mean—until the day he hit me. That's why I walked out. But he was the best thing that ever happened to me. He was handsome, masculine, and he wanted a monogamous relationship."

"What made you think of him now?" I said.

"The man who just walked by with that little girl."

"I have to go," I said, and stood up. "My train leaves at five forty-two."

"I'll walk you to the station," he said.

"How can you?" I said. "You're too bent over!"

"I can walk," he said.

Indeed, he could. Certain that I'd miss the train, I discovered that even bent over at the waist, scuttling like a crab, Miles walked remarkably fast, tapping his cane as if he were blind as we moved up Seventh Avenue. Halfway to Thirty-Third Street, a man I hadn't seen in thirty years came out of a convenience store and called my name. He'd sublet my apartment on St. Marks Place one winter with his partner, a handsome French architect who was a friend of a friend. The architect, I'd heard, had recently died of a heart attack and left an estate of nine million dollars, of which the man outside the convenience store was now the executor, though he lived in Fort Lauderdale and was back only to take care of the estate. In fact, he couldn't wait till he was back in Florida. "I hate New York," he said. "I just want to get out of here."

The man had always had an attitude, Miles told me after we said goodbye. "How can you hate New York?" he said.

"A lot of people do," I said. "Everybody has a city he's suited to, and New York isn't everyone's."

"Well, I couldn't have lived anywhere else," said Miles. "I can't imagine my life if I'd stayed in Philadelphia."

And that was true. At the train station Miles went to the men's room while I walked over to the big board to see if the track for my train had been announced, and when he didn't come back I looked across the lobby and saw him heading toward the escalator to the street—so I ran after him and said, "What are you doing?" He said he thought I'd left on the train. I said it was delayed. But we decided to say goodbye anyway, and I put the twenty bucks in his hand that he'd always asked for on previous visits but hadn't this time. Then I watched him go up the escalator, not even sorry to see me go, which made me feel both relieved and a little sad. The only thing more depressing than old friends calling you up is old friends when they stop calling you up. How funny Miles had looked scuttling across the lobby, leaving me there without saying goodbye. He's used to being alone now, I thought as I watched him disappear through the doors to Eighth Avenue. He's detached, at peace in some way, like George in the loony bin. He's reconciled to the fact that we are all alone, on our way out, just like a plane coming in for a landing. And with that thought I located the track number of my train and went down the escalator to the platform and got on the regional to Washington.

LI QINGZHAO (1084–1151) is considered the greatest female poet in Chinese history. During her lifetime, she defied cultural expectations for women by writing and persevering through war, exile, imprisonment, and the loss of her fortune. Li Qingzhao is renowned particularly for her ci (lyrics), poems set to music with predetermined meters and tones.

WENDY CHEN is the author of the poetry collection *Unearthings* and the novel *Their Divine Fires*, forthcoming from Algonquin Books. Her translations of Li Qingzhao's poems are also forthcoming from Farrar, Straus and Giroux in a collection titled *The Magpie at Night*. She is the editor of *Figure 1* and associate editor-in-chief of *Tupelo Quarterly*.

Three Poems

LI QINGZHAO
TRANSLATED BY WENDY CHEN

LATE SPRING

Late spring. Why still
such bitter homesickness?

Ill, I comb my hair,
my regret long as each strand.

All day long, the swallows
chatter on the beams.

A soft breeze carries the scent of roses
through my screen.

BY CHANCE

Fifteen years ago,
by flowers under the moon,

we composed poems together,
admiring the blooms.

Tonight, the flowers and moon
are exactly the same.

But how could my feelings
be like before?

SPRING AT JADE TOWER
Red Plum Blossoms

Soon red, silken petals
will break open
the jade buds.

Have the branches facing south
fully bloomed?

I do not know how much fragrance
stirs in these buds.

Yet I see each one filled
with measureless being.

I waste away
beneath the spring window,

listless and too sorrowful
to lean against the railing.

If you want to come have a drink,
then come.

Tomorrow morning, the wind
may rise.

CHINELO OKPARANTA was born and raised in Port Harcourt, Nigeria. Her debut short story collection, *Happiness, Like Water*, was nominated for the Nigerian Writers Award, longlisted for the Frank O'Connor International Short Story Award, and was a finalist for the New York Public Library Young Lions Fiction Award, as well as the Etisalat Prize for Literature. Her first novel, *Under the Udala Trees*, was nominated for many awards, including the Kirkus Prize and Center for Fiction First Novel Prize, and was a *New York Times Book Review* Editor's Choice. She received her MFA from the Iowa Writers' Workshop, and she is currently associate professor of English and creative writing at Swarthmore College. Her most recent novel is *Harry Sylvester Bird.*

Fatu

CHINELO OKPARANTA

The choice was between an injection harvested from the ovary cells of Chinese hamsters and one made from the urine of postmenopausal women, each filled with hormones that should stimulate my eggs to drop. The egg drop must be timed, the doctor had explained, so that he'd know exactly when to perform the insemination. After his reassurance that I'd have no side effects to worry about, I felt confident in my decision to go ahead with the trigger shot.

It was May in Pennsylvania, warm, mildly humid, but strangely odorless during the afternoons. In the mornings the aroma of the dew-covered fields mixed with the intense aroma of cow dung. Only a native Pennsylvanian or a vastly distracted person would not have noticed.

The smell must have been there that morning too, when Fatu wrote to me. I did not see her message until I was seated in the doctor's office, trying to decide which injection to choose.

I still see her words in the notepad of my mind.

Can we meet? I'm in the city. I know you're not too far away. It would be good to see you. A lot has changed . . .

Was I tempted by the invitation? Of course. I still had not managed to pick up the bits of my crumbled heart.

Yet even with my emotions stirring, I put her aside, tucked her away in the periphery of my mind.

I chose the concoction made from postmenopausal women's urine. Better to stick with humanity than introduce foreign hamster genetics into my system. But it wasn't just a matter of human versus hamster. I would also be injecting into my body the fundamental constituents of an entire other human life. Who was this woman whose hormones would soon mix with mine? Where was she from? Any chance she was anything like me?

I called Fatu that evening, hours after I left the clinic. We talked late into the night, and the following morning, there I was, drinking up the natural serenity of the village-like town where I lived, in an apartment from whose windows I could hear the melodic calling of the birds, and I thought to myself: whether the future pans out with Fatu or not, I have to give our relationship another shot. She couldn't come to me, she said, due to a work obligation. So it was up to me to go to her. I got in my car, wound down the windows of my worn-out Chevy Nova, and set off on the three-hour drive to New York, unsure if my beat-up car would even make it to the city.

There were things of which I should have reminded myself: The crescendo of my neighbors' moans, the way their coital flourishes still brought back memories of Fatu's infidelity. The resentment that surged in me each time I made ofe nsala, that soup for new mothers—each time I ground the uziza and thought of the seed that might have already been in me if not for the fact of Fatu's betrayal. The way her betrayal derailed our plans.

I arrived shortly after noon at her hotel. Inside, the room was softly dark, like dusk. Fatu sat at the desk, knees together, elbows on thighs, head propped on her hands, leaning in toward me. Out the window, above the tall buildings of the Lower East Side, I could have sworn I saw stars. Fatu's black hair, in loose Bantu knots, glowed like unexpectedly recovered memorabilia, and something about the doting in her brown eyes reminded me of my father. The way he looked whenever we had our little arguments, always keen to make amends. Old, sallow eyes, but always a father's love. Fatu was short, like my father, no more than five feet four inches. Perhaps I'd always projected all the goodness of him onto her. That night, after nearly three years apart, I might have been even more eager to project.

She looked longingly at me, and she said it again: *A lot has changed*. Meaning, she explained, that she was now aware of her own mortality. That she'd learned from seeing the dead body of her seventy-five-year-old mother that the dear ones in her life must be cherished. She was now a different person, had grown, and would do better, communicate better, be more sensitive.

I said, tired, sore with desire and with the agony of her absence, "I've missed you."

Hope is a funny thing, the way it sneaks up on you long after you think it's dead. There I sat with Fatu in the hotel room, and everything seemed possible again, a second life, a new beginning. "But how can I ever trust you again?" I asked.

She remained silent.

"If we are going to do this the right way, you've got to earn my trust," I said.

It appeared to me that her face dropped, and that the light in her eyes dimmed just a bit.

I said, "I don't mean it in any bad way, but I'm having trouble shaking the past. Can't you help me to trust you again?"

She said, "I'm sad that you feel that way. I've always had your best interest at heart, even if it might not have appeared that way."

I'd have to cut my losses if I were to make things work, this I knew. So, I said, "OK. The past is the past." It didn't feel like a giving-up or a settling. It felt, rather, like rejuvenation. Something in my mind was already doing timid cartwheels, and as it sprang on its hands, its voice was cautiously ululating.

I would have thought you'd have gone with an actual person," Fatu said, when I told her that I'd begun trying. "Why not an acquaintance, a friend—someone you know?"

"Too much risk," I said. "This way is far less risky."

"How long have you been trying?" she asked.

"Over a year," I said.

"And?"

"Clearly it hasn't worked," I replied.

I thought of how strange it was that the egg and sperm somehow continued to miss each other. Wasted vials of sperm. The last few times there'd in fact been no follicles at all, so the doctor had not bothered to try. No need to waste sperm without any viable eggs.

"I'm sorry," Fatu said. "I wish I had been there for you—with you."

I had wished the same thing, but I didn't tell her this. I was thirty-nine years old. I had watched two of my friends lose their window of opportunity, focusing on careers, or waiting to find the right partner, or even, catering to husbands who kept saying, "Maybe in a year or two." Waiting and waiting until the doctor announced that they had hit menopause. It was possible that my window was already well on its way to closure. However it panned out with Fatu, I would not now give up what I had already begun in her absence, because after all this time, I was beyond ready to mother a child.

We spent hours together—a shared meal, an evening stroll, staring into each other's eyes in the comfortable silence of the hotel, cuddling in a way that felt more intimate than sex—and then I returned to Pennsylvania, arriving home well past midnight. In a week, I'd be making another attempt for the baby, and if I were so lucky, Fatu would be right there by my side for the remainder of the journey.

Before you know it, we were as close as a knife and a fork, skipping over the catch-up stage of the relationship and cutting straight into the meat of our lives, acting like a couple once again, as if we'd never even been broken up.

We spoke hours on the phone every night. Throughout the day we shared text messages. The day before the insemination, at 4:30 in the morning, I rose from bed to take the injection of hormones created from the urine of those postmenopausal women. I was scheduled to take it at 5:30 a.m. I worked as a motivational speaker in those days. After giving myself the injection, I'd be headed back to the city, to visit a young women's high school in Queens, where I would give an anti-bullying speech and generally inspire young women to believe in themselves.

Even now I can see the day unfolding the way it should have: The gray morning clouds. The spring sun blanketed and napping in the sky. The scent of moist twigs and leaves and earth swirling in through just-opened windows. On the counter, the syringe, needle and all, and two small glass bottles the size of miniature spice jars. Powder in one of the bottles, a clear liquid in the other. The pharmacy instructions—a sheet of paper, half-filled with black print. And Fatu, by my side, running her palms across my arms to steady me, maybe even getting ready to administer the shot for me.

But Fatu was still back in the city, an early morning appointment she could not miss. Residency requirements. No way to be in both places at once.

According to the ultrasound, there had been a good number of follicles this time. Two fat ones racing to maturity. What with the growth hormone, I was hopeful that this time it would work. No reason for a fail.

"The hCG trigger injection must be taken within the proper time frame," the doctor had warned. "Ovulation usually occurs within twenty-four to thirty-six hours of the injection. Any mistake with the timing, and we might miss the ovulation window." If I missed the window, I'd have to wait yet another month.

My age was flashing like a neon sign before my eyes. Every month counted. Not to mention that sperm was not cheap. At around seven hundred dollars per vial plus shipping, plus storage and other fees, I'd spent close to ten thousand dollars on the sperm bank alone.

I stuck the syringe needle into the small liquid bottle, as instructed, drawing up the fluid. When it had filled to the correct measurement, I injected it into the bottle with the powdered hormone. I breathed a sigh of relief. All was as it should be.

The next step was to swirl the liquid and powder, very gently, so that the two became a nice mix. I picked up the bottle and swished it as if rolling a precious stone between my index finger and my thumb. No wahala. All done. I thought of Fatu with longing and resentment, but I could not fault her for not being there. My pregnancy plans had after all been made, a complete schedule and series of appointments set in motion before our unforeseen reconciliation. She could not have been expected to drop the last few weeks of medical school for a relationship that was just beginning afresh. But I wished she were there all the same.

I eased her from my mind. Just enough to be able to concentrate on the task at hand. Next step: Target the fleshy skin of your belly a few inches below or to the side of your belly button. Wipe the area with an alcohol swab. Pull up the mixture into the second syringe, and inject into the muscle of your stomach. (All of this while holding the needle and syringe at a ninety-degree angle to the injection site, and holding the flesh between your thumb and forefinger.)

There I was, having stuck the needle into the bottle, attempting to collect all the liquid, but no matter what I did, I could not get the needle and syringe to pull up all of the medicine. No matter how I moved the bottle, about a fifth of the mixture remained inside. I shook, twisted, turned it in my palm, and still, no luck drawing up the medicine fully into the syringe.

If Fatu had been there, she'd have known exactly what to do, doctor that she was. But she was three hours away in the city, in the middle of an important meeting.

At what point did the safety lock snap? I can't now remember. All I know is I let out a piercing cry when the needle disappeared from view. It was 5:15, and the needle was out of order. In only fifteen minutes I was to be on my way to New York, and yet, no growth hormone in me. My baby was somewhere in the nebulous universe, floating like faith, like a thing only existing in somebody's dream, a grain of sand that could easily be blown away by the wind.

I picked up the phone, dialed Fatu, important meeting be damned. If she could only offer some flash of insight, a way to fix what surely was a simple problem.

The phone rang and rang, but no answer.

I soothed myself with empty consolations: She's just at work. She's obviously busy.

Even now, there are questions I still long to ask her:

Whose interests was she protecting when she decided to hide the details of her relationship from me?

What *would* have been the right time, in her mind, to let me know that she was already in a relationship when she reached back out to me?

Did she ever genuinely care for me, or was I no more than a pawn in her game?

When her voicemail came on, I left a message, something brief, not wanting to sound paranoid, or like an already injured cat. "Fatu, are you OK?" I asked. The past is the past, I reminded myself as I hung up.

I turned my attention back to the syringe, pulled up the browser of my phone, and googled: BD Safety Glide syringe and needle.

I scrolled and clicked pages, trying to find any syringes that looked like mine in order to look at their instructions for use. I cursed the nurse, cursed the fact that she hadn't bothered to mention anything about the locking features of the contraption.

I switched over to YouTube. By now it was 5:45, and I still had not managed to inject myself with the medication.

I dialed Fatu again.

If I had gotten her on the line, I would have said, "Fatu, I can't do it. It's not working." I imagine she would have said to me, "Don't worry, it's fine. Just take a deep breath, and tell me what's going on." Or maybe she would have said, "Not to worry. Let me walk you through it." She would not have gotten on the next bus from the city or rented a car from Enterprise and come right to me. But surely she would have shown up in some way, the way I imagined good partners and lovers did.

I returned to my vials and syringe, attempting to bend the needle out of the safety latch. If only I could get the needle back out, maybe I could inject what was in the syringe straight into my stomach.

The needle was almost out when a good amount of the mixture dribbled onto the floor. I had now lost a large quantity of the medicine that was supposed to already be inside me.

In my bedroom, I threw on a simple black dress, and wrapped a scarf around my neck. I gathered the folder containing the printout of my speech, the one from which I'd be reading when I finally made it to the city. I grabbed the medicine and syringe, my wallet along with my driver's license. I said a prayer for this child whom I'd been wishing for almost all my life.

At that hour of the morning, darkness blanketed the road, and the air smelled fresh and yeasty, a mixture of the usual cow dung and a bread-like scent. Long ago I had begun to imagine that there was a bakery or a brewery the next town over, and that the wind, coming and going like it did in the crisp morning, must have carried the scent over.

I drove five miles per hour above the speed limit—fast, but not fast enough to have been pulled over by a cop if there had been one tucked away in a nook of the road. Bare as it was, I arrived at the hospital in a matter of minutes.

I have heard all the stories of women trying to conceive, and perhaps mine is just another one of them, banal in all its small and useless details: a dull or sharpshooting donor, remarkable or unremarkable motility, follicle availability or lack thereof. The story never fails to touch on these. But add to that a boulder, because there I was attempting to park my car when I slammed into one of the giant cement posts that lined the parking lot. I let loose the kind of wail that scared even me, a mourning woman's wail. There was immediately the scent of something burning, no longer the yeasty morning air, but rather the fiery, sizzling scent of burning rubber or plastic. Stepping out to inspect the car, I would have imagined a dent the size of the boulder's frame at the trunk area, but I was astonished. The engine was fine, the car unblemished, only the smell of something on fire, and of smoke in the air.

If you know stories like this one, then perhaps you are one of those people who have ideas about the kind of woman I must be. Maybe you are one of those who chastises me to my face, or who secretly speaks badly of me while smiling into my face. And all the while you are thinking just what a failure I am: utterly incompetent at completing basic pre-pregnancy tasks. It even makes sense to you that I have not managed to find and keep a partner. You think that I have surely brought this upon myself— that it is no one's fault but mine that I should have to go through the pregnancy journey on my own. You wonder how a woman like me could ever even hope to succeed at motherhood given all my prior failures. If you are that kind of woman, then you don't surprise me. Women are after all their own worst enemies, waiting in the background to pounce and tear each other down. But I suppose it is also true that they can be their own scaffolds, their own greatest support.

The receptionist was not the chastising kind of woman, but rather a gentle-faced redheaded woman, entirely too wide-awake for so early in the morning. She ushered me right in to see the nurse, who was just as kind.

It wasn't only the issue of the safety latch, I explained to her, like a penitent sinner at a church confessional. It was also the issue of the spilt medication.

First, she inspected what remained of the medicine. She proceeded to take out a fresh new syringe, suck the liquid mix into it, and flick the bubbles out. "About sixty percent," she announced. "Why don't we see what the doctor says?"

It's best we put away from our minds all memories of the painful encounters in our lives, but no matter how I try, and no matter how brief the meeting was, I cannot forget the encounter with the doctor. Even now, as the baby fusses in her stroller, and as I run my fingers softly over her, his image is clear. If I am gentle enough, soothing enough, she will fall back asleep, but his image persists: a moderately tall, gray-haired white man, hovering near the doorway of the examination room.

I long ago stopped correcting mispronunciations of my name (so much wasted time and effort only for it still to be mispronounced), but something about the coldness in his eyes made me do just that. "Anunobi," I said, repeating it correctly for him, somehow feeling the need to assert myself, to make sure he knew that I was a living, breathing person as valuable as himself. But already it seemed he might have felt me not so valuable, because he remained there in the doorway, not stepping any further into the room.

"There's quite a bit of the medicine gone," the nurse was saying. "Should she proceed with what's left or re-order a new set?" she asked.

The doctor looked with irritation at her, and then back at me. "That's your problem?" he asked, as if I had wasted his time in the worst kind of way. There he stood, in sky blue scrubs, looking disgustedly at me.

He shook his head, turned around, and left the room, and I thought of God. This doctor, just like God, turning his back on people who came desperate, at his mercy, begging for help. If God decided to withhold aid, it was certainly the person's fault. Who dared blame God?

The nurse must have seen the crestfallen look on my face. She walked the few steps over to me where I sat on the examination bed. Her face was slender and long. "I'm so sorry about that," she said. "He just has a lot on his mind."

Back at her stand, she lifted up the needle and syringe and looked thoughtfully at it.

"Here's what we'll do," she said. "You're quite tiny. I say we give you what's left here of the mixture. It should still do what it's supposed to do."

"You'll inject it for me?" I asked softly. Her eyes narrowed some more, her jaw slightly pronounced, with worry or with thought.

She let out a quiet, sympathetic laugh. "Of course. That's exactly what I'm here for," she said.

I had missed it earlier when she'd introduced herself, and now her auburn hair covered the name tag on her chest. As she stuck the injection in me, I asked her name.

What I meant by the question, and I told her as much, was: Tell me your name, so that I don't ever forget you. Your name will be the word that represents kindness to me.

She smiled even more affectionately at my words, but a bit shyly, like a woman not used to receiving compliments.

For the first time since 4 a.m. that morning, I felt a deep sense of relief.

By the time I walked out of the ER the morning sun had risen. The cedars and elms and white oaks stood tall like sentinels, silent witnesses to my fertility ordeal. I should have cancelled my school appointment, should have gone home and de-stressed for the insemination the next day, but I took my responsibilities seriously and continued on my mission to keep my appointment with the school.

I-80 East led me through 170 miles of relatively smooth-moving traffic, but then at the George Washington Bridge, everything stopped. Cars froze, even the clouds seemed immobile. Everything except time. I had hoped not to have to cancel the school appointment, but after half an hour stopped at the bridge and the certainty of arriving too late, I called the school principal. After three and a half more hours behind the wheel, I returned home and threw off my clothes, scattering them like flaccid petals all over the floor.

What happened next was not yet the beginning of the surprise, but it was only a matter of time. I picked up the phone and dialed Fatu, and when after a few tries she picked up, I announced to her that I had missed my school appointment.

"Sickness?" she asked.

"No. Stress," I said. "And bad traffic."

I told her all of it. The problem with the syringe. The spilt medication. She remained quiet as I spoke. "Everything is a mess. Even my house is now a mess, clothes scattered everywhere," I said.

"Don't worry about the mess in the house," Fatu said, after a brief silence. "I'll have Sithembile clean it all up for you."

Of course, there was no Sithembile. But the name belonged to the little make-believe house girl that Fatu liked to conjure up back when we were first together, each time she or I was too tired to do the housecleaning. Sithembile had become our inside joke.

"Sithembile," I muttered, trying to remember the meaning of the name. She had told me once, years ago when we were first getting to know each other. The sound of Fatu's voice was the last thing in my ears as I fell asleep, my clothes heaped around me.

On the afternoon after my insemination, the spring green tulips and climbing roses were in full bloom. I imagined cutting some stalks for Fatu, making a bouquet out of them.

That afternoon, she kept her word—she called in between her appointments to check in with me.

"So, the doctor was the one who put it in you?" she asked.

"Yes," I replied. "I've only ever had it done by him."

"That's good," she said. "But when I get mine done, I think I'd rather do it at home."

I said, "I can understand that. When do you think you'll want to do it?"

She said, "Depends on my partner."

And then I thought, Of course. Your partner. Me. Surely she must have been referring to me.

I said half nervously, half confidently, "I'm sure your partner will be open to it." At the very worst, maybe the whole partner business was just one of her silly jokes, like Sithembile, the phantom child house cleaner.

If it was a joke, I wanted to play along. I asked for her name.

Fatu cleared her throat, and said, "I'll tell you tomorrow."

By now there was a cold fear rising in me. Fear of the possibility that this was no joke. But I reasoned with myself that this was just my fear speaking.

Just to be sure, I asked again, "You really have a partner?"

She said again, "I'll tell you tomorrow."

"Why not just tell me now?" I asked.

"No reason," she said.

"So, where is she as we speak?" I asked.

"Under the bed," she said, without any hesitation, so casually that I was sure that if she weren't speaking of me, then the whole partner thing was definitely a joke.

The bleeding began on day five after the insemination—a passionate, angry, dragon-like red that left a stain like a crimson inkblot on the crotch of my underwear. With it, a lightheadedness, shortness of breath, diarrhea, swelling of my feet. But it did not spread. Just a spot.

I had never spotted before, so my mind perceived it as an incomprehensible burden—a stranger's burden. Whose blood was it anyway? An accidental misplacement of blood. But on day eleven, blood rushed out. I called the clinic, in the hopes that a nurse or doctor would somehow reassure me, but the voice recording announced that the offices were now closed, and directed me to call 9-1-1 in an emergency. I was not so eager to have another ER adventure, so I consulted the internet. Reports about the side effects of hCG. Severe pelvic and abdominal pain. Diarrhea. Lightheadedness. What kind of poison had I just ingested in the name of making a baby?

On Babycenter.com, I stumbled upon a discussion of a thing called implantation bleeding, women saying that they had also experienced some abdominal discomfort, perhaps related to implantation, and yet, some had gone on to receive a Big Fat Positive. Maybe this was the sacrifice of life: a little blood lost so that another being could live. Days later, I continued to cramp and bleed, but still I held on to implantation as my fortress, my beautiful red bastion of reassurance and hope. There was no room in my mind for doubt, at least I assured myself that there shouldn't be. If one doubted, one welcomed failure into one's life.

Meanwhile Fatu was getting progressively more and more difficult to reach by phone.

Two weeks after the insemination, I endured the worst blood loss of my life, far from a mere inkblot on the crotch. Again I consulted the baby forum and according to voices there the signs were no longer promising. I imagined the loss as a floating soul, like a bubble that simply refused to settle in me, one that refused to find its home in the warm, aching cavities of my womb. My precious, darling rolling stone. By now Fatu was nowhere to be reached.

* * *

Sometimes in my sleep I see a small bird—a finch being dragged by a larger bird by the feathers on its wing. When the finch finally hits the ground, a bright burnt-orange ribbon spills out from somewhere, landing precariously on the bird's delicate neck. I saw the finch in my sleep the day before my doctor's visit. The little bird fell to the floor from the force of the larger bird, but her small neck was a pillar that refused to be throttled. Her neck simply could not be severed by the larger, yellow-beaked bird. Even the band-tailed pigeons came, but could not put a peck-dent in the finch's neck. When I snapped out of the dream, it was clear to me that somewhere out there in the world, a larger, formidable bird would always keep trying to kill her but, always, would fail.

Some mornings after my doctor's visit, when I simply lay in bed, feeling the disappointment of not having conceived, of yet another fruitless journey to pregnancy, and thinking of my disturbing encounter with the doctor, my phone flashed and buzzed with a message from Fatu asking how I was doing. I imagined her eating lunch the way she sometimes did, back during our first time together, tendrils of okra stretching up from the soup bowl, the soup's greenish coating on the small swell of garri in her hand. She swallowed them always with her eyes closed, always so mindlessly closed, the little balls of garri slipping down the pathway of her throat.

It was 1 p.m., and I had not yet managed to brush my teeth, let alone get into the shower.

I could have typed back a meaningless response. Instead I picked up the phone and called. A brief exchange of the usual greetings, and then I asked her what had still been on my mind all this time. Was her mention of a partner to be taken seriously?

Who was the partner? Was she real? Or was it just a reference to me?

A lot can happen in a moment of silence. A simultaneous affirmation and refutation. A complete overhaul of things hoped for. A shattering.

"Thandi," she replied. A South African human rights attorney with a thirteen-year-old son. She had just emerged from a bad divorce from her husband.

"Where is she?" I asked factually. "Where has she been all this time?"

"Some people need their distance," Fatu replied. "Anyway, I'm sure she prefers the continent. Who wouldn't? These days, it's like someone put juju on America. America, like a book everyone is ashamed to admit they once enjoyed. America, the new third world."

She went on and on in that vein.

"How long?" I asked.

She made muffled noises, semi-hushed words like numbers, as if counting the months. "Over a year," she said, finally.

I grew numb, silent.

"I was waiting for the right time to tell you," she said. "It wasn't the right time."

Did Thandi know that we'd been talking so intimately for all this time? I asked. Did she know about me?

"She wouldn't care if she did," Fatu replied.

My heart sank like a thing too heavy to bear its own weight. How had she figured Thandi would not care if she'd never even given Thandi the option to decide in the first place? I imagined Thandi, sitting in a room alone, trying to dial Fatu and only getting Fatu's voicemail or a busy signal. All the while, Fatu had been on the phone with me, Thandi a buried secret. I, too, had once been that secret swathed in dark rooms, laced with hushed voices. I'd been the one she had probably claimed would not care as she spent the night with another woman. I, too, had once been the partner. And, now, out of sheer accident and vulnerability of heart, I had allowed myself to be duped into being the other woman.

I could not stay on the phone any longer with her, so I excused myself and hung up.

Afterwards, I called my father and wept. I was used to the warm hum of his voice on the thin, static line connecting Umuahia with Pennsylvania, the way his words still managed to pour out smoothly into my ears, mollifying me. That afternoon and long into the evening, trapped as I was behind a surprising but inevitable wall of sadness, he consoled me.

Months went by. I could not bring myself to return to the clinic. Seasons changed, but Fatu was as present in my mind as ever before.

I stopped completely trying for a child. There was too much disillusion in me to keep trying.

The year I turned forty-three, I found the courage to call and ask for repossession of my vials for home insemination. Otherwise, they might wind up sitting there for eternity. A perpetual stalemate.

The head of andrology listened without saying a word until I was done with my long rambling plea. Then he said quietly, "Oh, honey, I wish you had called earlier. All these years? Of course, that's always an option for our patients!" We could not go back in time, he said, but he offered me his name, Chad, and promised to take care of me whenever I was ready to get started.

Over the course of our correspondence, we devised a plan. For four months, I would monitor my ovulation with an ovulation predictor kit (OPK), note when I had my LH surge, keep track of those days in preparation for a self-insemination. The OPK monitoring would be a good substitute for the pelvic ultrasounds that had been a staple of all my fertility doctor visits. No need for the large plastic transducer to be thrust inside me every two weeks. Rather, a simple pee-on-a-stick test. Other instructions: Decrease stress (take a break from work if possible). Eat well. Forty grams of protein a day. Lots of leafy green vegetables. Liver and full fat dairy. Folic acid. Good hydration. Those sorts of things.

"Come directly through the double doors and you'll find me in the last room down the corridor," Chad said. I'd never met him before. In my mind I filled in his image with that of the kind nurse from the ER: narrow face, slightly pronounced jaw, auburn hair. If he had smiled, it would have been a shy, slightly startled smile, just like hers.

The afternoon I drove over to Chad in andrology, the GPS, perhaps simply by chance, took me on a new route by way of the highway and only a little via local roads. Maybe also simply by chance, all lanes were clear. In those brief moments when I was not on the highway, all the traffic lights on the local roads glowed green.

I arrived at the clinic just after 4 p.m. and found a parking space in no time. The sign read: RESERVED FOR NEW AND EXPECTING MOTHERS. I was certainly not a new mother, but I had been expecting a child for so many years—hoping to be expecting. I claimed the spot as my own.

Before leaving my car, I made preparations: I moved the front seats so that there was plenty of room in the back. I spread the pillows I had brought from home across the floor of the car, enough padding so that I would be at ease when I returned to it. Over the pillows I spread a large towel. Finally, to form a privacy screen, I taped sizeable opaque poster papers across my windows and windshield. As luck would have it, the year before, in advance of my knowing that I'd once again be embarking on another baby-making attempt, I had taken care to fix the air conditioner. Now I made sure to leave the car engine running so that it remained a nice moderate cool. It was summer, early July, and already the heat was frightful.

Chad was waiting for me by a metal table inside the treatment room. He turned out to be a gray-haired round-faced man, not at all what I'd imagined. He had the lean body of someone younger, but the poise and gravitas of a grandfather.

Looking up at me, he said, "You've confirmed with the OPK that you've begun surging?"

I nodded, assured him that I had.

"I'll read you a series of instructions. Please stop me at any time if there's anything you don't understand or would like me to repeat."

I nodded.

He began:

"Do not expose the vial to extremes in temperature. Do not put it in the fridge, for instance. Do not expose it to heat. Keep it at body temperature. Don't bring it near water or soap. Water and soap kill sperm. Only open the vial when you are ready to use it; do not expose its contents to air. Air dries out semen, which in turn kills the sperm."

I nodded.

"Make sure you use it within an hour of leaving."

I nodded again.

He handed me a brown bag with the vial inside and said, "When you leave, don't stop to say anything to anyone. Just go."

Before I left, he stretched out his arm and patted me on the shoulder, then handed me the insemination kit, which he'd explained would be complete with an insemination syringe. This particular syringe was a basic design, for which I was grateful. No safety lock involved.

"When you've taken in all the sperm with the syringe, remember to try and tap out the air bubbles. Just some slight taps. Air bubbles are the enemy."

I nodded.

"My sister was once in your shoes," he said, then added, "You have my very best wishes. Do let me know how it turns out."

Back in my car, I opened the insemination kit and the vial and put on the sterile gloves. This had been the plan all along: not to bother driving the twenty minutes home and risk the death of many of the sperm. Each minute counted, and already I had lost so much time in years of waiting.

I opened the vial and sucked the contents into the syringe. Such little fluid, in a vial less than one third the size of an average index finger.

I did my best to remove the air bubbles from the syringe, but each time I tried, it seemed I risked losing some of the sperm, so contrary to what Chad had advised, I made peace with the bubbles.

I lay down on the padded floor of the backseat, my waist a bit elevated on one of the pillows, legs up, leaning on the left back window.

Then I inserted the syringe into myself. Slowly.

I must have lain with my feet raised, my hips elevated for more than twenty minutes, because when I opened my eyes, the day appeared a little darker. I slowly rose up, packed up my paraphernalia.

I was forty-four years old, and in the two-week wait, there was no bleeding nor diarrhea nor swollen feet. Instead, a new life was beginning in me.

Hope is a funny thing, the way it fills you with purpose and allows you to create your own story and run with it, or puts a barricade between you and your story. There was no block this time. My daughter did come, after all those years of trying. I must have conceived that evening, a forty-four-year-old single woman with a pair of sterile gloves, a syringe, and a vial. In a car.

In all of the time that passed, I had begun to imagine that I would name my child after the kind ER nurse or Chad in andrology. But the moment the midwife handed me my daughter I realized that somewhere along the line, I had forgotten the kind nurse's name. It had been so simple. Something like Emily or Caitlin or Jenna or Nancy. I had ordered myself to remember, and for years, I had remembered. And yet, eventually, I had forgotten.

"Chad," I called out to my baby as I held her in my arms, not as a reference to any battle, but as in the lake, large and self-contained and full of small islands. The name tumbled out awkwardly and ill-sounding, and even if his was the name I remembered, Chad no longer seemed a good name for the child. Instead, for those beautiful intimate moments filled with hope that Fatu gave to me, when I believed anything to be possible— love, reconciliation, happiness—I named her Fatu.

All of this was over twenty years ago. My Fatu has grown, has even made a grandmother of me.

Whenever I'm in the city to visit with my child, I stroll by the hotel where Fatu the lover and I met that final time, just to remind myself how close I came to mending things with her. Also, to remind myself how easily one can deliver oneself to a rat, the rat blowing air at your feet, all the while taking bites out of you. At my boarding school in Umuahia, the rats used to eat the tips of the children's toes. But that is neither here nor there now; it's been decades since I've been in Abia State.

Out on the park bench where I keep an eye on the baby—my own Fatu's newborn child—something circles the sky, a buzzard waiting in the thermals, preparing to pounce on carrion, something already dead. Fatu the lover circles my mind; she'd probably been testing the waters the whole time, or playing around just for her own entertainment. These days I think of her as a bull terrier trying to catch its own tail. Going around in circles. Never reaching a destination. Never satisfied. Maybe, even now, she is still circling, pursuing new prey. I would allow all thoughts of her to drop out of my mind once and for all, but this is how it is some days: my mind folding, unfolding, and refolding itself around the memories of her. My mind, going back to her voice that day on the phone, pleading with me to give her another chance.

i am my own elder now

HONORÉE FANONNE JEFFERS

there is no old lady for me to seek
one who takes a blade
& hones my wild needs
& Lord do I need
oh I need
i am the old lady that I miss
i am my own elder now
no knees swollen to slowness
to lean against
as I sit on a pillow
as she parts & scratches my scalp
as she oils the strands
with tar baby's wisdom
oh the tools i thought i wouldn't
need for the many centuries
she would live

i am the girl who climbed
out of my own breaking bones
my flesh touched bright & soon

come love me come touch me

i am a girl
hear my insistence

i am a girl
i don't care that you see something
ancient greeting your world

you laugh & call me see-through
you sing that I no longer matter

> *come sing to me come strum my halo*

my grandmother is gone
her throat ejecting violence
upon dreams before she died

> *girl girl-child you ain't no mama*

oh my dames they have left me
veined hands bidding good-bye

> *but still you a woman now*

they pulled at my fingers
they stained me with strength

> *the blood done gone with no sign*

everything here
is the color of knives

OMAR EL AKKAD is a journalist and author based in
Portland, Oregon. His first
novel, *American War*, is an
international bestseller and
has been translated into more
than a dozen languages. His
second novel, *What Strange
Paradise*, won the Giller
Prize in Canada.

Pillory

OMAR EL AKKAD

My father was a cathedralist. He had no formal training in religion or architecture. He worked as an inventory manager at a company that imported pencil-top erasers and small toy cars from China. He explained this to me once, when I was very young, in that cautious, formal way men of limited import tell their sons what, if not why, their lives have come to be what they are. One day when a snowstorm closed the schools and my mother was running on empty, he took me to his office and showed me the filing cabinets where he stored the sum of his working days: dozens and dozens of beige ledgers, each one a nest of figures tracing the journey of smiling rubber squids and miniature Ferraris from somewhere in Guangdong province. He opened them carefully, delicate in a way I didn't associate with him. Their spines let out a soft knuckle-crack on opening and I saw him wince at the sound. He pointed to the numbers that filled every page, all snug in their columns. Without this, he said, without this work, the world would stop turning.

I asked him if I could have a race car. He said they didn't have any of those at this office, that's not what they did here. He closed the ledger, put it back in its place, and looked at me like I hadn't understood a thing he'd said.

In his spare time my father liked to visit the big cathedral downtown. He liked to take in the length of the nave, the intricate arching stone, the way the stained glass rainbowed the passing light. He liked to marvel at the grandeur of what people could build, given enough faith and determination, in a single life. With a single life.

I was six or seven the first time I overheard him explain what he hated most about being a parent. A few of his work friends had come over for dinner one night and afterwards they went out to the back porch and I sat upstairs in my bedroom with the window open, listening to them talk about nothing in particular. Just before my mother went to bed she asked my father to move the laundry to the dryer once the washer was done, and after she left my father said the worst thing about having kids was the laundry—not the amount or the frequency, but the smallness of kids' clothes, the way you couldn't ever get a basket of laundry folded and put away without little socks and underwear spilling everywhere, falling out from the legs of jeans and the insides of fitted sheets. You know it's coming, he said, but you can't do anything about it; no matter how hard you try, some tiny fucking thing falls, it always does, and you have to stop and pick it up. That's how all the days go now, he said, one way or another; with sudden stops, like a car that keeps slipping into neutral—is it too much to ask for a single uninterrupted day? I'm not asking for much, he'd say. He said that a lot.

We want impossible things. I always wanted to have known my father before I entered his life. As it was, I knew him only in his years of retreat, when he was already a member of that fraternity of underdone men who exist in silent, bitter conversation with the decisions they wish they'd made.

I suppose a therapist would tell you that's why I ended up doing the work I do. The work of starting over.

For the past seventeen years I've been an employee of the Department of Reincarnation Policy. No one stays still at the Drip—over the years I've held a half-dozen positions of no real consequence, as analyst or archivist or assistant, shuffling around from Legal to Adjudication to Statistics, the latter office being my final posting. Though I don't know it when I get up in the morning, this will be my final day at the Drip. By noon I will resign and leave the building so suddenly that my manager and an HR rep will chase me out the front door, yelling something about paperwork and liability. It'll be a bit of a scene, but that happens here sometimes.

Every morning I take the bus to work, though there's a man on the same commute who doesn't like me. Most days I find a seat far enough away from him; through a phalanx of limbs he might give me a dirty look before he loses interest. But every once in a while there's no room to sit or stand except right next to him, and that's when he'll pepper me with impossible questions: Where are the lives you're hiding? Who decides who comes back? Do you get to judge yourself, in the end?

I only know to ignore him, and most times this riles him up, sometimes to the point of shouting. Once, when this happened, an exasperated woman nearby stood up and marched to the front of the bus, where she asked the driver to do something. The driver shrugged and said, He's distressing. The woman nodded, thinking they were in agreement, but I'd heard the driver say this more than once before, and eventually I realized she meant "distressing" as a verb. I used to imagine the angry man on the bus as some kind of eighth- or ninth-go-round, his mind coming apart under the weight of so many half-departed lives. I used to do this with anyone whose way of being I couldn't understand. But now I find it comforting to adopt the bus driver's view of things—we are all of us going through each day, tired and tried and, with some grace or none, distressing.

The building I work at is unremarkable, a mildly fortressed thing. In the early designs the architect succumbed to the lure of metaphor and imagined a structure twisted into the symbol for infinity, but the bureaucrats eventually tamed this into a simple circular design, and the result is a squat, stale donut that looks like the Pentagon with its corners hammered in.

Inside the lobby, above the information desk to which all visitors are directed, is the only halfway interesting piece of decoration in the building—a digital counter, like the one in Midtown that tracks the national debt. It's a rule at the Drip never to celebrate any reincarnant, no matter what kind of lives they led. There's no framed photo anywhere of the fifth-go-round physicist whose hundred years of stubborn research helped solve the energy crisis, or the man who kept going back to volunteer at the same refugee camp every time he returned, dressed in the body of a child but with seven decades of altruism under his belt. The administrators consider it a violation of neutrality to honor these people, to litter the hallways with the faces of reincarnants who did good with their second and third and tenth chances, with the coin flips that went their way.

There is, in equal measure, a reluctance to commemorate milestones, and this year the Drip marks three of them. The first is known to all: one hundred and fifty years ago this month, a child named Ella became the very first confirmed reincarnant. Likely there had been many before her, and in the museum that sits across the street from this building there are a few clippings of newspaper articles detailing children who by the time of their third or fourth birthdays exhibited signs of some strange disease, riddled with phantom memories that belonged neither to them nor to anyone they knew, but to someone else, far removed and recently dead. But Ella, on account of where she was born and the vividness of her recollections, her impossible intimacy with the life of an octogenarian who happened to have lived and died in the very same town, is considered the first verifiable case, the one after which it could no longer be denied that our species had entered a new phase, a new mode of being.

The second milestone is purely administrative. This fiscal year, the Department of Reincarnation Policy will overtake Agriculture as the fourth-largest federal agency by budget size. And the third milestone is an informed guess. According to that clock in the lobby, ticking forever upwards in accordance with a heavily disputed statistical model, at some point this summer, somewhere in the world, the three-billionth reincarnant will be born.

Their last winter together, my parents fought over a dead rat. It latches onto your imagination, a thing like that, and likely if they'd gotten into an argument about anything else, an uncapped bottle of toothpaste or mud tracks in the hallway or any one of those stupid little fissures that in time do just as good a job of tearing up the landscape as any single earthquake, I'd have forgotten all about it. But this was a dead rat, and I thought about it for years, long after the split, like a nemesis.

It was a bad winter that year; probably the thing was just looking for warmth. That's how it ended up behind the cabin filter in our old Corrolla. For some reason, though I didn't know what a cabin filter did and had only seen the little bucket inside it where the rat died after my father finally removed it and cleaned it out, I cultivated a vivid impression of how the end must have come. I imagined that bucket spinning, which I learned many years

129

later is actually what it does, when the heater or air-conditioning is turned on, and I imagined the rat's leg caught in the bucket's gaps, snapped but not severed in the spinning. I imagined it stuck there for days.

It didn't take long for the smell to become unbearable. My mother opened the glove compartment and reached her hand deep inside, into the guts of the car. She took a picture, a clump of limbs and fur clearly visible under the flash. My father said he'd take care of it. Weeks passed.

Finally it blew up into their big argument. They never raised their voices at each other; instead I learned to gauge the severity of their fights by how much they seemed not to care whether I could hear them. That day I sat in the living room with them and it was as though I wasn't there at all.

I don't like the person I have to become in order to get you to do anything, my mother said. My father stared at the living room table, as though it might come alive, might try to leave.

Afterward my mother went for a walk and my father went to the garage and I heard these bursts of noise, a smashing and something like a scream and then nothing. When finally I worked up the courage to sneak outside and take a look, I saw shards of plastic on the driveway, the garden hose nearby, still running, a little rivulet snaking toward the drain, and wedged there between the grates a small, cashew-shaped thing, thick with decay.

My father stood by the back door, oblivious to me. He was staring at his reflection in the small squares of glass.

Just get through the day, he said. Just get through the day.

And then he smiled at his reflection, over and over again, like he was trying to commit it to muscle memory, like he was practicing.

*　　*　　*

130

It's a slow day, only two interviews on the schedule. Statistics and Archives occupies the east wing of the sixth floor, sandwiched between the offices of Religious Liaison and Educational Affairs. It is widely known that these two departments are, by a big margin, the worst places to work at the Drip, the site of constant confrontation. To get anything done, one must learn to tune out the sound of myriad clerics and concerned parents' groups who arrive almost daily to dispute one policy or another. It makes it very difficult to complain about the monotony of working in Statistics and Archives, a place designed to be invisible.

My first interview of the day is with an alleged second-go-round. She is seven, and was fifty-two when she died. The adjudicator in her case has given her an assessment of forty-five on legal and seventy-five on identity, which everyone at the Drip knows is a way of saying the adjudicator believes the applicant is a reincarnant, but there's a legal threshold for identity, and the evidence doesn't meet it. The standard of proof, developed over the years, involves a safety deposit box of sorts, a lawyer, and a list of ten specific details a person must draw up and keep secret in anticipation of the next life. Only if they're able to recite eight of the ten on the next go-round are they considered to have met the legal threshold. This proof of identity package is offered as part of almost every will, but a lot of people don't take advantage of it. The most widely accepted formula suggests that, upon death, there's a fifty percent chance of reincarnation, meaning a one in four chance of a third go-round, a one in eight chance of a fourth, and so on. Some people don't think the coin flip's going to go their way, others don't think about it at all. They don't get a proper verification package and without it, we're left with cases such as this one, a child of seven possessing the memories of someone generations older, but legally below threshold. Too much of herself, and not enough.

I start the interview the same way I always do, letting the applicant know that this is for archiving purposes only, and has no bearing on the case, which like most will wind its way through Legal, the single largest department at the Drip. I tell her about the classification requirement, which keeps this interview inaccessible to the public until fifty years after the applicant's death, barring renewal. I ask if she's willing to waive it; she agrees. I ask her standard questions about the conditions into which she was born and she answers them matter-of-factly. It's clear from the beginning she's not lying. There are all manner of semi-legal and entirely criminal enterprises that offer memory packets for people who want to fake it, who want to cash in on some unclaimed inheritance or shed themselves of responsibility for wrongdoing committed in their previous lives, and these cases take up much of the time and resources of the Drip's criminal division. But in the end you can always tell. It hangs on them, the past, it holds them in place.

I ask her about her home life and she says her second-go parents initiated the application, wanting nothing to do with her. There are so many policies related to parental obligations for reincarnants, options for both children who carry previous lives and the parents into whose care they arrive. She says for her part she has no interest in fighting her parents. She says she only wants a quiet life, that she isn't going to claim or continue any part of her previous one. I want to tell her that these things are more common than any other outcome desired by our applicants and the people into whose lives they have entered, that to this day, after so many years, a lot of parents can't comprehend the absence of newness in their newborns, and that most people who come back don't want to keep doing the work of their previous lives, that for every genius mathematician who returns aching to solve the Hodge conjecture, there are ten who just want to sit on a beach somewhere and drink.

Even the thing you'd most expect—reincarnants going to look for surviving loved ones from previous lives—isn't as common as you'd think. They run away as much as they run toward.

But I don't tell her any of these things. I'm not supposed to. Instead I thank her for her time and file the report. The database says it's the one-thousandth interview I've filed. I can't remember most of them. They blend into one another—an immortality of sorts, a single endlessly disputed existence.

The last interview I ever conduct at the Department of Reincarnation Policy is with a boy of fifteen. His application is another threshold case. His parents argue he's a second-go-round, but he's fighting it. Once again the adjudicator has put the case just below cutoff, ensuring it'll end up in court. Once again I can tell, before the boy says a word, he's lying. He fidgets, eyes me as though looking for a way around me. His file is full of little details too odd and specific to be anything but shards of a previous life. His parents list a litany of impossible memories: orderings of numbers, shipping routes, the insides of churches.

I tell him this interview has no bearing on his case.

Then what's the point, he asks.

I say it's for research, for statistical analysis, and to assist the department in future cases.

What about my case, he says. What about me?

I start to repeat myself, then I stop. I take another look at his file.

Why do you think they're trying to get rid of you, I ask him. It's not on the list of standard questions.

He shrugs. I don't know, he says. They just . . . they make stuff up. I just want a normal life.

There's a silence. I put the forms down on the desk. I close the file.

I'm not asking for much, he says.

It occurs to me he has better posture, this time around. He isn't slumping yet, doesn't have that worn-down air I remember, that reticence.

There's something I've always wanted to ask you, I say.

What do you mean *always*, he replies.

Sometimes when the guys at work would call up and invite you out to the bar, you'd say, I'd love to, but you know how it is with the kids. Even when Mom would tell you it was fine, go out, have fun, you'd still tell your friends that same thing—I'd love to, but you know how it is with the kids.

He looks at me the way I imagine the first person to ever see a mirror looked into it, suddenly conjoined to an impossible reflection. He says nothing.

I guess my question is, why did you always say, "the kids"? When you were complaining to your buddies about how hard your life was, how little freedom you had, why did you always say kids, plural? You only had one.

I can see him doing that thing he used to do, walking through his options, working out what someone who genuinely doesn't understand what's happening might say. I feel exhausted on his behalf. I push the little red button that's under every one of our desks in this building, the one you're only supposed to push if an applicant becomes threatening or violent. In a few seconds security guards come in and they don't ask questions, they simply grab the boy and lead him outside. He doesn't protest, doesn't stop looking at me until they've dragged him away.

I wait a while, then I delete the file. I pack my things. I get up and leave. My boss, who sees the boy dragged away by security, asks me what happened. I tell him I quit.

* * *

Once, a few years ago, I got to interview a twenty-go-round, at the time the only known one. It was back when I was in Special Division. There had been lots of talk about the first confirmed twenty, though it was far from confirmed and everyone in Special Division knew the interview would come to nothing. That many pasts don't live well together inside one mind, to say nothing of the fact that many of those lives we'd only worked out through supplementary evidence—shreds of concurrence, things overheard in early childhood by others, snippets of her own memory, blurred and thin—because so many of them ended so early: death in childhood, death in adolescence, sudden accidents, desperate misfortune. Best we could tell, she'd made it out of her teens just twice.

She spoke in puddles, all the ended parts of her rippling outwards, calm and ungraspable. I took down every word but could make almost no sense of it. By the half-hour mark the supervisor watching the interview had tuned out completely. I sat and listened to the woman meander through the entrails of memory, lucid and irreparably torn, graceful in her distressing.

At the end of the interview, I asked her one of the questions we're told never to ask the many-times returned. I ask her what she wanted.

Free, she said. I want good and free.

We want impossible things. The rest is only living.

HANNAH LILLITH ASSADI
is the author of *Sonora*,
which received the Rosenthal
Family Foundation Award
from the American Academy
of Arts and Letters and was
a finalist for the PEN/Rob-
ert W. Bingham Prize, and
The Stars Are Not Yet Bells,
named a best book of 2022
by the *New Yorker* and NPR.
In 2018, she was a National
Book Foundation 5 Under 35
Honoree.

Che si fugge

HANNAH LILLITH ASSADI

On the telephone from the hospital, my father tells me he wants a cigarette. He has fallen again. His once hearty frame is now so frail, I can hardly bear to look at him. The cancer is in his bones. The cancer is everywhere. A wise friend once said that gazing upon death is like staring at the sun. But it's worse than that. The last time I saw my father before this call, I was shocked by how thin he had become in the course of months, and he said to me, you look at me like I'm some strange man. I didn't say, it's far worse than that.

"But these people in the hospital," my father goes on, "won't let me smoke."

My father doesn't mention that his doctor has pronounced the end is no longer years away. That if we're lucky, we might have this season and the next. My mother tells me all of this instead. "Your father is dying," she says, in the same tone she uses when she wants to guilt me into doing something. Then she begins to wail.

As I talk to my father on the telephone—he in Arizona, me in the Berkshires—I watch the dusk fall languorously on a green sea of grass, brilliant with falling stars or just fireflies. My two-year-old daughter plays with the children of my friends and they chase after each other through the field.

"What if we went somewhere?" I ask my father, engaging in make-believe as I do so often now with him. "Let's go to Italy," I say. But it is the town of his birth that crosses my mind. I don't say its name though. It feels too late to talk about Palestine.

My daughter trips, and my stomach clenches even as she squeals with delight. "I fall down," she cries happily.

"I can't go to Italy," my father says after a while, but I am no longer paying attention.

The last time we were in Italy together was the summer after I turned sixteen. I still remember the twilight road descending to Bergamo the evening I drove us all back to the hotel in Fakri's Benz. In another life, Fakri and my father were two Palestinians studying engineering in Italy, though most of that time was spent sleeping with Italian women and drinking haram Italian wine. The consequence of so much nostalgia for that bygone era (the sixties!) was them getting very, very drunk at dinner.

My father was shouting, "Quant'è bella giovinezza che si fugge tuttavia," a beloved Italian saying, as I recklessly drove Fakri's beautiful Mercedes at speed downhill. I cringed at my dad's maudlin ravings, cringed at that man he once was, the one who always had a belly, whose cheeks were sometimes red from vodka, who smelled always a little of tobacco, cologne, the faint trace of pot, who was sometimes rageful, often hilarious, so alive. How much now do I want him back.

Meanwhile Fakri was hollering at me insistently: "Do you feel Palestinian habibti? Do you? Can't you feel it?" As if the night, or the drive itself, that drunken drive down the falling road, was a sort of baptism unto Palestinian-ness itself. Fakri told me to drive faster, chanting Falestine, Falestine, Falestine with duende, and then my father forgot his dulce youth and joined in, like the homeland might emerge from the Italian landscape a fata morgana.

I didn't feel Palestinian. (A sensation that is not particular to that night: I don't speak Arabic, my mother is Jewish, and I am American born and bred, so I have always felt disingenuous asserting belonging within such a tormented narrative.) But I did feel *something* as our descent hastened, as the view below dizzied and dazzled and tempted and sickened me. What I felt was that awful inclination that has always plagued me—not to Falestine—but to falling, a desire to fall, to no country but death's country. *L'appel du vide*, the French call it. The call of the void.

I have been told, in no uncertain terms, I will inherit nothing from my father in the material sense. In the immaterial sense, I wonder what it is I have inherited from him more profoundly: his Palestinian-ness or his propensity to fall?

My father has been falling all of his life. When he was a small child before the Nakba, playing on his roof in Safed, he dropped a story off the ledge. And there was that crash from bicycling down a steep desert hill in Arizona when he was middle-aged, and one of my earliest memories of him is in its aftermath with a big bloody bandage wrapped around his head. Still, nothing compares to the numerous times he's fallen since he's been ill. Observing him, it almost seems like he is giving himself up to the ground, with graceful surrender, with desire even. (He says it feels like he is being pushed.)

Years ago, when my father saw my face turn ashen as I drove down Highway 87—which descends thousands of feet from the Tonto National Forest to the Sonoran Desert in a seemingly endless (gorgeous) spiral—he spoke to me of the seventeenth-floor apartment in New York City where he once lived.

139

"What scared me about it," he said, "was that it made me want to fall."

And then he assured me it goes away, the falling thing, like a bad flu, or recurring nightmare.

There are two recurring dreams I have had most often in my life. One is a variation on the same theme: I am in an elevator as it rises out of its compartment. It just keeps going up. What terrifies me in the dream is not the uncontrolled ascent, but the inevitable, imminent fall from it.

The other recurring dream began at my old, beloved apartment on Macon Street in Bed-Stuy. In this dream, I was always waking up in a different apartment than the one on Macon, one with different walls (too white, too bare, in fact not unlike a hospital). I now lived in this lesser place and so I wept, head in my hands. I can still remember the deep relief of waking up and finding that Macon remained as it revealed itself before my opening eyes.

Why suffer these two particular dreams over and over again? What does falling have to do with home? Probably nothing, and maybe everything. We are born, we die, with a dream in between. We live in an apartment, a country, on a planet, in a galaxy of a rapidly expanding, darkening universe, in a body. Until we don't. Where do we fall to? My second daughter lives inside of me now, and I shelter her until she falls away from me. We lose Eden—Palestine, Macon, ourselves. Home is only a metaphor for life. Who are we but wandering spirits, refugees from the void?

Or perhaps, the answer is prophecy. In the end, the second dream is a dream that came true: I'll never wake up in that apartment on Macon Street again.

*　　*　　*

My daughter finds me in the green, dusky field. "I fall down!" she reports blissfully, pointing to the criminal grass.

"Are you okay?" I ask her, and my father, who is still on the phone, responds instead. He is okay, he says. But then he moans. I hear him vomit. My mother begins to shriek. It's not pretty, no it's fucking awful, and I'm a girl whose only religion is beauty and there is so much of it just beyond me so I say goodbye daddy, take care of yourself, and hang up.

But I'm still with him, staring across the distance at a field of cows, idyllically grazing and tagged for death, and I forget all about Italy as my daughter tugs on me, and I ignore her, and type in a question for Google and it informs me that my father's hometown of Safed and the Berkshire vista before me share the same elevation. And it strikes me that my father's five-year-old vision of leaving Safed—of the house where he says they left gold beneath the floorboards, from which my grandmother, a few days postpartum, walked with her children on the road to Damascus, away from her family's home since the sixteenth century for which there was no deed, no paperwork because theirs was a deed more imperishable than words, and so, they believed they would return, of course they would return, and then days, months, years, lifetimes (and now my father's) have passed—this childhood vision is also his last.

"No cry, Mommy!" my daughter screams at me. And I realize it is true. I am weeping at long last over this inherited, quintessentially Palestinian fact.

We leave the Berkshires and return to the city. The weekend away, alas, was just a weekend and we are always returning to the city despite our best efforts at leaving it. This time it is to yet another temporary sublet. (To put it discreetly, we are not in a position to sign a lease.) This place feels almost like home, more so than the others that followed Macon—that is until we come back to a leak that has, quite literally, caused the ceiling to fall through. Standing there, thirty-five weeks pregnant, tiptoeing around the crumpled plaster, observing the building's skeleton, its web of beams and pipes and ghosts, for the second time in a few days, I think of '48, of my tata pregnant as I am now, and begin to weep.

Days later, we are interrogated by the landlord. Don't we know that our sublet agreement with his primary tenant is illegal? What paperwork do we have? What are the terms of our contract? Let me stop there. This isn't truly tragic, this isn't war. We didn't lose the rite of centuries. Weeks later, I will observe a New York City sanitation truck destroy in broad daylight all that remains (a suitcase, a green chair, a vacuum cleaner) to a homeless woman as she cries, scratches her face with that unmistakable, desperate painkilling need. I know, this isn't that. Nevertheless, I feel a terrible lightness. And I have, on so many days, in the years since we left Macon. The same lightness that accompanies driving too fast down a steep road in Bergamo, the lightness of riding in an elevator as it shoots up through the stories (or in my dreams through the roof), the lightness of gazing at the sea sparkle over the rails of the Verrazzano Bridge, the lightness that presages a fall.

We move again. We've done it so often, we're almost good at it. Almost. Maybe it's in my blood. This time to the music of our daughter wailing, flinging herself at the doors, at the chairs she believes belong only to her, the screech of tape, sweep of broom, the ache of my back, the roaring vacuum, our kicking fetus, Clorox stench, we need more paper towels, the sound of keys on the countertop, and then our suitcases, our daughter's toys, our boxes full of so much what? are stacked around us in the morning parlor of my best (and most charitable) friend's beautiful brownstone. My partner touches my belly, says: "I feel like we've fallen so low. Like anyone can just get rid of us at will."

Is this what you meant, Fakri? Is this a pale semblance of what being Palestinian feels like?

Sometime between this move and our next, my father falls again, and I call to ask how he is feeling, and he lies, and when he asks how I am feeling, I also lie. My mother tells me what I already know—that he can no longer hear upsetting things. No talk of Palestine, no talk of my endless, temporary displacements, no talk of money woes. Khalas. Enough is enough. He just wants to meet his new granddaughter. So, we talk a little bit about the gabapentin, the oxycodone, the radium treatment. Then he says, "There are no miracles."

"You tried everything," I say. "You really fought." And a memory of him belting out "Fight" alongside The Cure returns and I think of the long fight of his life, as he moved from home to home to home so many more times than me, for so long without papers, or citizenship, facing arrest, and once even the threat of being thrown off a ship. But how can I even pretend to summarize all of that here? An entire life is no anecdote after all. Not his, not yours.

"I fell again," my father says. "It happened so fast, this falling. I just fall all the time."

And I say something useless in response.

"What day is it today?" my father asks. I tell him it is Tuesday and he expresses disbelief. I ask my father if he's watching the game in the hospital. The Warriors are on and Steph Curry is his favorite player. He says he doesn't care anymore who wins or loses the stupid game.

"But you love them," I say.

"I just want to go home," he says. His voice is so diminished now that everything he says sounds as if he is about to cry. But he isn't.

I don't ask what home he means. Then a sudden surge of joy in his voice surprises me. "You know what I have always loved?" he asks me.

"What's that?" I ask.

"Italy," he says. "Quant'è bella giovinezza che si fugge tuttavia . . ."

"Tell me what that means again," I say.

"How beautiful youth is," he says. "But how to translate che si fugge . . . ?"

I haven't had that dream of Macon Street in a long time. Instead, I now have a recurring dream in which we live in the penthouse of a tall building. Just like my father's storied New York City apartment, it is usually on the seventeenth floor. And then, for no stated reason, we are removed from the apartment itself and forced to live on the windy roof. I can't look down, both because I fear I will fall and because I might want to.

In the last dream like this, I realize that the entire world is ending. Our bright, fiery sun plummets without ado and then it is night in the middle of the day. I can hear the ocean swelling, the birds crying. The wind is too loud. My daughter is in the dream, too, and she clings to me and her chest is humming, warm, or it is me, and I am warm and humming with my mad love for her.

When we wake up again in another dream place, I wonder, is this it? Have we come home? Or, in other words, have we fallen to the bottom yet? But I know there is no such thing as either place. This is why we all dream of falling, and falling forever.

*   *   *

"No more falling," I say to my father on the phone before we hang up. This is the sort of make-believe we engage in, both in the beginning and in the end. And, I almost do believe it.

After all, how could I know that some weeks later, I would drive the 2,500-mile distance to him in his desert, with a newborn and a toddler, because the end was nigh, and bear witness to his trembling body, illogically thin, as he daily fret over the few steps between his bed and his wheelchair? How could I know that I would ask him in his final days to find a phone number up there for me to call him on? How could I know that I would be the one who would press my ear down onto his chest, and hearing no song, announce to my mother, he's gone. That in the aftermath of his passing, we would find ourselves moving yet again, my mother and ourselves, and once our furniture was all gone, sleep between the echoey walls of his last homeland, on two couches pushed together, and how I would wish there were such things as ghosts, a visage, a wail, clear articulate proof he remained rather than just wineglasses inexplicably breaking, coyotes howling, and dreams, oh the dreams, the dusk, its magical western palette. Yes, we would again find ourselves where we have been all of these years, not homeless, but not yet home, staring up at the stupid stucco ceiling, singing our daughters to sleep.

How could I know any of this would come to pass as I hang up the phone? The end comes so fast, and so soon. And there are no revisions. How could I know how deeply I would yearn for an unassuming phone call such as this—the one I am hurrying off of, the one which began as it always does with my father saying *hi Hannah, it's your daddy* disregarding a smartphone's inherent caller ID—this phone call which is now over.

"That's okay, habibti, I know you're busy. Have a good night."

145

No, I couldn't know. Back here, in this essay, it is still July and not December, and my father remains, and the warm sun has risen again so I take my daughter to a nearby playground, the swings so comfortingly familiar no matter their point in space, and she beelines right for them, and points to the empty one beside her. "Sit down," she commands.

I do as I'm told. It's been so long. I know I delighted in this once. This lightness, this fleeting sensation of flight, this casual forgetting of how easy it is to fall. "Whee," she cries. "Wheeeeeeeeeeee."

And up we go, into the sky.

GHAITH ABDUL-AHAD is
an Iraqi journalist. Born in
Baghdad in 1975, he trained
as an architect before he
was conscripted into Saddam
Hussein's army, which he
deserted. Soon after US-led
coalition forces took control
of Baghdad in April 2003, he
began writing for the *Guardian*. He has won numerous
awards, including the British Press Awards' Foreign
Reporter of the Year and
two News and Documentary
Emmy Awards. *A Stranger
in Your Own City*, his debut
nonfiction chronicle of Iraq,
was published in 2023.

Stars Aligned

GHAITH ABDUL-AHAD

One evening in early March 2015, I met with a tribal sheik as he settled for a picnic on the long sandy beach of the Arabian Sea in Aden. From the back of his armored Land Cruiser, his tribesmen bodyguards brought out white plastic chairs and a table, and busied themselves arranging glasses, plates, and apples before withdrawing to recline on the sand a respectable distance, chewing qat and keeping a watchful eye.

I was in Yemen to write about the slide to civil war, after the Houthis—an armed opposition group with links to the former president Ali Abdullah Saleh and Iran—had captured Sanaa, putting the Yemeni President Abd Rabbu Mansour Hadi under house arrest. He had fled to Aden a few weeks earlier, and now the Houthis were chasing him down and threatening to invade Aden.

The sheik pulled out a small knife from an embroidered sheath tucked behind his large tribal dagger and began slicing the apples. From a plastic shopping bag at his feet he removed a bottle of Djibouti-counterfeited London Gin, poured himself three fingers, added orange Fanta, and lifted his glass, saluting the sea and gulping half his drink.

"May Allah curse President Hadi and the Houthis." His eyes were moist, the skin tight around his mouth, and he spat his words with anger.

He tightened the thick scarf wrapped around his head against the cold wind that blew from the dark sea. The sheik's family, one of the most prominent in northern Yemen, had maintained a cordial relationship with the Saudis for decades, while in the 1970s and 1980s, he was part of the leftist revolutionary movement that swept through the Arab world. He fought alongside the Palestinian factions in Lebanon, and later lived in exile in Damascus where he formed ties with Hezbollah and the Syrian regime. And thus he was one of the very few people in Yemen who could still talk to both sides, as he tried fervently to stop the upcoming war.

He said that a few days earlier he had met with the Houthi leader and his military commanders in their mountainous stronghold in northern Yemen, who told him that Hadi was a Saudi and an American agent, and that if he managed to flee Sanaa before they got him, they would hang him from a pole in Aden. The next day he drove from the mountains to Aden, where he found Hadi surrounded by the same set of advisors whose policies had caused his downfall in Sanaa, talking about forming a new army from the southern tribes.

"One is an arrogant fool who believes he can do everything and the other is an idiot who can't do anything," said the sheik, adding that even the Iranians were telling the Houthis not to attack Aden and start another sectarian war in the region.

"If a war erupts, there will be no return and Yemen as we know it will be finished."

And yet, there were many who were excited about the prospect of war. The Salafis saw in the war an opportunity to avenge their defeat at the hands of the Houthis, who had captured one of their most important madrassas in the north and driven them out, along with their families. Al Qaeda took advantage of the charged sectarian atmosphere to expand and recruit among the youth, portraying themselves as defenders of the Sunnis of Yemen against a Shia Iranian invasion.

Sectarianism was sweeping across the region, and pan-Arabic TV channels in the Gulf used a language borrowed from the conflicts in Iraq and Syria, of Shia militias and Sunni tribesmen. The fact that the Houthis are Zaidis—an offshoot Shia sect that is closer to the Sunnis in jurisprudence than to the main branch of Shia Islam dominant in Iraq, Iran, and the rest of the Middle East—seemed to matter little.

The Saudis poured money into anyone who pledged to fight the Houthis. Tribes, always willing to take money and weapons in return for a vague pledge of allegiance, came to Aden in convoys of pickup trucks mounted with anti-aircraft guns and piled with fierce looking tribal fighters. They drove through the streets, their large banners beating hard in the wind. The delegations' chieftains gave speeches, threatened the Houthis with annihilation, and posed for photographs with President Hadi or one of his associates, then drove away laden with crates of ammunition and guns, cars, and money. No one would fire a bullet when the city fell a few days later.

Even members of the Southern Secessionist Movement—who for a decade had been agitating for southern independence and the restoration of the state of South Yemen through a largely peaceful grassroots movement, called al-Herak al-Janoubi (The Southern Mobilization)—started combining their regional zeal for independence with sectarian rhetoric, to appeal for support from the Saudis and other Gulf powers who until then had dismissed their calls for secession.

* * *

Late one night, in March 2015, in that fateful week before the war, I sat in the car with Abdul-Raheem al-Awlaqi, a friend and Herak activist I had known for many years. We were chewing qat and watching the silver light of a half moon shimmering on the foaming waves. Sweat beads gathered on his forehead, while his cheeks bulged with the chewed leaves. "For the first time in many years, the stars are aligned for the independence of South Yemen," he said. He told me he had met the president's son in the presidential palace, who informed him that his father did not trust his northern generals anymore, and wanted to form a new army of the southern tribes. The son asked him if the Herak activists were willing to support his father.

"Hadi wants to build an army and I told them that I will send my people to join."

I said that it was a strange alliance between a country's president and those who were trying to secede from it.

"Every soldier we train, every weapon we get, we will use later to gain the independence of the south."

I knew that Abdul-Raheem was a passionate believer in the independence of the south, and refused to acknowledge the divisions that crippled the Herak, but now his dreams were becoming dangerous, and would not only end in heartbreak and frustration as they usually did, but in civil war. When was the last time something good came out of a war, especially in this region? I asked him.

"The peaceful stage of the Herak is over," he said with excitement. The southern factions divided along tribal and regional lines would be unified in this war against the northerners. "Everyone will come together, the armed factions in the mountains, along with tribes in the east and the people of the city of Aden."

How would he take the gunmen off the streets once they'd acquired a taste for fighting? "Look at Iraq and Syria," I said.

"Don't worry, Aden is not Aleppo," he answered.

The first time I met Abdul-Raheem was in August 2010 in Aden. I had gone there to write about the emerging new branch of Al Qaeda in Yemen, called Al Qaeda in the Arabian Peninsula.

When I arrived at Aden International Airport it was dark, empty, and smelled of mold and diesel fumes. Men wearing sarongs in cheerful colors and patterns clambered over bags, bundles, and cardboard boxes while women in long black robes sat silently on a bench.

Next to the glass exit door stood a man with a thick mustache, dyed black hair, and sunglasses. He would make a perfect villain of a Bollywood movie, I thought to myself. In the street a stifling heat swallowed me, like I was in the belly of a giant whale. A new city, a new story, and a childish joy filled my heart. That evening I took a walk along the seafront. Puddles of water formed in the sand, dark and thick like oil.

The next day when I walked out of the hotel lobby I saw another man with Bollywood mustache and dyed black hair, and I thought, what a coincidence, it must be the fashion here.

I went to meet a journalist in a seafood restaurant, who was to connect me with some former jihadis, who promised to take me to meet the Al Qaeda guys. Scruffy cats scuttled between the tables dragging fish carcasses.

We ate, talked, and discussed the story. Halfway through the meal the journalist pointed his chin toward something behind me.

"Someone is filming us."

I turned and saw a third Bollywood mustache, this time protruding from underneath a phone. You are being followed, you are being followed, you are being followed, I repeated to myself.

Reality was suspended for an eternity, as I broke into a cold sweat and felt a shiver in the midday heat.

What's next? I thought. I wait? How petty my plans were, how stupid to think I could outwit the mukhabarat, a Middle Eastern intelligence service, how petty I was because I was scared.

Then came the paranoia. Who betrayed me?

Were they listening to my calls?

Was one of my friends in Sanaa spying on me?

Why was the journalist in front of me grinning instead of panicking? Was he part of it?

I stared stupidly at the half eaten fish in front of me and tried to calm myself, thinking I was not arrested, maybe there were three men in Aden who all had the same Bollywood mustache.

The next morning, when I saw one mustache waiting for me faithfully at the lobby of the hotel I felt relieved: as long as they were following me, they were not arresting me.

An absurd game ensued in which the mouse waits for the cat, and I made sure that he didn't lose my trail while I plotted how to escape from him. I knew that a poet friend of mine was visiting Aden, so I called him and we made a plan.

I walked to the reception desk and asked for the name of a good restaurant, with Bollywood mustache standing next to me realigning the hotel's business cards. I took a taxi, and he followed me through the crowded streets in a red Vitara, getting stuck in traffic four cars behind. I stopped the taxi and went into a restaurant, waited until he left his car, then came out and jumped into a new taxi. The poet picked me up later that day in his cousin's rickety minibus. I crouched in the back seat imagining the streets of Aden filled with red Vitaras.

The poet and I moved into a flat in the former red-light district of Aden. The apartment was large, dusty, and very hot. The kitchen was so large that its remoter corners lay under a thick layer of unexplored must and cobwebs, and I had an eternal fear of the mice that lurked in the cupboards.

The poet was short, with delicate features and a gentle soul. With his sharp nose, dark eyes, and handsome face, he resembled one of those ancient Himyarite sculptures in the National Museum in Sanaa. He was a brilliant orator, a moody writer, and a broken artist.

He was like many young people in Damascus, Baghdad, and Beirut who read Borges and Kafka and frequented the cafes of the French cultural centers—and, when drunk or high, spoke of great projects and books that evaporated by daylight. They inhabited a no-man's-land between creativity and stasis. Their hopes and dreams were constantly shattered and their creativity became a monster eating them from inside. The poet would spend an hour talking of a short story he wanted to write about the old streetlamps in Aden that date back to British Colonial times. He would stand animated, smacking his head with excitement, and narrate the piece in the middle of the room until enough hashish and cheap vodka soothed his creative monster and he slumbered back into inaction and stasis.

He woke in the afternoon, grumbled until his cousin—a slithering smooth operator—picked us up in his minibus. We went to the same restaurant every day to have the same lunch of rice and fried chicken. After lunch we drove to the qat market, a huge dark warehouse with light bulbs hanging from its perforated metal roof. The poet and his cousin spent a good hour negotiating with traders who sat cross-legged on raised metal benches, tasting, rejecting, feigning insult, tasting again, bargaining, and finally purchasing three bundles of the bitter-tasting green leaf. In the darkness, and the shoving and shouting of the qat market, I felt safe.

We chewed qat with a very colorful group: a shark fisherman, a former government functionary, and a businessman who owned a ship that smuggled Iraqi diesel to Somalia. Night after night, the fisherman and his friends spoke of the days of the communist People's Democratic Republic of Yemen, when Aden was one of the most progressive cities in the south. They told stories of social justice and free education, of cheap rents and guaranteed government jobs, of presidents driving old cars and of traffic policewomen standing in the middle of the street, erect in clean uniforms. Under the communists it was a time of frugality, they said, when they had to queue for hours to get an orange, but no one went to bed hungry. They said they had been reduced to the status of second-class citizens when their country was absorbed, through war, into the Republic of Yemen. Their state crumbled and was replaced by the kleptocratic regime of Ali Abdullah Saleh and his northern tribes.

They pointed to a string of grotesque buildings that blocked the sea and said they were built on public property taken over by rich northern sheiks and army officers. They spoke of two decades of unemployment and of a once proud education and health care system reduced to waste.

They pointed to equally impoverished northerners selling vegetables from the street stalls and said, they have taken all our jobs and left us and our city to rot.

Like Abdul-Raheem, the poet hated the regime in Sanaa, accused it of corruption and human rights abuses, and he belonged to a clique of northern intellectuals and journalists who sympathized with southern grievances, but unlike Abdul-Raheem and other southerners, they did not see the solution in secession, but in forming an alliance that would work to bring democracy to the whole of Yemen.

※　※　※

Everyone said that Aden was now like a haggard old woman. In the loose folds of her shriveled leathery skin lay streets and alleyways laden with the scum and grime of centuries. The city smelled of fermented baby shark fins, of sweet milk tea, of jasmine, mangos, and incense mixed with diesel fumes and sweat. Allegedly the old woman had taken many lovers, as men visited her from all over the world when she was beautiful and elegant: Indian nawabs and Bedouin tribesmen, British officers, Turkish coffee traders, Somali sailors, and Levantine merchants.

Now the children of Aden look back at their mother and ask, Who is our father? Is he an Arab? An Indian? A Somali? Was he a tribesman or a merchant?

I visited a coffeehouse wedged inside a small dark room within a colonialist era stone warehouse. The roof was high and vaulted, the space lit by a single bulb, and the entrance decorated with curtains of mangos hung on strings to ripen. Two old grey-haired men wearing sarongs, and with neatly clipped mustaches, sat playing dominos and stared into the distance while thin and emaciated young men in low-cut jeans stood outside laughing, chewing, and spitting paan. The owner was invisible behind a huge copper kettle, lifting his arm high to pour condensed milk into glasses before filling them with masala tea.

The two men were silent in the midst of shouts and general cacophony. They only spoke when they called for more tea. They showed me a stack of postcards of old photographs, artificially colored, of once white, stout concrete buildings that were supposed to usher in an era of hope and progress when they were built in the fifties, and now sit in the middle of lagoons of rubbish, sewage, and the carcasses of motor vehicles. The white plaster has long peeled off their facades. Another postcard showed a romantic sunset on barren, volcanic mountains that were now covered with shanties of cinder block and blue plastic sheeting.

157

All the current misery and wretchedness were emblazoned with the symbols of authoritarian rule: the Republic's eagle, the green-clad policemen, and pictures of the president in Ray-Bans.

What the fisherman, his friends, and the two old men didn't tell me is that South Yemen, that communist utopia, had collapsed when feuding party bosses went back to their regions and tribes to recruit men to fight for their grab of power, all the while masquerading as communist visionaries with their Stalinist and Maoist terminology. I developed a passion for that mythical South Yemen and the romantic Secessionist movement, and it was while covering one of their demonstrations that I met Abdul-Raheem. He hailed from one of the tribal confederations of the south, and was a distant relative of the American preacher Anwar al-Awlaqi. We traveled across the south together and met the jihadis in the deserts and mountains to the east of Aden, where Al Qaeda was spreading among feuding tribes. And he introduced me to the youth agitating for a free south.

While Abdul-Raheem was aligning his stars that fateful spring of 2015 in the mountains northwest of Aden, secessionist leaders commanding small armed bands were attacking and capturing Yemeni Army camps, stripping northern soldiers from their weapons before sending them home on foot. Grey-haired, retired officers from the former People's Democratic Republic of South Yemen mounted old Russian tanks and drove them to mountain hideouts, skidding over the tarmac roads and leaving a thick trail of dust and smoke in their wake, while young people cheered and waved flags and guns.

In Aden, metallic grey clouds hung low over the city, and a gale blew across the Arabian Sea, sweeping the streets of their suffocating, humid heat, bending the tops of palm trees, and whirling rubbish and plastic bags in the dusty air. Thousands of unemployed young men poured into the newly opened recruitment center, pushing their faces against window grilles and shoving paper files into the hands of clerks, who noted names, ages, and home addresses, and promised jobs in the new army.

An old southern general came out of retirement to head a division and stood watching the young men. He was short, lean, and dressed in a threadbare safari suit and Zanzibar round cap. His leathery bronze-colored skin pinched in tight creases around his eyes and mouth and a silver-white goatee framed his paan-stained teeth. "All of this is a joke," he told me as we stood in the shade observing the youth running around, clutching their recruitment files. "I was a general in the old south army. In 1994 we had jet fighters, tanks, and ships, and all our officers were trained in the Soviet Union, and yet the northerners crushed us and invaded Aden in less than three weeks. These young men won't last for two days against the northerners."

Early the next day, a unit from central security forces in Aden allied to the Houthis tried to capture the airport.

Men poured into the streets to resist them. Tanks from loyalist army units led by the wiry minister of defense surrounded their camp, firing volleys of shells. Hundreds of men, among them Abdul-Raheem and his youth activists, clutched guns and fired, hiding behind cinder block walls and tin doors when snipers positioned on high buildings fired back. Bullets flew overhead and exploded in the sand around them. They cowered and moved in the protection of Soviet-era tanks until they reached the gates of the enemy's camp, driving their opponents out. Abdul-Raheem stood watching in disgust as crowds stormed the camp looting everything they could lay hands on—weapons, ammunition crates, mattresses, discarded clothes—stripping grilles from windows and pipes from toilets. Despite the looting, he was cheerful: after twenty years of occupation, Aden was finally liberated.

For three days Abdul-Raheem and other secessionists celebrated their victory. Hadi and his men declared that Aden was now protected by rings of defenders. Popular Committee fighters drawn from his own province stood in their tribal sarongs with guns, manning checkpoints and harassing northerners, those poor who had been drawn to Aden for generations, working in restaurants and groceries toward a better life.

On March 27, 2015, when the Houthis marched on Aden, the wind had stopped and the stifling heat had settled back on the city. The poet had come down to Aden to visit me, and we heard the rattle of heavy machine guns echoing in the distance, while black columns of smoke rose above the horizon. The rings of defense that Hadi and his interior minister had spoken of had vanished. The Popular Committee militiamen had packed their pickup trucks with whatever they could lay hands on and run away. The charismatic and highly respected minister of defense was captured, and late in the afternoon Houthi fighters poured into the center of Aden.

I found Abdul-Raheem standing in the middle of an intersection in front of the Mercure Hotel. The ambassadors of Qatar, United Arab Emirates, and Saudi Arabia had been staying there for the past couple of weeks, distributing money and building an anti-Houthi alliance.

Toting a Kalashnikov, he blocked traffic as the convoy of armed white SUVs carrying the ambassadors sped from the hotel. He jumped into a pickup truck and followed them with a few of his men, as their security detail. The convoy sped through the streets, climbing curbs and squeezing through narrow alleyways. Crowds that had gathered outside buildings and warehouses ready to loot thought that the convoy was ferrying President Hadi to safety, and started pelting the gleaming armored cars with stones, flip-flops, and shoes that only bounced off them, as they cursed a president fleeing a war he had brought on their city.

(In fact, Hadi was evacuated later that day by helicopter to a Saudi frigate off the shores of Aden.)

The ambassadors, trapped between advancing Houthis and angry mobs, scuttled from one port to the other, their private bodyguards looking nervously around, desperate to find a safe evacuation point. They were lost in a city consumed by the sounds of gunfire and looting mobs.

Abdul-Raheem watched the ambassadors depart in silence. We hugged and he said farewell in the tone of someone committing his life to war. Then he drove away to join the fight in one of the neighborhoods that was still resisting.

While some of the locals fought the advancing Houthi units, others simply began looting. Hundreds stormed the massive weapons depot built inside the volcanic Hadid Mountain by the British in the nineteenth century, looting machine guns, crates of ammunition, rockets, and grenades, millions of dollars of a poor nation's wealth squandered for decades on armament. The next day, an explosion ripped through the warehouses, killing one hundred and ten people. Hundreds of inmates broke out of the Mansoura prison, among them dozens of Al Qaeda members.

I drove with the poet back to Sanaa, and woke in the middle of the night to the sounds of Saudi jets dropping bombs. The city shook with reverberations from the explosions, and I listened to the crackle of anti-aircraft guns and knew the war had begun.

I returned to Aden a few days later, though Abdul-Raheem had fled to Djibouti after the Houthis overran the Herak positions. I was stopped at a checkpoint on the outskirts of the city, where the Salafi fighters who found my Iraqi passport accused me of being a Shia fighter pilot who had come to fight the Houthis. I tried in vain to explain that I didn't even know how to drive a car let alone a jet fighter, but they were convinced and took me to a small mosque to execute me. While walking with them, I managed to get hold of one of Abdul-Raheem's activist friends who vouched for me, and I was released.

The Houthis had not managed to fully occupy Aden. They controlled the main roads and some of the city's neighborhoods, but the largely poor working-class suburbs remained out of their control, and little islets of resistance formed there.

I spent the night in the heart of old Aden, in one of the concrete shanties that clung to the volcanic mountain slopes surrounding the neighborhood of Crater. My host was a tall, handsome, broad-shouldered car mechanic turned commander.

He was a Herak activist leading the neighborhood youths in their loud demonstrations. He had risen to the rank of commander after capturing a few heavy machine guns and an armored vehicle. A dozen or so kids from the neighborhood joined his newly formed battalion, resisting the Houthis and jealously competing with other kids over the status of their commander and their battalion.

But since then, his turf of liberated territory had shrunk to a few streets. Houthi snipers had taken over the surrounding hills, and Houthi soldiers were a few blocks away closing in on him quickly.

He laughed. "We had three days of independence."

In the crammed room, piled with bedding, pots, and ammunition boxes, his flatmate, unconcerned with the upheaval outside, busied himself preparing dinner and blaming the young commander for not taking care of himself. The former car mechanic denounced the resistance commanders of other neighborhoods for not attacking the Houthis and coming to his rescue. All day, he pleaded with them for help but none came; each jealously protected whatever turf he had and whatever weapons he'd hoarded, and they accused each other of cowardice, betrayal, and selfishness in scenes reminiscent of Aleppo or Tripoli.

All over the city, men had picked up arms, gathering in schools, government buildings, and squares. They ranged from unemployed youth, Herak activists, Salafis, and even Al Qaeda members. There was no structure; friends, activists, neighbors, and relatives coalesced around a charismatic neighborhood leader, a financier, or a thug. Often there were no clear lines separating these groups. A commander could be both a Secessionist and a Salafi. Many of the youth who joined the jihadi groups did so not for ideological reasons but out of hatred of the Houthis and admiration for the jihadis' discipline and ample weapon supplies.

In the street outside the car-mechanic-commander's tiny independent enclave, Houthi fighters manned checkpoints. Some dressed in military fatigues, others wore a dark blazer over their white dishdasha. Some of the fighters were in their early teens, small and scrawny, serious and curt, carrying Kalashnikovs adorned with slogans and pictures of their dead leader, Hussein al-Houthi. Beyond the Houthi checkpoints, the road was desolate and vulnerable to ambush—until another checkpoint appeared.

They were southerners at this one, and they too, were children, barefoot, in T-shirts and jeans. They inspected papers and scrutinized faces and accents looking for northerners. Overnight a craze had swept the city that married regional xenophobia to sectarianism. Every northerner was a Houthi. Next to the checkpoint, two jihadi fighters in shalwar kameez stood on the back of an armored vehicle, one of them fixing a heavy anti-aircraft gun. They smiled and laughed with the kids; gone were the days when they had to hide in the mountains, shunned and avoided.

Now they poured into the city, they manned checkpoints, and they fought with everyone.

The Houthis' occupation of Aden lasted four months. They were driven out by a coalition of Yemenis trained and equipped with US-made armored vehicles by the Emiratis, and assisted by teams of Emirati special forces and local resistance fighters. Other units poured into the city from the mountains. The swift victory only meant the quick collapse of the Houthis. Now all these units would advance north and link with other resistance movements in Taiz, Baida, and Marib, and combined they would encircle Sanaa, bring the war to a swift end, and chase the Houthi as Hadi had promised to the caves of their mountainous stronghold.

Meantime, Aden would resume its former glory; its port that had been stagnant even before the war would reclaim its status, its ships, businesses, and embassies. This is what the enthusiastic governor told me, a former general who had returned from London to help rebuild the city. With electricity, water, and jobs restored, Aden would become the next Dubai. Companies would pour into the city. A few weeks later, the governor was blown up by the jihadis.

Liberated Aden resembled other civil-war-torn cities of the post–Arab Spring wars. Burned and rusted-out tanks and armored vehicles were perched on hills overlooking a city of scarred streets and gutted facades. Buildings fell like crumbled concrete wafers on top of each other. Already impoverished people were left homeless by the war and turned into refugee squatters in their own city. The fighting may have been over, one militia defeated, but it was replaced by dozens of other militias. A city without water, electricity, or a sewage system was overflowing with weapons and fighters on the back of pickup trucks mounted with heavy machine-guns, and war was becoming the main employer. Commanders from the disparate, disunited resistance groups were demanding their share of the spoils from a broken and impoverished city.

The most powerful of them started imposing their protection racket, "securing" the ports, the factories, and whatever income-generating institutions there were. The smaller commanders contented themselves with looting public and private lands, especially those belonging to northern owners, and running their protection rackets over the neighborhoods and markets.

Three years later, in 2018, I drove out of Aden along the Red Sea coast toward the ancient port of Mocha. The roads were deserted but for Ethiopian and Somali migrants dumped by smuggler's boats early in the morning up the coast. They moved in small groups of three or four, sometimes individually, one after the other, in long human trains. They were barefoot, each person's worldly possessions consisting of a plastic bottle and a sarong draped across their chest; not a bag, not a sack, nothing else with them as they took the deserted road, littered with the skeletons of burned tanks and pickups, down to Aden.

The sea shimmered behind them like a giant mirror under the scorching sun.

We passed a military base that had been captured, and lost, many times. It resembled an ancient ruin, with tank turrets lying among blasted trees and fallen branches. The buildings were perforated with shell holes of different sizes, and everything was covered in a layer of grey film. A convoy of five destroyed Emirati armored vehicles stood outside. Their tires had melted into the tarmac and made a large black puddle. Metal sheets that had peeled off the vehicles lay twisted like banana leaves.

165

In Mocha, all the Emirati private armies had congregated. There were Sudanese mercenaries, beturbaned and jovial, sitting atop their technical trucks mounted with artillery pieces and bedding. There were also Salafi brigades, a unit of defected northerners, and even some Colombian mercenaries.

The town had been captured a year earlier, but it was still in ruins. Close to the harbor, once the world's leading port for coffee exporting, old buildings stood with their facades sheared off, revealing wooden rafters and walls riddled with bullet scars. Rubbish was piled on the shore between flipped sailing vessels and fishing boats where children swam and paddled.

But Mocha was a war boomtown, and among all the scenes of bleakness and desolation, poverty and wealth jostled together. Hundreds of brand-new Toyota Land Cruiser pickups tore through the narrow streets kicking clouds of dust and jockeying for space with American MRAPs, mammoth armored vehicles designed to withstand explosions. Amid this chaos, children begged for bottles of water.

One of the commanders I met that day told me he was a bus driver in Aden when the war started, and now he commanded a unit of a hundred men, and a dozen armored vehicles. How had he learned to be a commander? I asked him. The war had taught him. "War is the best teacher," he said.

SARA ELKAMEL is a poet,
journalist, and translator
living between Cairo and
New York City. She holds an
MA in arts journalism from
Columbia University and an
MFA in poetry from New
York University. Her poems
have appeared in *Poetry*
magazine, the *Yale Review,*
Gulf Coast, Ploughshares,
and the *Cincinnati Review,*
among other publications.
She is the author of the
chapbook *Field of No Justice*
(African Poetry Book Fund &
Akashic Books, 2021).

Cairo After You

SARA ELKAMEL

for my friends

Routinely, the city trims the limbs of trees as if to leave the view of the Nile unobstructed. We wake to green clouds, electric saws cleaving ficus; one more reason to lurk like strays in the house. It is here we say things the city cares very little about. *Your hair is very beautiful*, he said the first time I lay with my back in his chest. Like a shrub in a dust storm. Around noon, bird bones sometimes appeared on the carpet. Most days he kept his instrument encased—afraid for the strings. Just days before he left, his once-stray kittens became mothers. One sang, the other did not. I have already forgotten the name he gave the one he loved less. I recently learned crows can remember human faces; they can even hold grudges. So I wave to the same two crows as I drape old underwear over the oxidized clothesline. They do not wave back from the necks of our decapitated evergreens. They do not sing like kittens. All day I am thinking there must be a green necropolis somewhere—but where? At night the city acquiesces to the heat. The question of where trees belong is not straightforward. Every time I love something I carry it on my back. All our friends have gone. I am closer than ever to the earth.

The Endlings

TANIA JAMES

Iva's family wanted to see a Neanderthal, but the weather had them stuck in the cabin. Her brother-in-law suggested a hike in the rain, but Iva refused on account of her five-month-old. "She'll be fine!" said Vinod. "She's one of us—she's a Pagidipati!" The last time Iva went along with that logic, she found herself hunched in a raft of Pagidipatis, the only one singing herself hoarse to a screaming infant in a life jacket.

The cabin sat in the foothills of the Shenandoah Mountains outside Luray, Virginia. Until a few years ago, Vinod had had trouble renting it out year-round, but that was before a pair of Neanderthals were discovered along the banks of the Shenandoah River. They were sisters, billed on *Nightline* as "the product of a bizarre and illegal in-vitro experiment." *Nature* magazine took a more compassionate stance, referring to them as "endlings," the last of their kind.

Tourists descended overnight. The bids on Vinod's cabin spiked. The guest book was filled with testimonials from all over the world—*Thank you we will never forget this noble species. / Incroyable!*—that made no mention of the fire pit or the Carrara marble jacuzzi. People came for a glimpse into the Pleistocene

171

past. They left with T-shirts that read: SURVIVAL OF THE SEXIEST.

"Well," Iva said, trying not to sound hopeful, "why don't you all go without me?"

"Z wants to hike, don't you Z?" Vinod reached for the baby, who whipped around as if interested in the wallpaper.

"Sorry," said Iva, secretly pleased with Z's powers of discernment.

"Yeah, yeah," said Vinod. "Stranger danger."

While Vinod went to find his rain gear, Iva planted Z on the play mat, under the mobile that would provide about three minutes of entertainment, just enough time for Iva to wolf down a croissant.

Her husband called. Jai had caught the flu the day before they were to leave for Luray; he'd urged Iva to take Z and go without him. At least Iva and Z could enjoy some leisure time and avoid infection, and when was the next time they would get an all-expenses-paid vacation? Vinod ran a thriving urology practice in Chevy Chase, Maryland, but he was mercurial in his charity—stingy one minute and magnanimous the next. Jai was a middle school principal in downtown DC. Pride kept him from asking his brother for anything.

"Heyyyy," said Jai, his head filling the screen, his nostrils plugged with twists of tissue. Looking at him made Iva feel fluish. "How're my girls?"

She caught him up on the morning's debate, how Vinod's family was going hiking while Iva and Z would stay put.

"You won't be lonely?" he asked, using a congested version of his parent-teacher conference voice. "What'll you do there all alone?"

"I won't be alone. I have Z."

"And what's it called? Moms Love Chocolate?"

"It's not Moms Love Chocolate. It's . . ." Iva lowered her voice. "Chocolate Mommy Luv."

Chocolate Mommy Luv was a WhatsApp group of mothers of color from across the nation, a sisterhood of night owls, an altar upon which to rest their extremes of emotion unless the moderator deemed the offering harmful or off-topic. Chocolate Mommy Luv was unfortunately named.

A month ago, she'd turned to Chocolate Mommy Luv for advice on why Z was waking up every two hours at night. Mama-LlamaDingDong had blamed bed-sharing, saying Iva should never have pulled Z out of the crib, that this practice, in Mama-LlamaDingDong's experience, had led her baby to graze on her milk all night long. PurpleRain said this was ridiculous, that she'd bed-shared with all four of her babies, concretizing their bonds and reifying their independent spirits. Sometimes, Chocolate Mommy Luv was a confusing place, which was comforting in a way, to know that no one really knew anything for sure, no matter how fiercely they expressed themselves.

"I haven't posted anything lately," Iva told Jai. "We've been keeping busy."

"Huntin' for Neanderthals?" said Jai, in a bad Virginia drawl. "Just kidding. You already told me what you'd do if you found them."

"What did I say?"

"You don't remember?" He looked concerned by her poor memory, recent conversations simply frittering away as a result of her perpetual sleep deprivation. "You said you'd break them out somehow."

"Huh." She brushed the pastry flakes from her fingers. "What would you do?"

"I don't know. It's pretty fucked up what's happening to them, but I wouldn't go rogue. That's not really my style."

A stampede of feet overhead. Vinod was hollering at his kids to find their rain pants, ponchos, moisture-wicking socks. "I should go help," Iva said by way of goodbye, though her only intention was to help herself to another croissant.

Iva waved from the porch, waiting until Vinod's SUV had turned the corner at the end of the lane. Then she shifted the baby to her left arm and passed through the galley kitchen, grabbing the leftover plate of pancakes, and followed the paving stones to the coach house.

Iva had volunteered to occupy the coach house so as not to wake the whole family with Z's nocturnal shrieking sessions. The coach house was about the size of her apartment in DC, with a ceiling that soared over the living room and not one but two chandeliers—a massive wrought iron crown over the dining table and a smaller tiara over the king-size bed.

Z was whimpering by the time they entered the bedroom. As soon as Iva released her to the floor, she sprint-crawled to the walk-in closet. Iva did the secret knock—*tap-tap* with her fingernail, *thud-thud* with her knuckle—and cracked open the door.

The Neanderthal sisters were huddled by the shoe shelf, glowering up at her. (*Were* they glowering, Iva wondered, or was the glower produced by their prominent browbones?) At the sight of Z, the younger sister broke into a grin and patted her knees as Z climbed into the nest of her lap.

The older sister was squatting with her back to the full-length mirror, wrapping one of Iva's elastics around the end of her braid. (Iva's brush was on the ground, clouded with coppery red hair, evidence that she would have to dispose of.) Both sisters were covered in fur capes and pelts, the costumes they'd been wearing when they escaped their compound. The furs were in fact blankets from West Elm, made to look authentically brutish and matted by their employer, Rustic Adventures LLC.

"They're gone," Iva said.

Tossing her braid over her shoulder, the older sister rose to her feet. The younger followed, carrying Z. Iva stepped aside for the three of them to venture into the living area.

"I brought pancakes," Iva said, pointing to the dining table. Neither sister responded verbally; Iva had read that the sisters could not speak, that their voice boxes were buried down low in the chest, too low to make more than grunting utterances. Their lack of speech, she found, caused her to emote with excessive cheer. "No syrup this time!"

The older sister shuddered at the memory of syrup from their first breakfast together, almost two weeks before. She joined the younger on the rug, rolling the pancake into a tube before biting off the end. Z reached, but the older held it away and wagged a finger.

Watching the sisters eat seemed sort of rude, so Iva tidied her bed. Here and there she snuck a glance, wondering whether their paleontologist mother used to make them pancakes.

The sisters, Iva had read, were taken as adolescents from their mother who had taught them to read and write basic English. After the mother was institutionalized, the court assigned the sisters to a series of guardians. According to the older sister, the most recent guardian had tricked them into signing a ten-year contract with Rustic Adventures. At first, the sisters did as they were told, wearing fake furs, cleaning hides and turning spits of turkey meat while tourists watched from golf carts. The sisters grew to hate both roasted turkey and Rustic Adventures, and the night tours that left them vulnerable to ogling even as they slept under trees.

And so, in early June, the sisters fled their compound, traveling by night from one dark and uninhabited cabin to another until one day, they glimpsed a pair of headlights creeping up the driveway. They raced to the coach house, hoping to hide in a closet until they could flee in the night. The bedroom closet was crammed with suitcases and sleeping bags, but Iva glimpsed them as soon as she opened the door. They were crouched behind a space heater, their eyes the pale hard blue of rock crystal.

Her initial reaction—"Ohmygod shit shit!"—caused Z to cry hysterically. Before Iva could make a move, the younger sister stepped out of the hanging coats, waving her arms, hopping from foot to foot. Z went slack-jawed. The younger sister pulled a face, making Z laugh.

Slowly the older emerged and raised her palms in a pleading way. She mimed writing on her own palm and pointed to the kitchenette. Iva stepped aside, allowing the older to take the magnetized Post-it pad and pencil from the fridge and write in cramped capital letters: I CAN EXPLAIN.

Iva was mesmerized by their story—told in fragments and hand gestures—about the cruel guardian and the vultures of Rustic Adventures. When she asked where the sisters ultimately wanted to go, the older wrote: MOTHER.

"Yes, but where?" Iva asked, thinking that the older had misunderstood. The older underlined MOTHER. And it was true, Iva realized, a mother was a place as much as a person—in their case, a whole world.

They asked Iva not to tell anyone of their existence—not even the family members in the main house. Iva said nothing at first, still coming to grips with whatever the fuck was taking place in her kitchenette. She was ashamed, too, of screaming at the sight of the sisters, who were really just two orphaned girls of, what—seventeen? eighteen? The same girls she'd claimed she would

176

find a way to save. Guilty, uncertain, she allowed them to stay that night, telling herself that by morning, she'd know what to do.

As the days went by and Iva was forced to spend more time with Vinod, she grew convinced that no good would come of telling him about the sisters. He would insist, arms annoyingly akimbo, on notifying the authorities. Iva herself was skeptical of authority. Such skepticism was practically a job requirement at the immigration rights coalition where she used to work, in Maryland. The work had been constant and draining, calling lawyers to take on migrant children, visiting deportation centers, lobbying for stalled legislation. And though she had quit to take care of the baby—daycare being too costly—helping the sisters fired up the old engine of indignation, the sense of purpose that had once given shape to her days.

The sisters showed their gratitude by leaving her little bundles of wildflowers or wineberries on the kitchenette counter and keeping themselves confined to the walk-in closet. At night, Z's screaming tested all reasonable limits of gratitude. It was the younger who emerged from the closet one night and offered to rock the baby in her arms. Exhausted, zombified, Iva watched as her daughter turned calm in the younger's arms. Something about the younger's smell or sway or strangeness had Z entranced, Stranger danger be damned.

After the sisters had polished off the pancakes, Iva poured them coffee.

The older held up the notepad: HOW MANY MORE DAYS?

"Till we leave?" Iva asked. "Three, I guess."

The younger rested her cheek against the top of Z's head. She seemed saddened by the prospect of parting. The older wrote: WILL U HELP US?

"Do what?"

GET OUT

"Sure. Wait, what do you mean?"

BUY COATS HATS HAIR DYE

"Hair dye? Really?"

DRIVE US TO CULPEPER TRAIN STATION—5:35 TO HOUSTON

"Wow. How'd you figure out the train schedule?"

The older pointed the pencil at the nightstand, where Iva's phone lay atop a stack of magazines.

"How'd you unlock my phone?"

FACE ID WHEN U WERE SLEEPING

Iva imagined the older holding the screen to her snoozing face, waiting for the device to read her features. "That's kind of invasive."

U HAVE MANY OPEN TABS

Iva's face warmed. Clearly the older had gotten a glimpse of Iva's Neanderthal obsession, searches to do with clothing, honey-gathering, and one about intersexual relationships between Neanderthals and early *Homo sapiens*, a theory that explained, in part, the erasure of Neanderthals as a species. A valid question, Iva believed, possibly invalidated by her search query: *neanderthals sex homo sapiens?*

"Sorry." Iva winced. "I was trying to learn more about you."

WHY

"I'm just curious, I guess."

The younger swatted at the older's knee and signed something. The older nodded emphatically.

SAY NOTHING ABT US TO ANYONE PLEASE

"No, of course not."

4 EVER?

"I won't. I promise."

The older wrote down the address of a twenty-four-hour Walmart where Iva could obtain the clothing and hair dye. Tonight, after everyone went to bed. The younger offered to watch Z, but Iva said the baby loved being in motion and would be fine in the car seat. In truth, Iva had no idea how Z would react to being strapped into a car seat at three in the morning, but she preferred gambling on a tantrum than handing her baby over to sitters who were not only untested but another species altogether. She couldn't exactly check references.

A few hours later, Iva was breastfeeding Z when she heard the slamming of car doors. Her breath caught. She'd expected to hear the SUV rumbling up the drive, forgetting it was a hybrid that only purred at low speeds. She darted a look at the sisters. They were already shutting the closet door behind them.

In seconds, Vinod's twin boys were charging into the coach house—Iva scolded herself for leaving the front door unlocked— while she tried to snap up her nursing top.

"We saw the sisters!" they yelled as they ran to her chair, hopping in place with six-year-old fervor.

"When? Where?"

"On the hike," said Kush.

"The hike, right." Iva nodded, relieved. "Cool!"

Z twisted around to look at her cousins, delighted by the interruption. She reached for Luvh, who seemed momentarily hypnotized by Iva's cleavage.

"So!" Iva said, trying to draw his attention upward. "What were they doing when you saw them?"

After a long vacant pause, Luvh said: "They were naked."

"Yeah," said Kush. "Up top."

"The Neanderthal sisters were naked up top?" Iva said.

"And they had big ones, like yours," Kush said.

"Okay," Iva said briskly, "I have an idea: why don't you guys wash up before dinner?"

"Nah" and "we're fine," they said in overlapping voices.

"Well, I have to finish feeding the baby, so."

Kush asked if they could watch. Iva looked sternly at both boys, who looked sternly back, and said no.

In the evening, the adults convened on the deck. The rain had cleared, leaving behind a damp leafy smell that joined with the charcoal smoke of the grill. Vinod was flipping steaks, which he had jovially told Iva were not for her, as if she'd forgotten she was a lifelong vegetarian. Iva was just happy to take up a corner of the hot tub and spread her arms along the marbled sides. Her breasts were drained, her veins running with malbec. Her T-shirt puffing like a windblown sail.

Sitting on the edge of the tub was Myung, Vinod's wife. She was holding Z, drifting her chubby little feet through the water, which they'd cranked down to a reasonable temperature. At one time, Myung had carried the twins, but years of intermittent fasting had whittled her hips to arrowheads. Her cheekbones glowed with a balm she once shared with Iva called Au Naturel, and that was how Iva thought of her, a natural at everything.

"Z's loving the water," said Myung, arching her eyebrows at the baby. "She's remembering the womb."

Iva nodded, feeling similarly enwombed. "How was the hike?"

Myung rolled her eyes. "The twins insist they saw the sisters."

"I wish," said Vinod. "The last three reviews on TripAdvisor were two out of five stars because apparently it's my fault they didn't see a Neanderthal."

"I just hope they're safe," said Myung, beautiful natural Myung. Iva loved her. Iva loved everyone gathered here, maybe even Vinod,

180

until he said, "Once we get them back, we need to build a wall. Not a brick wall. Something with gaps they can see through."

"You can't do that," Iva said. "It's inhumane."

"Hello, it's for their own protection? An eight-lane interstate wraps around the park. I bet they've never even seen a car before—"

"What about more security cameras?" Myung suggested.

"We have cameras," Vinod said. "They keep smashing them. Do you guys have any idea how freakishly strong they are?"

Iva hadn't considered their physical strength. She'd always assumed them to be fragile, childlike, in part because she was at least six inches taller than both of them.

"I got some new surveillance cameras," Vinod said. "Spy quality. I'm gonna install them where no one can see."

"And where's that?" Iva asked.

"Where no one can see." He winked at her.

"Well, don't rig them up during our vacation," Iva said. "I don't want to be surveilled."

"Nothing to worry about if you've got nothing to hide," Vinod said.

"He's joking," Myung said. "He couldn't install a nightlight without help."

Hotly, Vinod listed the many things he had assembled and installed around their house. Iva took the opportunity to side-climb out of the tub.

"I'm tired," she said. "Think I'll go back to bed."

"You okay?" Myung asked.

"I'm fine. Just dehydrated, probably."

"Have a steak then!" said Vinod. "Just kidding, I have some corn on the cob and baked potato for you."

Iva said she'd have it all: the corn, the potato, and two steaks.

"For who?" Vin asked.

"Me."

Iva could feel the spotlight of their surprise. The two times Iva had eaten meat in the past were by accident; once informed, she immediately went to the toilet and threw up. And now here she was with a paper plate practically bleeding into her palm.

"Yeah," Iva said, trying to sound tired. "I've been feeling weak from all the breast-feeding."

"You could have low blood pressure," Vinod said. "Steak would definitely help with that. I bet it even helps with milk, you know, stimulation. Rare or medium rare?"

Iva gambled on rare.

"Attagirl," said Vinod, draping two glistening slabs on her plate alongside a foil-wrapped potato and corn on the cob.

"Should Vin take your blood pressure?" Myung asked, watching her with concern.

"No one is taking my anything," Iva said. "I'm just going to watch some TV and eat in bed. But I'll come back for the baby."

Iva strode away, her jaw tight. A fucking *wall*? Had everyone lost their minds? She stood on the porch of the coach house for a moment, breathing deeply against competing waves of anger and worry. She wondered if she should call one of her former colleagues, someone she trusted, to offer the sisters legal counsel. Iva wasn't a lawyer. She was just a mom in the middle of nowhere, bearing a paper plate of steak. Then again she knew the sisters would refuse any offer of outside help. *Homo sapiens*, they believed, were not to be trusted.

YOU ARE DIFFERENT, the older had written. NOT LIKE YOUR KIND.

Conferring with her sister, the older added: MORE LIKE MOTHER.

Iva knew they'd meant this as a compliment, but being compared to a woman under psychiatric surveillance—well, it troubled her.

182

*   *   *

Only later that night could Iva relax again, after returning from Walmart with several boxes of hair dye in French Roast. Each sister held her head over the sink, a towel draped over her shoulders, as Iva worked the dye through their coppery roots. The younger applied the rest of the dye to Iva's head, though Iva knew the brown wouldn't show up in her black hair. She enjoyed the scalp massage, their strange little sorority of stained towels and oil-slicked heads.

While waiting for the dye to set, they tried on their new clothes: cheap jeans, bucket hats, fleece coats. WHY MOM JEANS? the older asked, after reading the tag. Because the waistline is so forgiving, Iva had said. Because of all they hide. Because they were half off. Fully dressed, the older sashayed across the rug, then paused to swipe a finger across her palm. They all shared a laugh.

After rinsing and drying their hair, the three of them went to bed. No sooner had Iva fallen asleep than Z began to whimper. Only half-awake, Iva heard the younger pick up the baby, making a little grunting sound as she jostled and rocked her. Soon Z had drifted off again, and Iva mumbled something by way of thank you or how'd you do that, before descending back into a dream that was remarkably anxiety-free, in which Patrick Swayze was begging her to leave her life behind and run away with him into some sexy, sweaty beyond.

The next morning, while Vinod was out kayaking, Myung and Iva took the kids to Luray Caverns. Iva volunteered to drive so she had some excuse for holding onto the keys. At dawn, she would load the sisters and Z into the SUV and drive to the Culpeper train station. Just in case, she'd leave a Post-it on the fridge: *took car, driving Z to get her to sleep.*

The prior night's slumber party had Iva buzzy and exhausted, but she managed to take note of the highway signs, including the exit that led toward Culpeper.

"You okay?" Myung asked warily when Iva's mouth fell open again.

"Oh. Yeah." Iva shivered. "I was up all night."

"Z give you a hard time?"

"No, it was just me. Couldn't sleep for some reason."

"Do you think," Myung ventured, "that you might be spending too much time on your phone? I know that Chocolate Mom group means a lot to you, but you can also call me or your mom if you want to chat."

Calling her mother rarely ended well. Every conversation led back to the same Nike-inflected statement motto: "You all"—meaning the entirety of Iva's generation—"think too much. We just did it."

Fighting a yawn, Iva said, "Thank you. I appreciate that."

A silence ensued, the kind that usually precedes some sort of emotional bloodletting. Iva decided to cut to the quick. "I used to talk to my colleagues," she said. "I miss them. I miss my job."

"But, Iva, being a mom is the most important job there is."

Iva glanced at Myung, who gave a brain-dead grin.

"See, that's called *acting*," Myung said. "Did I tell you I'm trying out for a play next week?"

They talked about the community theater in Chevy Chase, the upcoming adaptation of *Steel Magnolias.* Four Southern women, but multicultural this time. Myung would be trying out for the Darryl Hannah character, a born-again Christian.

"I didn't know you could act," said Iva.

"I used to, in college. That's how Vinod and I met, doing *Pygmalion.*"

"Vinod was in *Pygmalion*?"

"He did the lights. So he says. To be honest, I don't remember meeting him at all—isn't that terrible?"

"It's weird," Iva said. "Vinod is pretty memorable."

"I know," Myung sighed. "To be honest I barely remember anything from college, from yesterday even."

"Yeah, the other day, I forgot my cell phone number."

"That's nothing. I've forgotten my kids' names."

They named other outlandish things they'd forgotten: the lead singer of Queen, half the lyrics to the national anthem, how to spell "banana." They laughed at how dumb they'd become, how functional they made themselves seem.

Just as Iva was beginning to relax, Myung tilted her head and asked, "Did you color your hair?"

Iva tucked a lock behind her ear. She'd thought her black hair would subsume all signs of French Roast. "Maybe a week ago? Before we came to Luray?"

Myung nodded. "It's subtle."

Iva curled her fingers around the steering wheel to hide her dye-stained fingertips.

In the caverns Iva forgot her own exhaustion, as awestruck as the first spelunker to worm down a hole in a Virginia hill and find himself on another planet entirely. Pleats and drapes of glistening flowstone. Ceilings bristling with stalactites, practically glowing as they narrowed to meet the stalagmites. The tour guide called the ones that merged in the middle "a marriage."

"See that?" Iva said to Z, who was strapped to her chest. "A marriage. It takes hundreds and thousands of years to form." Subdued by the shadows, Z was already nodding off.

Iva fell in step with the tour guide, a well-tanned young man with a pleasant drawl. He stopped the group by a chasm where, he said, a Neanderthal woman's remains had been discovered two decades ago, her skullcap so perfectly pickled in a pool of water that a paleogeneticist was able to extract its DNA, which was then inserted into a hollowed-out human egg cell, which in turn was implanted in the womb of the paleogeneticist. That single fertilized egg split in two, resulting in the birth of the Neanderthal twins, whom the paleogeneticist raised until they were discovered and turned over to the State, which allowed them to remain in their native habitat under park supervision, while their mother was in a mental health facility somewhere in California. "So although Dr. Collier displayed some questionable medical ethics, thanks to her, we have the sisters."

Rustlings of unrest. A man behind Iva declared that he hadn't seen the sisters, separately or together, during the entirety of his ten-day stay. "You guys should advertise when it's low season," he said. "That's why we came down here in the first place."

"I bought a special camera for this," said a woman.

"Actually," said the tour guide, "photography of the sisters is prohibited. In the past it's led to some violent confrontations."

The woman insisted that it was a telephoto lens, the kind that nature photographers use to capture wildlife from far away.

The sisters had told Iva about certain VIP tour groups that had been allowed to get uncomfortably close, so close that the older once heard a donor talking about her ass. She gave him the middle finger, earning herself a sharp rebuke from Rustic Adventures. The sisters were not to respond to tourists, forbidden from letting onto the fact that they were equal parts *Homo neanderthalensis* and *Homo sapiens*, the latter half inherited from their mother. This was not what modern man wanted to hear, said Rustic Adventures. Modern man wanted the authentic experience of stalking another species of human—familiar and yet essentially, impossibly, different.

But that was hardly a violent confrontation, Iva thought, annoyed at the tour guide for making the sisters sound so savage. Unless there was some other incident they hadn't told her about.

At the cabin, in bed, Iva nursed until Z dozed off with the nipple still in her mouth. Transferring Z into the travel crib would only cause her to gasp awake—some primal fear of falling that kicked in no matter how gently Iva lowered her onto her back. Soon Iva had surrendered to her own fatigue, and the harmonic rhythm of their breathing, and fell asleep.

In the seconds before Iva opened her eyes, she could hear the steady breathing of someone standing close by.

"Weird . . ."

Iva opened her eyes: it was Luvh, kneeling by her bedside, head cocked to examine the juncture where Z's mouth met Iva's nipple.

"It's not weird," Iva said groggily, deciding to turn this awkward moment into an even more awkward teaching opportunity. She explained that the milk was coming out of her breast, and that Luvh had also drunk from his mother's breast for a very, very long time. Luvh tried to process this information, but it was clear that milk flowing from a breast was about as logical to him as Kool-Aid pouring from a doorknob. Meanwhile Z's gaze was awake but unfocused, on the verge of a postlude Iva called "singing into the mic."

"Can we talk later?" Iva asked Luvh, snapping up her nursing top.

"But I have to tell you a secret," he said. "You can't tell anyone."

Iva assured him his secret was safe. They went through the motions of double and triple-promising before he confessed: "We didn't see the sisters on our hike. We lied."

"That's okay." With a pat on the shoulder, Iva asked him to keep Z from rolling off the bed and went to look for a fresh nursing top. The cups on her current top were stiff as papier-mâché. "I mean lying isn't great." She sniffed a bra. "But your lie didn't hurt anyone, so it's fine."

When Luvh didn't reply, Iva turned. He was letting Z grasp his finger and wag it up and down, a worried look on his face.

"I did see her though," he said quietly. "I came down to drink grape juice in the night and I saw her. She was in the kitchen, going through drawers. But then this morning I thought maybe it wasn't her. Cause she was wearing jeans and Neanderthals don't wear jeans. I told Mommy what I saw but then she got mad at me for making things up and also for drinking grape juice at night. She says that's why I have cavities but I just get so thirsty . . ."

Iva released the breath she'd been holding throughout Luvh's testimony. "It was probably just a dream, sweetheart."

"It wasn't!" he shouted tearfully, dropping Z's hand. "I'm telling you, I saw her!" He ran away, slamming the coach house door behind him.

Iva turned the lock and watched through the blinds as he stormed across the lawn, his hands buried in his pockets. Once he was safely out of sight, she put Z in the travel crib and charged into the walk-in closet. The sisters were passing a stick of string cheese between them. "What were you doing in the main house?" Iva said.

The younger bowed her head. The older chewed in defiance, swallowing before taking up her notepad.

NEED $$$

"So you tried to steal it? I told you I'd give you money."

HOW MUCH

"I don't know . . . a hundred and fifty dollars. It's the max I can withdraw from the ATM."

The sisters looked disappointed.

"I already bought the hair dye, the clothes, all of that . . ." Iva watched the younger pick at the hem of her distressed mom jeans. She imagined them wandering around Houston with their bucket hats pulled low. Where would they live, what would they eat? "Okay, look, I'll get you a hundred and fifty more when we get to the train depot. There's probably an ATM around there. Just promise me you won't take anything from the house. Agreed?"

The younger nodded. The older offered her sister the rest of the string cheese, but the younger shook her head, as if she'd lost her appetite. The older shrugged and shoved the rest into her mouth before lying down with her back to Iva.

After dinner and a movie with the family, Iva retired to the coach house with Z, carrying a bag of soup cans and ramen cups. All day she'd been hoarding non-perishable pantry foods for the sisters to take on their trip. Halfway down the paving stones, Myung caught up to her.

"Need me to watch Z?" she asked. "Or I can help you pack."

"I have to feed her," Iva lied.

"You just fed her, I thought."

"Not much," said Iva. "I can tell she's hungry."

Z smiled at Myung in the least hungry-looking way possible. "Just let me keep you company for a while," said Myung, and took the baby into her arms.

Leading the way to the coach house, Iva braced the bag against her body to keep the cans from clanking. "Here we are!" she sang out as they entered, hoping her falsetto would reach the sisters.

Myung wandered around the sitting area with Z on her hip. "I almost forgot how cute this place is. I think it used to be where

189

the horses were kept—not by us," she added quickly. "The original owners."

If Iva was supposed to take offense, she'd missed the opportunity, too busy trying to shove the bag of cans into a cabinet. "Yeah, I've loved staying here."

"Oh, you wanna show me your crib?" Myung said as Z lunged toward the bedroom threshold.

"What's there to show?" Iva asked, but Myung and Z had already crossed over, and she could hear Myung naming the crib, the window, the bed, the closet.

"Yes, that's the closet," said Myung. "What's up, baby? You wanna look inside?"

Iva closed her fists, sickened by the squeak of the door hinges, the flick of a light switch. She waited for Myung to scream.

Iva screamed first. "Myung! *Myung!*"

Myung rushed out of the bedroom with Z. "What—what is it?"

"You should leave," Iva said. Myung looked bewildered and annoyed. "I think I have a sore throat."

"Why are you screaming if you have a sore throat?"

"I just remembered—don't you have that audition coming up?"

Myung's face fell. "Oh shit. I mean shoot." She returned the baby to Iva's arms and took several steps back. "Do you think you have what Jai has?"

"Possibly. Probably."

Iva watched Myung rewind over all the time they'd spent together, the entire car ride of shared infected air. "And you're only telling me *now*?"

Iva began to apologize but Myung waved her off. "It's okay, I should go. I'll make us some golden milk and leave it on the stove."

Iva thanked Myung and locked the door, then hurried to the walk-in closet, Z on her arm.

The door was open, the sisters nowhere to be found.

"Hello?" Iva called, her voice cracking. The sisters were gone. They'd left without telling her. Had she done something to upset them? Was it the money discussion?

Z gave a grown-up sigh and rubbed her ear, a tired sign. Time for a nap. Time to get back to life as Iva had known it, taking care of her child, just the two of them again.

One of the suitcases, lying on the floor, moved slightly. Iva's heart leapt. She flipped back the lid, and there was the younger, barely able to sit up before Iva had embraced her.

It was midnight. The younger had gotten Z to sleep in the travel crib where she would probably stay for the next three hours, until Iva would have to feed her before the journey to Culpeper.

For now the sisters were asleep in the closet. Iva should have been sleeping too. Instead she was in bed with her phone, catching up on Chocolate Mommy Luv threads, trying to make up for her silence by remarking on old comments. BlueLotus lamented the fact that she was still pureeing foods for her LO (Little One) who refused to chew his food, leading her to wonder if she should accept the gastroenterologist's advice and subject her LO to a scope. Iva joined the twenty-one other mothers who gave this idea a thumbs-down. (*Your LO will figure out how to chew eventually*, wrote MamaLlamaDingDong. *He won't be drinking his food in college!*) Iva treaded gently into the perennial bed-sharing debate. She offered her vocal support of paid leave for new parents and her neutral comfort to SailorMoon75, whose husband had maybe slept with the housekeeper.

Immediately Iva received some private messages: *Glad you're back! . . . We missed you! . . . Where ya been?* Vague as they were, these messages lifted her up.

Sorry to be out of touch, Iva wrote back. *We're on a vacation . . .* She changed "vacation" to *in the mountains with in-laws*.

Some of these women were deep in the sleepless trenches and in no state to hear about other people's getaways.

Has it been fun? BlueLotus wrote back. *Ready to say goodbye?*

No, not ready, Iva thought. Not ready at all.

And here Iva paused, struggling to find the words, just as she struggled whenever she tried to describe her interactions on Chocolate Mommy Luv to Jai. He always nodded, slightly tuned out. This was the loneliness of having a life online. To everyone else, it was a mirage.

And now Iva had gone a level deeper into unreality. She couldn't even explain to her Chocolate Mommy Luv friends how meaningful the last two weeks had been, how unexpected and exhilarating. How could it be coming so quickly to an end?

She closed the app and lay for a long time listening to the white noise machine. It swallowed sound the way her mind would swallow memory in the weeks to come, when the nights would unfold as they had before, unending, inevitable. Sometimes it seemed that the only memories she could claim were the ones captured by her phone.

And then she had an idea.

Switching the phone to silent, she stepped softly to the walk-in closet and opened the door, the hinges mercifully quiet.

Moonglow fell through the skylight, washing the sisters in blue. They lay on their sides, the older's arm over the younger's waist. Iva raised the phone, opened the camera app, and centered the sisters in the crosshairs. Three taps. She stepped back and closed the door.

As she returned to her bed, guilt gave way to a little burst of joy. She had them now. She would always have them.

Iva was still staring at the photo when she felt a tap on her shoulder and wheeled around.

There was the older sister, holding Z.

Iva stiffened. Shoving the phone in her back pocket, she gave a sheepish smile. "Sorry, was she fussing?"

The older didn't move. Z was deep asleep against the crook of her neck, emitting a wheezy snore that Iva could almost feel caressing her own throat.

Iva reached for her baby. The older twisted away, angling herself so that Z was just beyond Iva's grasp.

Slowly Iva's arms fell to her sides. She understood the threat, could feel it in her womb, where sometimes a movement ghosted through her as if the baby had never left her body.

Now the older held out a hand, palm up. Her fingers made a summoning motion.

Shaking, Iva tried not to drop the phone as she placed it in the older's hand. Once more Iva reached out her arms, she and Z falling into each other.

She watched the older swipe through photos. One picture, presumably of the sisters, made the older look up at Iva with a peculiar expression, as though Iva had turned into an object of curiosity, a stranger of uncanny likeness.

After deleting the photos, the older set the phone on the nightstand and went back to the closet, shutting the door behind her.

Iva swayed from side to side. She dipped her nose into Z's neck, the baby's pulse flitting against her lips as she whispered words of comfort the baby didn't need, so primal was her trust in the arms that kept her from falling. Iva herself wouldn't sleep tonight. She would be counting the minutes until she could drive the sisters to the train station, where she would tell them to ride to the end of the line, then get off and keep going and never come back.

LOUISE ERDRICH, a member of the Turtle Mountain Band of Chippewa, is the author of many novels as well as volumes of poetry, children's books, and a memoir of early motherhood. Her novel *The Round House* won the National Book Award for Fiction. *Love Medicine* and *LaRose* received the National Book Critics Circle Award for Fiction. Erdrich lives in Minnesota with her daughters and is the owner of Birchbark Books, a small independent bookstore. Her recent novel, *The Night Watchman,* won the Pulitzer Prize.

Blessings, Suspect and True

LOUISE ERDRICH

1

One night on my birthday I
put my hand into the air
and a luna moth landed on my wrist. A

birthday blessing?

Though spectral and ravishing a
luna moth has no mouth
because it doesn't live long enough to eat.

> I refuse to consider the
> implications.

2

Once I was very poor and slept
beside my brother in the stairwell of a
shopping mall.
When we woke up there were
muffins and coffee at our feet. The
coffee was so hot and good.
Thus, after enduring shame and contempt
were we humanly restored.

> Though after we ate the muffins things
> got worse.

3

One morning my horse-loving daughter
came home from a barn where she had helped attend
a foaling mare. She told me
that she had spent the night in a sleeping bag with the
smaller of the twin foals,
her warmth keeping it alive.

                  Blessed were we all.

4

A man with beautiful work-hardened hands
made a tree house for us
that was open to the sky.
In the middle of the night he and I went into the
structure and made love,
the Milky Way so bright over us it was visible even
in the city. We floated
up, traveling beyond this world.

            Thus were we forever connected, taken together into
            the river.

5

On a night of sorrow, I finally lay
at peace beneath the black
sky and stars. A thousand fireflies
surrounded me and up I floated again.

In the fervor of pure darkness the
stars and the insects signaled
indecipherable longing. Thus forever
and endlessly was I blessed beyond measure.

            Really? Was I blessed? I
            still don't understand
            desire.

6

I saw my grandson fall in love with a small white pine.
He kissed its soft needles. Another grandson cradled his
brother's hands. A third cried the name of his beloved every
day into a toy telephone.
Thus was I healed by the trueness of baby men.

At least
to some degree.

7

On a day of anger, I was given a bird
to hold. It huddled tender in my
hands and asked me not
to crush it. Was I delivered from my
anger by caring for my anger?
The bird came back to me many times.

What is this?
A poem or
a fortune cookie?

8

I took a snowy walk with my daughter.
She was pregnant in the beauty of the lord.
And I, who do not believe in
any lord but the Lord of Life,
bowed down to her in my heart.

9

My daughter waded into the cold lake with
her white wolf dog.
Nobody else spoke their language for
many years. Finally they taught me a
few of their words.
They are the only words I
will ever need.

197

10

Through a forest draped with moss of
electric green, I walked with my ancient
twin, who returned
to me as my child. We sat on a
fallen log.   She put her hand
upon mine. Don't die, she
said.

Okay, I answered.

SAYAKA MURATA is the author of many books, including *Earthlings* and *Convenience Store Woman,* winner of Japan's Akutagawa Prize. She was chosen for inclusion in *Freeman's: The Future of New Writing* and was a *Vogue* Japan Woman of the Year. Her latest book is a story collection, *Life Ceremony,* published in 2022.

GINNY TAPLEY TAKEMORI is the award-winning literary translator of Japanese authors Sayaka Murata and Kyoko Nakajima, among others. Her most recent translation is *She and Her Cat,* by Makoto Shinkai and Naruki Nagakawa. She lives in Japan.

Transmogrification

SAYAKA MURATA
TRANSLATED BY GINNY TAPLEY TAKEMORI

Everyone here is nice and friendly, I thought. I'd just started working part-time, after a long hiatus, at a restaurant in the neighborhood. I'd done this sort of work as a student, but I never imagined I'd be doing it again in my forties.

My husband had suggested a part-time job since I'd been moping around the house now that there was no need for me to look after my parents anymore. My mother's operation had gone well and her recovery had been smooth, so I no longer needed to rush back and forth between the hospital in Yokohama and their home to wash my father's underpants since he was utterly incapable of doing any housework. Now that she'd been discharged from the hospital, she needed to be active to help her body to heal, she told me, so there was no need for me to come so often. I'd left my job in order to care for them, so this left me hanging. I'd been busying myself going between the hospital and their house for over two years and lacked the courage to return to society. My husband was worried about me fretting at home all the time.

"Makoto, you always liked going to work rather than staying home doing the housework, didn't you? How about getting back into your old life? There's no rush, you can take it at your own pace."

The only people I'd seen over the last couple of years were my husband and my parents, so this made me feel better.

My husband and I had known each other since college. He was a calm sort of person, and being an emotional type myself, I felt saved by his easygoing personality. Thanking him, I got an interview at a nearby family restaurant, and started working the morning shift.

My hours were from 8 a.m. to 1 p.m. The restaurant was busier than I'd expected, and as the lunchtime peak approached, we were all running around preparing tables and dealing with customers, and I ended up exhausted.

The moment of calm between the mini breakfast peak and the lunchtime rush had become the highlight of the day, as we would chat about this and that while changing the place settings and menus. That was the only time we weren't running around, and it was refreshing to talk with people outside my family. I often shared a shift with two college students, Takaoka and Yukizaki. At first I felt uneasy about the age difference, but they were both nice people, hardworking and reliable, and took the trouble to show me the ropes. I soon felt quite comfortable around them.

I first began to feel something was off when some drunk customers came in one morning. I'd just changed into my uniform and had gone into the dining area to find an ebullient group of middle-aged men who looked like they'd been drinking all night in a local izakaya giving Takaoka a hard time.

"Hey, this parfait is different from the picture on the menu. You a student? Stop taking me for a fool!"

"I'm so sorry, but this picture is of the Strawberry Special Parfait. The one you ordered is the regular Strawberry Parfait. It *is* a bit confusing. I do apologize."

"It's your mistake. Go and make it again. Hurry up."

"Certainly, sir. So I'll cancel your order for the Strawberry Parfait, and make a new order for the Strawberry Special Parfait, okay? The price will increase from 850 yen to 1,600 yen. Is that okay?"

"It's your mistake so do it for the same price!" one of them roared.

"Stop following the damn manual! Idiot! Look, it's all melted now. I don't want that! Bring the other one! Hurry up!"

"I do apologize. I'll check about the price for you. Please wait a moment," Takaoka said with a smile, and bowed.

He went behind the counter and started making the Strawberry Special Parfait, then noticed me staring open-mouthed. "Oh, good morning," he said, and nodded a greeting.

"Amazing," I blurted out. "Those customers are being horrible, but you don't look even slightly annoyed."

"Annoyed?"

He didn't appear to understand what I meant. He quietly finished making the new parfait and took it to the rowdy table. For someone so young, he was pretty mature, I thought.

A few days later, I was taking breakfast to a regular customer when I heard a man shout, "Just apologize, dammit!"

The atmosphere in the restaurant instantly changed and became threatening. My customer frowned and sent me a look as though to say, go and do something about it, quick.

I apologized to her for the disruption and went over to where an elderly man I'd just taken an order from was shouting at Yukizaki.

I worried that I might have made a mistake with his order, but it turned out to be that the doria gratin he'd ordered hadn't arrived yet. I hurried to the kitchen and asked them to hurry with the doria gratin as the customer was angry.

"I've been waiting an hour!" I heard him roar.

"I'm terribly sorry, sir," Yukizaki told him. "I'll just go check up on it."

"Don't bother about that. You should stay here apologizing until it comes."

I rushed over to them and told the customer that I'd confirmed the order with the kitchen and that they were making it right now, but still the old man kept complaining.

Even after his dish arrived, he looked dissatisfied. It hadn't even been ten minutes since he'd placed his order and here he was shouting. I started to feel angry.

"Hey you, there isn't any cheese. Bring some now!" he bellowed, pointing at the self-service counter for condiments.

I was the one who'd taken his order, but he wasn't addressing me—he was shouting at Yukizaki, who was busy taking an order from a customer at the next table. He was picking on her because he wanted to give a cute young girl a hard time, I realized with annoyance.

I was going to protest, but even when he added, "You thick or something? Bring some Tabasco too!" Yukizaki didn't look at all put out and simply smiled. "Certainly, sir," she said and went to get him some.

She was so professional, I thought, impressed. Once the old man had paid and left, I couldn't help telling her, "Wow, Yukizaki, you're such a pro at dealing with customers. You never even made a face and just kept smiling as you dealt with him. That's so amazing! You're so mature. I really admire you!"

"What? But what do you mean, Kawanaka san? It's not like that at all!"

"Neither you or Takaoka ever look in the least disgruntled when dealing with horrible customers, do you? I always lose my temper. If anyone talked to me like that I'd feel irritated and end up in a fight."

"Lose your temper?" Yukizaki looked at me, bemused. "You use the oddest words sometimes, Kawanaka. A bit old-fashioned—I mean, like, they come up a lot in movies and manga and things, but they're hardly ever used in real life . . ."

"I know just what you mean, Yukizaki," put in Takaoka. "You see them a lot in school textbooks too, don't you?"

He was putting out the day's lunch menus and had overheard our conversation.

"You said something weird the other day, too, didn't you? Um, not anomaly . . ."

"Annoyed?"

"Yes, that's it!"

"Ah, I've seen that word in books," Yukizaki said, nodding.

I burst out laughing. "What, you mean neither of you has ever felt that way yourself? If you've never felt irritated or got angry, you must be a total saint! Ha ha ha!"

The two just looked at each other. Then Takaoka looked at me, a puzzled expression on his face.

"Angry? Oh, it's one of those one-vowel words. You do see it quite a lot."

"Well, yes, but . . ." I was beginning to feel irritated. I had the feeling that the two of them were making fun of me.

"You see it a lot in schoolwork and old books and things, don't you? Of course we learned it at school and I know what the dictionary definition is, but . . ."

"Yeah yeah, it's like something I've never actually felt myself. A sensation of heightened emotion, but it's different to feeling moved . . . more like, um—oh, I remember, a churning feeling in your stomach or something, wasn't it? However much I have it explained to me, it's difficult to really get a sense of it. I find it hard to follow angry scenes in old TV dramas and films and the like too. I mean, when they're angry, I always wonder why they don't just explain how they're feeling logically and discuss things, rather than go to all the trouble of screaming. It doesn't really make sense, does it?"

"Same here. In my case, my parents are also from the generation that doesn't understand anger, so when we went to school and saw the head teacher shouting, we were really shocked. Instead of explaining things properly, why do they have to open their eyes and mouth wide and shout?"

I was beginning to feel a bit scared, and took a step back as though to escape the two of them coming at me with their pure questions.

"What's wrong, Kawanaka? We just want to know!"

They came closer, gazing at me with innocent smiling faces that I now found scary.

"Now that you mention it, there've been lots of TV specials lately about how young people are losing the emotion of anger," my husband said.

"They don't get angry?" I was flabbergasted.

As soon as my husband had come home from work, I'd accosted him and started ranting about what had happened today. As he removed his suit he'd said blithely, "Young people in my company don't really get angry either. And there don't seem to be any angry scenes in TV dramas anymore, apparently because there are so many people who don't understand it."

I wasn't satisfied so easily, and grabbed his arm as he loosened his tie. "I mean, I know you occasionally get people like that, but is it really possible that all young people have suddenly stopped being angry all at once?"

206

"Well, I don't know. Maybe it's catching or something, because whenever I'm talking with young people angry feelings don't really well up in me either. Actually, to be honest I've never really gotten all that angry, ever since I was little. My parents were the types to always lose their temper, but I got sad rather than angry. And these days I always say 'sad,' not 'angry,' since that best describes what I feel, and young people can understand it too."

Come to think of it, I never had seen my husband get angry. I'd always thought of him as a calm sort of person, but maybe that was only because he didn't have much sense of anger to begin with. Surely it couldn't be true, I thought. I recalled the few young people I'd come into contact with over the past two years, like the nurses in the hospital and my local supermarket staff, but I could only remember them all smiling. And I couldn't really tell what it had been like before because I'd always been the youngest in the company I used to work at. When had things started to change?

"But isn't it a good trend? Like that college student said, it's healthier to discuss things calmly than get angry. It means society is getting more peaceful, you know."

"I guess. But don't you find it a bit scary? Anger's an important emotion, isn't it? I suppose getting into fights and yelling at each other isn't sensible, but surely there's more to anger than just that. Isn't it a beautiful feeling, the sort of power you have when your true self is on fire? A marvelous emotion that shows you will protect what's important to you. Isn't there more to it than just sadness? Look, don't you think you should be teaching them that?"

"Eh? Teaching them what?"

"About getting angry. Young people are so gentle and have so little life experience, it's probably just that they don't quite realize they're actually angry. Our generation knows what anger is, so shouldn't we be teaching kids about it?"

My husband had finished changing into his loungewear and laughed uncomfortably. "Well, teaching them about something they don't feel for themselves will probably just confuse them. If what you're saying is true, surely they'll realize it as they grow. I don't think you really need to become an anger missionary and preach to young people about it. Anyway, aren't you tired after being on your feet all day at work? The Indian restaurant I went to at lunchtime was so delicious that I dropped in again on my way home from the office and got some takeout. Let's have that for dinner."

"But Yuji, that means you'll have curry for lunch and dinner."

"No problem! I had mutton for lunch, and I got spinach and butter chicken for tonight. You like spinach curry, don't you, Makoto? Let's try it. The restaurant is really good."

I had a feeling the issue was being obfuscated, but it was also true that I had always been drawn to his easygoing nature. It was infectious, and I always felt saved by it.

He was smiling brightly. True, he'd always had a gentle nature, but had he always been this gentle? Had he been changing without my noticing?

While I'd been shut off from society, could it be that I'd missed the chance to change myself?

My husband was humming to himself in the kitchen. The aroma of delicious curry hung in the air. I was seized with the urge to scream, but I suppressed it and said as brightly as I could muster, imitating my husband, "Wow, thank you! It's been ages since I last had Indian curry. I'm so happy!"

"It's been so long since I last came over to your house, Makoto. It hasn't changed at all!"

I'd contacted Junko to let her know that things had finally settled down at my parents' place, and she'd replied right away, "Let's meet up! I haven't seen you for ages!"

She was a close friend from university, and when I'd been stressed out caring for my parents, she'd cheer me up by sending photos of yummy food or cherry blossoms near her office by message app.

Her hairstyle and fashion sense had changed somewhat since I last saw her. She had always been quite flashy, but now she was perfectly coordinated in natural beige.

"I'm sorry, something suddenly came up for this evening. I'd have loved to see Yuji after so long too."

"Not at all, I'm happy that we can chat together just the two of us after so long."

We'd initially arranged to have dinner together with my husband, but I'd just made the reservation at the restaurant when she called to say that some work thing had come up that evening, so could we possibly meet for lunch instead. Having already made the reservation I was disappointed, but it couldn't be helped if she was busy, and so I proposed a light lunch at home with some alcohol-free champagne. Yuji already had a lunch appointment with a friend and couldn't come, so it was just the two of us.

I poured some of the champagne into glasses and we raised them and smiled at each other. Wiping away a smudge of beige lipstick off the glass with her thumb, Junko asked, "So how are things? You're working part-time at a family restaurant?"

"Yes, I thought I was used to that kind of job, having done it in college. But there are quite a lot of rude customers so I sometimes get fed up. And you know what? The other day . . ."

When I told Junko all about how Takaoka and Yukizaki had meekly apologized, she sighed.

"That must have been a nasty experience. Older people picking on young student part-timers . . . it makes me feel really sad."

"Sad?" Junko too?

She sighed and leaned back on the sofa.

"I guess the different sensibilities of the generations leads to that kind of trouble. I mean look, not many young people these days get angry, do they? But that's kind of beyond the grasp of older people, isn't it? The current sensibility, I mean."

"Um, to tell the truth, I'm the sort to get quite angry, really," I said, laughing and doing my best to not sound too serious.

"No way! Come on, Makoto, you have to keep up with the times, you know!"

"I guess I've just been too tied up with things at home. Somehow I can't keep up with the world," I said, laughing again.

"That won't do at all! You have to get out of the house and talk with other people. Come to think of it, next week there'll be a Public Next Spirit Home Party. Why not come along?"

"Sorry, but what's a Public Home—er, thingy?"

"Oh, didn't I tell you? My husband presides over these Public Next Spirit Home Parties. They're a kind of meeting to raise spiritual awareness to another stage, and they're held once a month on Sunday. Actually, tonight's business is a management meeting. Uh, don't get me wrong, it's not like those weird culty organizations that were popular for a while. Perhaps I'd better explain it. It's not run by one central conspicuous founding leader like a cult—that's an old-fashioned idea, and is pretty boring content-wise too, right? In our group, everyone has charisma. Everyone is a spiritual leader. That's the policy of our Public Next Spirit Home Parties."

"I see," I said, nodding vaguely.

"Oh Makoto, you think we're a bit dubious, don't you? I can tell by the look on your face! I mean, have you really never heard

210

of us? Nowadays everyone with an interest in self-improvement belongs to a Public Next Spirit Home Party somewhere, you know. Even though my husband presides over one, I myself belong to three Spirit Parties. That way I get to experience various worlds, and it's more effective. It's like my soul is opening up."

"Wow, that's amazing! Sounds like magic, ha ha!"

"Membership of our group is cheap too, at sixty thousand yen a month. Surprisingly reasonable, huh? I bet you're wondering how we can possibly get by on that kind of deal, but we manage thanks to our large membership. Our Family is somewhat fluid, but we currently have over a hundred or so members. In our case, 'Family' doesn't refer to any personal household, but to an existence that goes above and beyond that. The sudden plan for a meeting this evening is for the management committee to discuss a proposal for the whole Family to go on a trip abroad together."

"Really?"

I felt somewhat hurt that she had prioritized some weird meeting over our dinner plans. I smiled and took a sip from my glass.

"Look, here's our business card. You see this little red sticker? That entitles you to attend once for free. You'd be really welcome, Makoto. Give some to those kids at work too. It'll definitely be a good experience."

"Wow, thanks!" She gave me ten or so of the cards, and I pretended to look at them admiringly before placing them carefully in a corner of the table.

"Come on, Makoto, stop being so woolly-headed. You'll never get to a higher spiritual stage like that. You'll end up being like, um . . . hey, remember her? When we were at college and doing that part-time job—Orgasmic Isogawa! Ha ha ha ha!"

"Orgasmic Isogawa?"

"Don't you remember? Back then about eighty percent of college students had never had sex. That was a spiritual movement too, or rather a revolution, wasn't it? Anyway, we were working at the family restaurant and there was that annoying old bag who would get hysterical over how all young people should experience orgasm. Remember? We all called her Orgasmic Isogawa behind her back."

"Aahhhh!!! Yes, I remember!" I shouted, as a vivid image of the woman's face rose up in my mind.

"Well, we shouldn't have used the term old bag to counter the negative power of the previous generation, but we were young. Anyway, it really was annoying how she was on some kind of weird mission to inform all young people about the joys of sex when *she* was the one who wasn't keeping up with the times. If you're not careful, Makoto, all the young people at your restaurant will start calling you Angry Kawanaka behind your back, you know! Well, I don't know—young people these days are so well-behaved that they probably don't do that sort of thing. Ha ha ha!"

"Ha ha ha ha!" I laughed, suppressing my anger.

"But look, if you have any life problems, I recommend you come to our Public Next Spirit Home Party. Now and then we get old people who can't control their anger or who can't forget experiencing orgasm when they were young, that sort of people. But they understand right away how stupid that sort of karma is. Honestly, you'll quickly move on to the next spiritual stage. Do come, Makoto! I understand how you feel. I was the same five or so years ago. I'm not sure how to put it—I hadn't yet found the new me, or maybe I was possessed by karma. I was always fighting with my husband. But then I went to a Spirit Party and my eyes were opened. So this is how a new age is born, I thought, and I was completely awestruck! It was like a path had suddenly opened up for me, and ever since then I've only ever had really great fortune slips whenever I go to a shrine. The gods are watching over us after all, eh? They can see what spiritual stage a person is at, you know. You'll be the same in no time, Makoto, trust me!"

I wasn't really listening to her. If I did I would end up yelling at her, and if I yelled at her I'd be marked as an uncivilized person haunted by old emotions and she would just laugh at me, so all I could do was sit there smiling vaguely.

To change the subject I cleared away the empty glasses, poured some tea, and took the cake out of the refrigerator.

Junko enthusiastically picked up the plate I'd put the cake on. "Hey, where did you get these? So pretty!"

"Aren't they? They're Swedish, a souvenir from one of Yuji's colleagues."

"Really? So lovely! Oh, this teacup is cute too! We hold Spirit Parties every month and never have enough crockery."

"I bought that one at an antique shop that just opened recently. They had a lot there, so it's probably a good place to look."

"Oh really? I'll have to go check it out! So cute!"

I always thought Junko and I were very similar, but that may just be because we spent so much time together, copying each other, sympathizing with each other, being infected by each other's sensibilities. Now that anger had disappeared, though, all we had left in common was our taste in kawaii. If kawaii disappeared too, what emotions would still be left for us to share? Maybe sadness, or fear, or happiness—but then what if all that had gone?

Feeling uneasy, I pointed at her yellowish green nails and purred sweetly, "Oh Junko, your nails are so cuuuute!"

I went onto the balcony for a vitamin vape. Vitamin vapes weren't harmful like the old nicotine cigarettes, but I didn't like the way the distinctive lemony smell clung to the cushions and walls so

I always smoked on the balcony. As I exhaled the yellow smoke, I wasn't sure whether it was a sigh or smoke from the cigarette.

Orgasmic Isogawa used to smoke nicotine cigarettes, I thought absently.

It had been twenty-two years since Junko and I had worked in the same restaurant as her. Junko and I had both just started college, and at first we'd just talked about our experiences at the same university, but we often found ourselves on the same shifts and started going out somewhere on our way home to eat and grumble about customers and other staff members, and had quickly become best friends. It was really as fast as falling in love.

The year we started college, over eighty percent of students had never had any sexual experience. This was widely reported in the media, and scholars and commentators were in uproar about it, but we didn't feel any fear or doubt. Rather, we laughed scornfully at all the adults making a fuss.

"Why do they care so much about our private lives? I mean, really, does it matter if that sort of thing disappears?"

"It's bit gross, after all!"

We used to laugh at the middle-aged people urging us to have sex, calling them ecstasy zombies. One middle-aged guy at work even offered to teach me, which made me want to throw up. I was revolted by the touch of his hands on my shoulders and my favorite shawl felt dirtied by him. In tears, I'd told Junko how I felt, and she'd been furious.

"How dare he, the ecstasy zombie bastard!" she'd consoled me. "The next time he tries anything with you, Makoto, I swear I'll punch him. I'll cut off his dick!"

"Thank you, Junko."

Our anger created a strong bond between us.

What had really got us riled up, though, more than blatant male harassment that just made us despair, was Isogawa, who was in her late forties and despite being a woman like us would lecture us endlessly about how we should be having orgasms.

She would always frown whenever men pestered us and tell them to fuck off, yet still she would lecture us that we mustn't die without having had an orgasm.

"Oh no, I'm on the same shift as Orgasmic Isogawa tomorrow."

"Ugh, pulling a sickie would be worse. You'll be lectured again."

"Sexual harassment is bad enough, but Orgasmic Isogawa is really wrong in the head."

"Yeah, she's totally nuts."

"Fuck off and die, Orgasmic Isogawa!"

As we sat drinking beer in the park, Junko suddenly shouted, "Right! You can piss right off, Orgasmic Isogawa!"

"Fuck off!"

"Piss off!"

"Fuck off!"

We felt great cursing loudly like this, and the more formidable our enemy was the more strongly we bonded.

That was probably our own version of orgasm. As it was, nowadays hardly anyone had sex anymore, just a few old people who still came every now and then. We'd triumphed over Orgasmic Isogawa by majority vote.

What was she doing now, I wondered. Had she abandoned orgasms now that she'd become part of the minority? Or maybe she was living somewhere out of sight secretly still having them.

Where had *that* Junko, the one who'd raged with me that day, gone? Why hadn't she made me change along with her?

It was night and a cold breeze was blowing on the balcony. A lot of lights shone in the night, from windows, street lamps, and car headlights. Most people use tools to emit light when night falls. There were always people lurking behind that light— exchanging words, just like Junko and I did back then.

In those days, in the restaurant, in the park, in izakayas, Junko and I were incandescent with rage. In the light, we embraced each other tightly with anger.

What sort of emotions were mingling in the light coming from condos now? Sadness, or fondness, or calm asexual love? Or was something of anger or ecstasy still left?

Or was it nothingness?

"Makoto, it's cold! How come the window's open?" my husband's carefree voice rang out from the light behind me.

"Coming in now," I chirped softly back at the light, enveloped in a calm nothingness.

First thing the next morning, a little girl with a schoolbag on her back came in with her father. He hurriedly ordered a chocolate parfait for the girl, then without ordering anything for himself paid the bill and left, leaving the girl behind.

"Is that girl okay?"

I was worried she might have been abandoned there, but Yukizaki appeared to be unfazed.

"Oh, haven't you seen them before, Kawanaka? They come in from time to time. It seems that when her mother isn't around, she has breakfast here then gets a train to school."

The girl quickly polished off the parfait. The staff and other customers indulgently watched over her as she sat looking bored, swinging her legs.

I was at the cash register attending to a customer paying their breakfast bill when out of the corner of my eye I saw something glisten.

"Oh no, will you stop that? You're not supposed to do that here in the restaurant!" I heard Yukizaki say gently, half laughing. I turned to look and gasped when I saw lots of shiny spheres floating there. The girl had somehow got hold of some soap bubbles and was blowing them around.

I hurried over to the girl and gently warned her, "I'm sorry, you can't do that because there are other people around. Not in the restaurant, okay?"

She nodded obediently, then she hoisted her schoolbag onto her back and, ignoring me, ran through the restaurant blowing bubbles and left, leaving a trail of soap bubbles floating in her wake.

I was just wondering whether I should get the mop for the floor, when next to me I heard Takaoka murmur, "Oh no, I'm omifying."

I looked up, startled at the look of rapture on his face.

"Omifying?"

"Didn't you super omify just now? It really took me by surprise."

"I know, I really omified hard," Yukizaki agreed.

"Whenever I omify, I feel great for the rest of the day."

"Yes, I think omifying is the most important thing in life. I always try to omify once in a day."

"I totally get you. It makes life worth living, doesn't it? You could say it adds sparkle to the daily routine."

"Yes, it does!"

It seemed to be a word popular amongst young people, and I didn't know what it meant. But seeing these two talk so enthusiastically about being inspired by something to "omify" and achieve some kind of special state somehow made me feel left out.

Here I was still getting angry and unable to omify, and this made me wonder if I'd been left out of step with the current model of a standard person.

What would Orgasmic Isogawa say, I suddenly wondered. She must be about seventy years old now. What would she say to them? Would she still yell that if they had the time to omify, they should have sex and experience orgasm? Even though nobody these days had sex. Had she spent the last twenty-two years of her life yelling all the time?

In my college days I'd been so angry with Orgasmic Isogawa, but strangely enough now I missed her. I almost felt she might rush out of the back room at any moment wearing her lipstick and curled bangs.

I went home and turned on my husband's computer to look up the meaning of the word "omify," and discovered that it was trending now.

> To become unusually imaginative, to become disoriented, to have an increased desire for abnormal behavior; accompanied by enhanced creativity and the desire to express oneself by drawing pictures and singing songs. Not used to describe mere emotion or sentiment, but some heightened urge to do something. However, exceptions apply when the subject is a child.

What the heck was this idiotic word salad? Given that it was trending, couldn't they come up with a better definition? Feeling irritable and angry, I closed the computer.

At dinnertime, I asked my husband, "Hey Yuji, do you know what 'omify' means?"

"Eh? What makes you ask that all of a sudden? Now that you mention it, I was really omifying on the train not long ago."

"What? It's a word you use, Yuji?"

"Oh, is it dialect? Don't you use it, Makoto?"

"Whether I do or not, that word didn't exist when we were young, did it?" I shouted, surprising even myself, and my husband hurriedly got up and came over to rub my back. "What's up, Makoto? Calm down . . . did something happen at work today?"

"No! It's just weird! Suddenly you're all changing, and I've been left behind, and that's because I've been shut up at home so I wasn't exposed to it!"

"Exposed to it? What are you talking about?"

"Why didn't you use 'omify' at home? If you'd done that I'd have been infected too. I've been spending my time between home and the hospital, so you're the only one who could have infected me with that word."

"Come on, what are you so sad about?"

"I'm not sad, I'm angry!"

I was so hysterical that I knocked over a vase of flowers. My husband calmly handed me a towel and a change of clothes.

"Calm down, what's wrong with you? I never imagined you'd be so sad . . . er, angry, about me not using 'omify' at home."

"We as animals transform, you know. To fit in with the community we belong to, we are infected, we imitate, and we transform. If you don't infect me with society, I get left behind."

"That's true, but there's still time. People quickly change to match their environment. It'll happen before you know it."

"I hope you're right . . . I've never even felt what it is to omify."

"Don't worry. Trust your ability to forget and transform. I mean, we've never had any problems doing so before, have we? What about that pitch-black foreign frozen health soup that you go out of your way to buy online and have for breakfast every morning? No way you'd have gone anywhere near something like that two years ago, right? And that fashion of wearing a bellyband over a dress, would you have even contemplated that a year ago?"

"Well yeah, I guess . . ."

"Look, it's fine. We are simple, easygoing, superficial creatures and we're infected by our surroundings before we know it, without any place for will on our part, living our lives readily transforming. Have faith in your simpleness. Our genes have been constantly repeating this since long before we were born!"

Finally I was beginning to calm down and recover my composure thanks to my husband's words. I fell asleep there on the sofa with him rubbing my back, without even cleaning up or having a bath. I was strangely exhausted, perhaps because I'd been so worked up.

Just before I fell asleep, my husband picked me up, and I felt myself swaying as I lightly floated up from gravity. I fell asleep with the fervent wish that the next morning I would wake up having been properly transformed.

When Junko invited me again to one of her husband's home parties I decided to get serious about seeking out Isogawa.

I searched Facebook for everyone who'd worked at the restaurant back then, and contacted them one by one. When one of them told me that they'd invited Isogawa to their wedding and would probably be able to find her, I was so excited that my hands shook.

"But you and Junko never got along with her, did you?"

"You're such a kid, really. Women have a bond that men don't understand," I said after a moment's thought, giving the sort of answer that Isogawa would have given twenty-two years ago, reflecting the ideal woman of fifty years ago.

"What are you talking about? That's just gross. Well, suit yourself . . ."

That night I couldn't sleep as my heart was beating so painfully, almost as though I was in love. My husband and I slept on separate futons in the bedroom. We had never seen each other naked, or even kissed. What would Isogawa say if she knew that, I wondered. Would she yell "Have an orgasm!" like she did back then? I'd avoided her like the plague back then, yet now I was desperate to see her wild with rage.

Just then my phone beeped. I picked it up with my heart in my mouth. A new message had arrived.

"Kawanaka, of maiden name Okamoto? Apologies if I'm wrong."

I felt as if all the pores in my whole body had opened, and found it hard to breathe. Even without looking at them, I could tell my eyes were bloodshot. The temperature of my blood rose throughout my body, and I felt as though I was being reactivated as a living creature.

"That's right!"

"So it *is* you. I remember you. It's been a long time."

"Can we meet and talk?"

A while passed and I began to worry that she was annoyed or had fallen asleep, but then my phone vibrated and lit up. As if catching a firefly, I gently covered it with my hand and picked it up. Light leaked through my fingers and faintly lit up my futon. Within the small machine, Isogawa's words seemed to be glowing.

"I can do Monday."

"What's up, Makoto? Can't you sleep?"

I jumped at the sound of my husband's voice and started shaking.

"I'm fine. I just can't stop playing this game."

"Oh, sounds great. It's bad for your eyes, though, so if you're going to be at it for a long time then best turn on the light—it won't bother me at all. But don't stay up all night, okay?"

I wasn't sure why I'd tossed out that lie. "Thanks, but I'm going to sleep now," I told him, and he seemed satisfied. I was relieved to hear him snoring a while later.

"Thank you. Tomorrow I'll get back to you about where and when. I'm sorry to have disturbed you so late at night."

I'd been racking my brains what to write so that she wouldn't think me either rude or standoffish, but that was the best I could come up with.

I put my phone down by my pillow and closed my eyes, but my body was still worked up. I'd never felt that worked up even with my husband or with lovers at college.

I arranged to meet Isogawa in a hotel lounge.

I'd put considerable thought into finding a place that was decent enough not to appear rude, in a location easy to find, and relaxing so as not to put her on her guard, and in the end I booked a table in the lounge at a recently built foreign-owned hotel. I'd never put so much thought into where to meet someone in my life. Even when I was dating my husband, I'd felt that we should be able to talk about anything and if our interests didn't coincide then it would be fine to split up. But now I was completely set on Isogawa. I really wanted to keep her hooked, and I tried hard to think of ways to please her.

I also put a lot of thought into what to wear. What would be the best outfit to make her want to see me again after today—not too flashy, yet not too staid? After a number of trips between the closet and the mirror, I settled on a simple dark blue dress. I wound a bracelet with a humorous capybara pendant around my wrist, and attached a soft kokeshi doll key chain to my bag, thinking Isogawa would love them. Maybe she'd laugh and point at them, *What on earth are those?* I would have done anything to get a reaction like that from her.

I even got my nails done elaborately with a koala painted on my right index fingernail, and a skull on my left thumbnail, thinking it would amuse her. On the way to the hotel, I worried that I might have overdone it a bit and threw the bracelet in my bag.

I arrived at the hotel lounge thirty minutes early. After searching on my phone for the best seating arrangements, I chose the seat with the best view for Isogawa, and sat down opposite it to wait for her.

Isogawa appeared fifteen minutes before the arranged time. The moment she walked in, I could see at a glance that she hadn't changed at all. She wore a flashy suit with shoulder pads and her long hair was dyed light brown and fluttered in the breeze. Even her fashion sense hadn't changed. She was like a fossil, out of place there in the hotel lounge, but I found that reassuring.

"Long time no see," I said timidly.

"Wait, what about her? The one who was always with you. I thought she would be here today too," Isogawa said in the same tone of voice as before.

"You mean Junko? No, she isn't coming today. We are still friends, though."

"I suppose you are. You two always had fun badmouthing me, didn't you?"

I cringed.

"To be honest, I almost didn't reply to your message. I knew the two of you always hated me." She sighed.

"Oh no . . . I mean, we were young then. I'm sorry we were so rude to you."

"Well, never mind. I always thought you should have said things to my face. It was the fact you were so cowardly about it that bothered me."

"I really am very sorry . . ."

"Don't think you can make it all right just by apologizing!"

"Are you still angry, Isogawa?"

"Well it doesn't really matter. It was a long time ago."

"No really, are you angry? Are you still angry now?"

"As I said, don't worry about it. It's in the past."

"That's not what I'm asking. I'm asking whether you get angry lately!"

Even I was surprised at how loud my voice came out.

"What the hell are you getting at?"

"There's something wrong with me, Isogawa. I thought I was shallower. I was good at transforming myself. I was good at taking in the influence of my surroundings, and would rapidly change with the times. But now . . ."

Isogawa lit a cigarette. Not a vitamin vape, the tobacco sort they used to sell in the old days. It reminded me of those awful Jintan mints that my grandfather used to like. I had no idea if those weird candies still existed.

"And now, Kawanaka? You got married, I see."

"Yes, that's right."

"Hah. Congratulations. But is your relationship really that of a married couple? It was already like that back then, but young couples nowadays don't seem to have sex at all. I suppose you don't either? If that's the case, as far as I'm concerned calling yourselves a married couple is, to be blunt, a fake marriage."

"We do," I lied without a moment's hesitation.

She glanced at me incredulously for a moment, then her expression visibly softened.

"Really? Oh, I see. Well, that is unusual for young people today."

"As far as I'm concerned, it's like the foundation of the marriage, something that is absolutely necessary. Back in college it was like, how to put it, youthful impetuosity or something, I just went along with what everyone else was saying. But I'm an adult now, and I totally think that what you were saying back then was right."

"I see. It's true, isn't it? My son's wife is just hopeless. Can you believe it, they haven't had sex even once?"

That was the norm these days and there was nothing odd about it at all, but I'd decided I would do anything to get Isogawa to like me, and so I said flatly, "That's just terrible!"

"It really is! You've actually turned out to be a decent adult, haven't you? I wish I could get my daughter-in-law to listen to you. But my son and even my husband take me for a fool and just laugh at me. They tell me I'm old-fashioned, like a bitch in heat that's missed the boat."

"You are absolutely right, Isogawa."

She sighed in relief and leaned back in her chair, her expression gentle. "I bet it's hard for you, too. Young people nowadays are really unbelievable. Even though I'm just living a respectable life, they treat me like a fossil. I totally get what you're saying. So now it's not just orgasm, but anger has gone too? I mean, like that's even possible! It's one of the fundamental human emotions, even a baby gets angry. Scholars say that it's just a temporary absence of emotion in them too, it's not like it doesn't exist. They never listen, though, they're all a bunch of fools."

Seeing Isogawa getting more and more worked up, I felt a shiver of excitement.

Isogawa still got angry even now! She still got angry!

Meeting up with someone who was angry after so long was raising my spirits.

"I mean, what the hell is Public Next Spirit Home Party anyway, for fuck's sake?" I raged. "If it's public then what's so 'home' about it?"

"You think so too? My son's wife has been taken in by that bunch of weirdos too. I can't bear to watch! She's even gone into debt! I slapped her so hard for that."

"Seriously, I can't believe it! I mean, how the hell can they charge sixty thousand yen a month! Are you fucking kidding me?"

"What? You're getting off lightly with that. The place my daughter-in-law wanted to go to charged three hundred thousand yen a month! I slapped her face when I heard that. *Oh but Mom, you just don't understand with your old ways of thinking*, she said, grinning like a monkey at me. It creeped me out, I tell you!"

"Well done, Isogawa. I swear I'll do the same to Junko and make her wake up. It's her husband that's creepy. I thought so from the start, and I should have stopped her then. She's been totally brainwashed by the creep, that piece of shit with his stupid little mustache!"

"Oh, is that so? You'd better get them to split up as soon as possible! I'd give him a good piece of my mind. What a dick."

Sharing our anger gave us an unbearably sweet sense of excitement. Spitting out foul-mouthed curses for the first time in ages, we gradually got more and more heated.

My body became flushed, sweat erupted all over me, and I took off my cardigan. Isogawa also looked worked up and rolled up the sleeves of her blouse.

Our eyes shone, our nostrils flared, and our voices got steadily louder and shriller, and our breathing rougher. Our body temperatures rose moment by moment, and sweat was breaking out on our foreheads and necks.

"I totally get you!" Isogawa almost shouted. "I'm also furious with my daughter-in-law, just furious! And *she* looks down on *me*! *It's because you're at the bottom spiritual stage that you feel anger, I hope you can grow quickly*, she says. Give me a fucking break! And my son takes *her* side! Even my husband just smiles at whatever I say lately. A bunch of grinning monkeys is what they are. It really gives me the creeps. But all my yelling just goes to waste, straight down the drain. Assholes!"

"Isogawa, you are absolutely in the right. The fucking shits! Why do you have to go through all this? I'll come over and sort them out for you. I'll shout at all of them, and keep beating them until they accept the anger they have inside themselves!"

A member of the hotel staff quietly came over and gently warned us, "There are other customers here too, so could you please keep your voices down?"

"Oh, do shut up! We're having an important conversation here. It can't be helped, we're getting a bit heated so of course our voices are going to get loud! You youngsters just simply lack this heat!"

"That's right! We're paying a lot of money to be here, so leave us alone! I mean, twenty-five hundred yen for a single cup of coffee! I've a good mind to report you to the Consumer Center. What a rip-off!"

"Very well, madam. I do apologize," the young woman said, and bowed her head deeply.

"Why the heck are you backing down now? That's the trouble with you young people, you just don't have any spirit."

"I totally agree! You shouldn't take back something you've said so easily!"

I always thought anger was an important but unpleasant emotion, but I was now taken aback by how great it felt. Our wave of pleasure was unstoppable.

"Let's go and hijack that public party thingy together!"

"Yes, let's! We can do it! Let's fight—we'll fight together!"

We held hands, feeling like heroes. We were sticky with each other's sweat, but we didn't care. It didn't bother us in the slightest.

We were bonded by this cozy pleasant feeling. I then realized that anger actually blossoms. Right now anger was blossoming,

I thought. Making the flower of anger blossom was our purpose in life. It was definitely wrong for anger to not exist.

I was possessed by the fervent thought that scattering the blossoms of anger within us throughout the world was what it meant to live.

"Oh wow, sure, I'd love to go to the Public Next Spirit Home Party!" Yukizaki said.

For a change we'd finished work at the same time, and as we chatted I casually mentioned it to her. I handed her one of the business cards Junko had given me and her face immediately brightened.

"I heard that having been to one of these is really useful at job interviews, so I've been wondering about them. Is it really okay for me to go along?"

"Sure, I mean Junko gave me several cards and told me to invite as many people as I like. Also, the first time is free, she just wants people to get a feel for the atmosphere."

"That sounds great!" Takaoka said as he came in on his break, so I had to tell him about it too and he was as excited as a child. "Wow, that's amazing Kawanaka. You're connected to these incredible people! A Public Next Spirit Manager for a job title is super cool."

Seeing how innocently pleased they were, I felt a bit guilty about taking such pure kids to such a dubious event. Of course I'd look out for them, but I was worried they might easily be sucked into the whole thing.

"That's how you learn about life!" was Isogawa's swift reply when I emailed her about my concerns.

We now messaged each other more frequently and more intimately than we did our own husbands. We were more closely bonded than family. Orgasmic anger was that powerful.

I couldn't help feeling that discarding that sort of power was clearly mistaken. I wanted to guide pure, brilliant young people like Takaoka and Yukizaki to the correct path. To that end, some amount of risk was inevitable, like a bitter medicine.

My husband was concerned about my relationship with Isogawa.

"Isn't it a bit weird to suddenly get this close to someone you used to hate so much? Makoto, are you sure stress isn't making you mentally unstable?"

"Shut up shut up shut up! Don't talk to me. Stop trying to brainwash me!" I shouted at him.

He looked as though he didn't even understand what it meant to shout and just gazed at me looking puzzled.

Suddenly I realized that my husband had long gone somewhere far away, and that Isogawa was the only friend left to me.

Sunday was a clear sunny day. I met up with Isogawa, Takaoka, and Yukizaki at the station, and we headed to Junko's house together.

The reason Isogawa and I had been speaking on the phone so often was to refine our plan to hijack the Public Next Spirit Home Party. We intended to remind everyone of the importance of anger.

We thought it preposterous that anger, one of the basic human emotions in existence since forever, could have suddenly disappeared.

"They must be raking it in, so I bet they live in a showy high-rise condo," Isogawa said indignantly.

I thought it was a bit old-fashioned of her to equate being rich with high-rise condos, but I went along with her. "Absolutely! It really pisses me off."

I used my phone to search the address I'd been sent on the map, and it took us to an old house that had been tastefully renovated.

229

We slid open the front door to find a reception desk, and a young woman looked up our names on a list.

"You're here as visitors, aren't you? Please wear these badges."

We put on the white badges and were shown into the living room.

"Please keep your shoes on."

It felt weird walking along the corridor in our shoes, but the moment I stepped into the living room I understood why. The floor of the room had been packed with earth, and it had the nostalgic smell of a walk in the mountains. At the center of the room was a big tree. I went up to it wondering whether it was real, but it was fake.

A lot of people were sitting on plastic sheets spread on the ground under the tree having a picnic. All the windows were open, and outside was a small garden with lots of real plants growing in it and also packed with people. It was a strange space, but everyone looked like they were enjoying themselves.

Placed on top of all the picnic sheets was what looked like Junko's homemade food and expensive champagne.

"Looks a bit cheapskate to me," Isogawa said disappointedly, but Takaoka and Yukizaki looked delighted, exclaiming "Wow, this is cool," and "It looks so relaxing."

"Are your friends a couple? Are they having sex like they should?"

I thought it was a bit vulgar how Isogawa had immediately come out with her orgasm talk, but went along with it anyway. "No, they're not—but they should! Young people should be having orgasms!"

Just then, the place suddenly erupted in applause. Junko and her husband had come in.

"Hello, everyone, are you all having fun?"

"Of course!" "Come and join us, Junko!" people responded.

I could see that she was pretty popular with the "Family."

"Today we have quite a lot of newcomers too, so I'll briefly explain a bit about our Public Spirit Party. Of course it's a party, but it's also an important meeting to discuss the next generation, and you should also be inspired and learn through the discussion so you can move up to the next spiritual stage. That's also the sort of place this is."

Everyone nodded vigorously at Junko's words. Only those wearing white visitor badges were glancing around in bewilderment.

"Um, when you say a meeting, what's it a meeting about?" Yukizaki asked, timidly raising her hand.

"Nice! Good question! The meeting here is about the standard model for people's character."

"Standard model?" Takaoka repeated, looking puzzled.

"That's right. It's like with fashion, but with people's characters— what character is in fashion. Let's take you, for example—come out here with me for a moment."

Takaoka looked a bit uneasy, but he got up and went to stand next to her. Junko smiled, revealing a smudge of beige lipstick on her teeth. Raising her voice, she continued, "Sorry to ask a personal question, but do you have a partner?"

"No, I don't."

"Do you ever feel anger?"

"No, I've never felt it."

"I see. I expect you often omify in daily life, do you?"

"Yes, a lot!"

"That's wonderful! So you all understand, don't you? He's a prime example of the standard model for twenty-year-olds nowadays. Hardworking and gentle, kind, doesn't get angry, and easily omifies. He probably doesn't spend much, and is reliable. Of course he doesn't fall in love or have sex, and isn't even interested in adult videos. Something like that, right?"

"Yes, you are absolutely right." Takaoka meekly nodded. I thought it amounted to harassment, but he wasn't in the slightest annoyed.

"This is a typical standard model for twenty-year-olds today. The character in fashion personified."

There was a round of applause. Takaoka bowed, looking embarrassed.

"It's just the same as food and fashion, there are trends in people's characters. What's more, it's not like that happens naturally. It's because people hold meetings to decide it."

The Family members were all nodding, while the visitors were looking at each other in confusion.

"Trends don't happen naturally, they are started. Someone always starts them, and they grow into a movement. It was already decided in a meeting years ago that this sort of character should become the trend to set the standard model for twenty-year-olds now. Everything is started intentionally by unsung professionals."

There was a stir. Junko continued, holding her hand over her heart, "I'm an example of the standard character model of twenty-year-olds twenty years ago. I don't have sex, but I am in love, and I value friendship, and I have a lot of anger. Rather than expensive brands I hanker after a more tasteful natural fashion and lifestyle, and I prioritize living life as myself over career and money. I never doubted that it was my own character, my personality—not realizing that someone had set it up."

I did a double take. The characteristics that Junko had given were exactly mine twenty years ago.

"The character you download from society at twenty becomes the base, and then you grow through the standards for thirty and forty. Since your character at twenty is the base, what type of character was trending at that time is extremely important."

Junko paused and looked around at everyone's faces.

"And what I want to do now is discuss what to do next. Take fashion, for example. Natural colors are booming this year, and hardly anyone dresses in colorful clothes. Plastic crossbody bags, knee-length sneaker boots, and beige lipstick. Plus a camel-colored bellyband worn over a dress—everyone does this now, right? But a few years ago nobody had ever heard of this fashion. Likewise, people also have designers, and we are those designers. What next? That is our motto. All of us are designers. That is the objective of this party."

There was a round of applause. Junko smiled and patted Takaoka on the back.

"So what do you think? Do you understand?"

"Yes. It's incredible! I'm so moved to have the opportunity to be here. It's an incredible honor."

I looked at Yukizaki next to me, and she too was nodding her head delightedly.

"Okay then? Let's begin! This meeting is held at every Spirit Party with more than a hundred members. The character decided here will be presented to the management and representatives, who will hold a number of further meetings at higher levels to eventually decide on the latest standard model. Once Japan's standard model has been decided, there will be a show at which other countries will also present theirs. I attended one in Italy two years ago, and it was very stimulating."

Everyone sighed when Junko said this. It seemed that everyone in the Family longed to attend one of these shows.

"Well then, let's start. Of course, this is basically a home party, so let's enjoy the champagne and relax while we talk."

Junko clapped her hands twice, and the meeting started.

"So when will this standard we're deciding come into effect?" Yukizaki asked.

"Oh, how could I? I forgot to explain something really important," Junko said as she poured champagne for a Family member. "On the whole, we think of character trends in terms of five-year periods. The next five seasons are already decided, so what we are discussing today is the character for twenty-year-olds in thirty years' time. What character for twenty-year-olds will be best for humanity thirty years from now? Please use your imagination and discuss amongst yourselves!"

"In thirty years' time? What would be best, I wonder. Probably best if they don't fight too much, really."

"But it would be good if they spent more, wouldn't it?"

Lots of people started talking to Junko.

"It would be good for humanity if they like working, wouldn't it? They should want a career and be ambitious, and happily work overtime until late at night."

"Breeding is also important for humanity, though. The more we breed the better, right?"

"But if you don't have money, you can't breed, can you? Of course, getting the economy going is more important."

"How about placing importance on motherliness and liking kids, irrespective of gender? Like doting on other people's babies and being supportive with their upbringing?"

"Sounds good, but it might leave room for criminals to take advantage."

Champagne corks popped as people exchanged opinions. I looked around at everyone, bewildered. The character that would be fashionable thirty years from now? Did that mean that my character when I was twenty had been designed by someone thirty years before that? For the sake of humanity? I was just wearing the character that somebody else had designed? Just like I was wearing a bellyband over my dress now?

I was beginning to panic when Isogawa suddenly stood up.

"Stop this RIGHT NOW!!!!"

The room fell into silence at the sound of her shouting.

"This is insane! You bastards! Stop this crazy meeting right now!"

"Oh, perfect timing. Please look, everyone. She is a perfect example of a standard model of a twenty-year-old fifty years ago," Junko said, pointing at Isogawa. "She likes love and sex, mates frequently, gets wildly happy and angry, and richly expresses her emotions. She loves flashy things, and she likes high-class brands, whether restaurants, clothes, or bags. This is what the highly popular standard model of fifty years ago now looks like fifty years on!"

The place erupted in applause at Junko's words.

"Wow, that's great! If you like love and sex, you can breed a lot!"

"In fashion you often get things that were all the rage fifty years ago making a comeback and becoming popular again, don't you? How about reviving the character popular fifty years ago with a little customization?"

"Good idea!"

Everyone around Isogawa was getting more and more excited.

"Stop it! Close this meeting now!" Isogawa kept shouting, her entire body turning red.

"Wow, I'm really omifying now . . ." Takaoka murmured.

"It's true. I omify just looking at her."

"I haven't seen anyone get this angry for a long time."

"I'm totally omifying."

"Me too, really omifying."

In the middle of them, Isogawa stamped her feet and roared, spittle flying, "STOP OMIFYING!!!" She was almost dancing in her rage, waving her arms around and stamping her feet loudly. "Stop omifying right this minute! Stop using other people to omify!"

I couldn't say anything. I couldn't say anything *because I was omifying*.

Seeing Isogawa shaking with rage, for the first time in my life I was omifying. I was omifying out of control at the sight of Isogawa with her shoulder pads and curled bangs shouting and spraying saliva and sweat.

"Say something, Kawanaka!"

Suddenly hearing my name, I was startled and began shaking.

"Well it's not your fault, you can't help omifying at a scene like this, can you?" Yukizaki said, rubbing my back and smiling.

"You're omifying?" Isogawa gaped at me. "Kawanaka, are *you* omifying?"

Her voice was trembling and she stared at me as though I'd betrayed her.

"No, I'm not!" I shouted, hugging myself and trying to bring it under control. "I'm not omifying!"

"Raptaphoria," Yukizaki murmured as she stroked my back. "Seeing the two of you, somehow I'm in raptaphoria."

"What's that?" Takaoka asked, mystified.

"I'm not sure, but it's like the word omify isn't enough. There's more respect, more like worship, that sort of special feeling."

"Raptaphoria . . . somehow it really does seem to fit it perfectly."

"I think I understand what you're saying. This feeling really is raptaphoria."

"Raptaphoria," I murmured in spite of myself. Isogawa was so unbearably darling, and I wasn't so much moved as I felt an acute awe at something pure, a sort of deep emotion of worshipping the miracle of being alive now. This was what it was called, I understood in my soul.

"Raptaphoria!"

"Yes, raptaphoria is the perfect word for it."

Everyone was excitedly murmuring the word.

The reason I had longed for Isogawa to contact me, had put so much effort into choosing what to wear so that she would like me, was not because I was in love or was scheming. I could only explain it with the word raptaphoria.

It was something that had been in my subconscious all along. Before uttering the word just now, I had often experienced raptaphoria in my life. When Junko and I had been slagging off Isogawa, how even our lukewarm beer had tasted utterly delicious. When I was a child, the moment I learned that my best friend was moving to another school. The moment I met my husband and felt for the first time that I wanted to become family with someone. It was raptaphoria that I'd been experiencing at these defining moments in my life.

"I'm sorry, I just can't stop feeling raptaphoria . . ."

I recalled all the raptaphoric moments in my life, tears streaming down my face.

Isogawa was staring at me, stunned.

This word would definitely spread like wildfire. Raptaphoria would surely become an essential word of the new era.

I could only describe the feeling of having witnessed the very moment this word came into being as raptaphoria.

Isogawa alone was left behind, dumbfounded.

"Isogawa, deep down you too must be experiencing raptaphoria . . ." I said quietly, holding my hand out to her. I wanted to show her this beautiful emotion as soon as possible. I was certain there must be a lot of raptaphoria overflowing within her. Her life must be full of wonderful raptaphoria. I had to infect her with it as soon as possible.

Isogawa went pale. She alone remained uninfected, steadfast in her anger, blooming magnificently in our midst.

KELSEY DAY is a poet from southern Appalachia. Their work has been nominated for the Pushcart Prize, the Penrose Poetry Prize, and Best of the Net. Their next poetry project, *Field Notes from the Anthropocene*, is a collection that explores the intersections of queerness, decay, and environmental violence in the rural south.

Samson Mythologies

KELSEY DAY

It is, first, an inconvenience
this fundamental delight of
being many.

Last night I kissed the salt-dew between
each of Delilah's fingers,
while she pulled the worms from my eyes

one by one.
It takes four tries before I admit to having
multiple bodies.

The evidence is in my hair—see how
the ends are frayed and split
from moving between myself?

The scarecrows double over drunk in the cornfields
and a litter of mice spread diseases
in the engine of a combine harvester.

At night, I plant a desk fan by my bed
so my body is left
watched and cooled while I multiply

into a handful of beetles, all sight-starved and
antennas blinking, a nest of nests,
they, they, they—

I give myself away, in so many small and careful ways.

In the kitchen, in the bent-up corners of a Tuesday
shading our eyes against the fluorescents
like we are saluting to one another.

In bed, rippling into
something new every time she
touches me, my face a glitching television screen.

The perpetual retreat, when I enter a room
and my body must climb out the
window of my body.

The loosening proof, a voice baked into
every conversation, each new and ancient risk

of being seen

MIEKO KAWAKAMI is the author of the internationally best-selling novel *Breasts and Eggs*, a *New York Times* Notable Book of the Year and one of *Time*'s 10 Best Fiction Books of 2020. Her other novels, translated by Sam Bett and David Boyd, include *Heaven* (2021), shortlisted for the 2022 International Booker Prize, and *All the Lovers in the Night* (2022), a finalist for the 2023 National Book Critics Circle Award for fiction.

HITOMI YOSHIO is associate professor of Global Japanese Literary and Cultural Studies at Waseda University. She specializes in modern and contemporary Japanese literature with a focus on women's writing. Her translations include Natsuko Imamura's *This Is Amiko, Do You Copy?* (Pushkin Press, 2023) and Mieko Kawakami's forthcoming short story collection, *Dreams of Love, Etc.*

Embroidery Thread

MIEKO KAWAKAMI
TRANSLATED BY HITOMI YOSHIO

Pain. Masako is in pain. Even though she's never been hit before, she's been in pain for a long, long time. From the outside, the scars aren't visible. But if you could wrap her body in a large piece of white cloth, there'd be a number of purple marks on it, as if on the inside were a bunch of rotting grapes, dripping with juice.

Because of the pandemic, Masako was laid off from her part-time job at the deli. There was nothing she could do about it—it wasn't just her, others too. But she couldn't tell her husband. Whatever the reason, she knew it would only make things worse.

So, Masako leaves the house at nine in the morning as usual and kills time until evening.

She's grateful for the warm weather so she can sit on a bench. Coffee shops are difficult. She has to keep ordering drinks to stay, and what's more, she's afraid of the staff who stare at her. Benches, on the other hand, are much more comfortable. No one pays attention to her, and no one complains when her water bottle is empty.

When her back starts to ache, she stretches and walks to the Uniqlo store, twenty minutes away. She walks through the entire store slowly and thoroughly, and then she moves on to the drugstores. She goes from one store to the next, reading each label and noting the price in her head. Whenever she comes to an intersection, she takes time to watch the traffic lights change color. Then she returns to the bench and eats a rice ball wrapped in plastic.

Her husband, five years older, had drifted from one job to another until he finally gave it all up four years ago to start an izakaya bar, which went out of business this past spring. He was always losing money with the few customers he had, but the business was brought to an abrupt end by the pandemic, leaving behind only debt.

Masako somehow knew that things would have gone wrong with or without the pandemic. Her husband was good-natured and daring enough to think about starting his own izakaya, but he was also a helpless coward. As soon as someone pointed out his ignorance or mistake, he would lose his temper and lash out. He couldn't help hurting others as much as he'd been hurt himself.

Masako didn't know why she was living with this man, or how she came to live with him in the first place. She must have gone through the relationship with open eyes—she just couldn't recall how it all happened.

There were countless times when she felt regret. She felt pain in so many places. But she kept reminding herself that it was because she was weak. She'd never been hit, after all; there was not even a trace of blood. The pain must be her own fault.

So much of what her husband said to her seemed right. *Useless. Incompetent. Why can't you do such a simple thing? Stupid. Bad luck. Totally worthless. You don't understand anything.*

Still, in the early days of living together, Masako felt a contradiction in her husband's endless sermon one night and timidly pointed it out to him. At that moment, he put his fingers around her neck and tore off the necklace, a memento from her late mother, which she'd always kept close. Masako had bought the necklace with her first salary as a gift for her mother, who had raised her single-handedly and couldn't afford any luxuries. Her heart stopped then and there.

Sitting on the bench, Masako hears all kinds of voices. Mothers playing with their small children. Lovers peering into their smartphones. Students chatting away.

"If you get infected, there's no point telling anyone. You'd have to quarantine, of course, but it's better to keep quiet. Think about how your child would get bullied."

"I know, I know. Honestly. You just pretend it's a cold and stay in bed."

The two women look around to see if anyone is listening, but when they see Masako, they ignore her and continue talking. Masako, too, pretends not to hear. It's still only two o'clock. How many hours are there in a lifetime? She'd tried to count them as a child once and came up with a number, but now she couldn't remember it.

The wind blows so strong it sweeps everything upward. Torn pieces of wrapping paper, scattered leaves, plastic bags. They all float away somewhere, somewhere other than here, but no matter how strong the wind blows, Masako's body doesn't move.

"Don't forget to call my brother." She remembers her husband's words. Masako had no siblings. Her mother was dead and she was all alone. Now that her husband had lost his business and had nothing to do but stay home all day, he'd instructed her to call his older brother and ask him for money. "It's better if you do it. Easier for him to help you than me." She stares at her phone screen. *If I tap the number with my finger, he might pick up. But what would I say? How do I bring up such a thing? How much money do I ask for anyway?* "Don't mess it up," her husband had told her. "Just get the money. He owes me big-time, you know. At least I have someone to ask for help. Look at you. There's no one you can depend on, not even one relative or a friend."

She can't get herself to press the call button. When Masako graduated from a vocational school, she couldn't find a job and had to work part-time to make ends meet. She had no money. It's not like she had spent it all. She lived day-to-day, just getting by. She was honest and never cheated anyone. The jobs she held were not complicated, but she worked as hard as she could—in factories, in dry cleaners, in noodle shops. One day led to another, and here she was. She never made her own choices, but she never refused anything either. *Was that a bad thing? Is that where things went wrong?*

"Lucky you. You have it easy." Her husband mocks her when he gets drunk. She recalls his words. Lately, it's been happening a lot—his lectures would last for hours, even an entire night. "You tell me what I'm supposed to do. I'm going crazy. You have it easy, you know. You lived your whole life without using your brain. That's the thing about you women. No responsibilities. Have you ever seen a homeless woman? That says something. Women have it easy."

Maybe he's right, Masako thinks. *I can go out on a walk. I have a house that shelters me from the wind and rain. I'm not injured or bleeding anywhere. I can breathe. There are people in worse situations. People who are suffering more than I am.* Masako thinks about how lucky she is that she has nothing or no one to protect.

It's almost time. Whether she comes home late or early, her husband will be in a bad mood. Masako gets up and walks back the way she came.

Something catches her eye by the side of the road. As Masako approaches, she sees that it's a skein of embroidery thread—new, shiny, and white, with the binding still attached. Someone must have dropped it. Masako stares at it, hesitates for a moment, then picks it up. As she walks, she unravels the thread. She wraps it around her index finger more and more tightly until the circulation stops and her fingertip turns purple. Then she chuckles to herself. *No luck dying with embroidery thread.*

JULIA ALVAREZ has written novels, collections of poems, nonfiction, and numerous books for young readers. Best known for the novels *In the Time of the Butterflies* and *How the García Girls Lost Their Accents,* her most recent work is *Afterlife: A Novel,* and a new picture book for young readers, *Already a Butterfly: A Meditation Story.* The recipient of a National Medal of Arts, Alvarez is one of the founders of Border of Lights, a movement to promote peace and collaboration between Haiti and the Dominican Republic. She lives in Vermont.

Amenorrhea

JULIA ALVAREZ

The page is blank.
The ark caulked shut.
Lazarus won't get up.
My body, meant to signal every month,
goes dark.
My progeny sit
like passengers in a choppy plane,
both engines out,
their doomed heads tucked between their
knees.
Fetal and in position, they tense
as the plane drops down,
an egg with no membrane
woven to catch it.
Month after month
I neither bleed nor bear.
This woman's barrenness
revives the poet's fear—
the line stops here.

DAVE EGGERS is the author
of *The Every* and *A Hologram
for the King,* among other
books. He is the founder of
McSweeney's.

Everyone at Dinner Has a Max von Sydow Story

DAVE EGGERS

Suze, short for Suzette-Joy, had made fettucine Alfredo, and the Larkins, Tim and Frida, were there, on either end of the table because they liked to look at each other by candlelight. The Pulaskis were there, and everyone was glad they had not brought their sullen teenager, Andre, a vacuum of all contentment.

Suze had enhanced everything with candles and cats. The cats, with cream-colored fur and sea-glass eyes, were undersized and underfoot. The candles were everywhere—on the table, on the mantle, on the windowsills. The windows were open an inch on this February night, but everyone was warm and content, happy to see each other after many years apart.

After dinner, someone brought up the new *Dune*, and someone else mentioned the old *Dune*, and then Max von Sydow was conjured and Tim Larkin, who rarely had a good story, said he had a good story about the tall Swedish actor with the bottomless voice and the long, long face.

"I was in London," Tim said, "shopping for a hat," and instantly everyone knew this would be a good story, because no one at the table had ever shopped for a hat, much less in London. "I saw this very tall man in the corner," Tim said, "and at first I mistook him for a coat rack." There was laughter and then anticipation, for so far it was very exotic and magical, the idea of Tim Larkin from Terre Haute, Indiana, in a hat shop in London, with Max von Sydow in the corner looking like a coat rack. No one could guess where this story would go.

It went nowhere. That was it. Tim had been in the hat shop, and Max von Sydow had been in the hat shop, too. Tim said he left the store without buying a hat, and had no idea whether or not Max von Sydow had bought himself a hat, or had even tried one on. The only interesting twist to it all was that von Sydow, while shopping for a hat, had already been *wearing* a hat. "That was an extraordinarily windy week in London," Tim noted, as if that made the story any better, which it did not.

"I have a Max von Sydow story, too," Indira Pulaski said, and no one was surprised. Indira had lived in New York in the nineties, waiting tables in Tribeca, and seemed to have met and served just about everyone. But no one had heard her Max von Sydow story.

"I was in Stockholm," she said, and this produced a brief murmur of astonishment. First a story set in London, now one in Stockholm! The guests around Suze's table thought a bit more highly of themselves than they had when they walked in that night. "You all know how Stockholm is pretty much an archipelago," Indira said, "where you ferry between islands a lot to get to the various parts of the city?"

Half the heads nodded, though no one of the people at that table had been to Stockholm, and no one knew this news about it being an archipelago. If any of them had imagined Stockholm at all, they imagined it like Prague, or Berlin—a landlocked city with electric trams and bright modern shops set inside old stone buildings stained with soot. No one had pictured water, or ferries, or islands, much less an archipelago.

"I was taking the ferry from Gröna Lund," Indira said, "which is this really terrible amusement park on one of the islands. And I saw this man sitting on the upper deck of the ferry, reading a newspaper. He looked like a commuter. But this was a Saturday afternoon, and the ferry was full of drunken idiots coming back from the amusement park. Because it was unusual to see a commuter at that hour and on that day, I looked closer. And that's when I saw that the commuter was Max von Sydow."

There were murmurs of approval, and more sips of sancerre. Because Tim's story had been so brief and without payoff, the guests assumed that was the end of this particular Max von Sydow story. But it was not the end.

"You know how I'll talk to anyone," Indira said, "so I walked across the deck and approached him. And just as my shadow overtook him, he folded his newspaper and looked up, as if he'd been expecting me."

Indira's eyes twinkled. "And then we talked a little about Bergman. I was headed to Bergman's island, and he thought that was interesting. He'd never been there! And then the ferry arrived at his stop, and he got off. You know what he said to me when he left?"

No one knew.

"He said 'Ciao.'"

Murmurs of astonishment and approval overtook the room, and Suze took the opportunity to pour everyone more wine. She hoped that no one cared that she'd forgotten dessert, and hoped her guests would stay past ten, for she'd heard that if guests left before ten, the party was a bad one and the host was boring.

"I have a Max von Sydow story," Charley said, and Suze thrilled, because this would certainly keep everyone past ten, and perhaps ensure that her party leapt from average to extraordinary.

Everyone settled in, for Charley's stories were infrequent and sometimes rambling but occasionally very good.

"I was in LA with my dad," she said, and the faces around the table grimaced sympathetically, for Charley's father had died when she was a child, fourteen years before. "I already knew he was sick. He'd just told me, and I remember having a very adult sense of how much time he had left.

"We were walking somewhere in Culver City. It was a really bland part of town then, mostly industrial buildings, anonymous studios and such. A door opened to one of these buildings, and a man emerged. Immediately my dad said to me, 'That's a Swedish actor named Max von Sydow.' My dad knew the name of every actor, every role. It was a quirk of his. So he quickly listed a bunch of von Sydow's movies I didn't know, because I was ten years old and hadn't seen, you know, *Pelle the Conqueror*.

"We stood there, and I could tell my father had no intention of saying anything to Max von Sydow. My dad was not forward that way. But then the actor looked at us and smiled, and I guess that opened the door for my father. He didn't move, but just said from our respectful distance, 'Thank you, Mr. Von Sydow.'"

Charley's eyes were wet in the candlelight. Half the room held their breath.

"There was something very sweet about how my father said that," she continued. "I remember thinking, right then, that he'd said it in such a nice way. Just flat, plain, simple; he said it in a way that was clear he didn't expect anything in return. I figured that, at best, von Sydow would wave, and then get into the car that was waiting for him. But after my father said his thank-you, von Sydow came to us, and extended his hand to my father, and then bent down and shook my hand, too. It was very formal and grandfatherly. His hand was very old, very bony. Enormous and cold.

254

"Then he stood to his full height, towering over my father, and they talked for a bit about why he was in town. Apparently he was in Culver City to record some voice-overs for a *Ghostbusters* video game. Isn't that funny?"

The guests chattered for a second about this game, if anyone had ever heard of it. Peter had owned it, and confirmed it was real.

"Anyway," Charley continued, "he and my dad talked for a few minutes more, and then von Sydow excused himself. He mussed my hair and told me to be good. He shook my dad's hand again, and got in the car.

"And from then on, I remember having a new peace with everything. My father was dying young and I would be fatherless at ten, but then again, Max von Sydow, this giant of a man, was in Culver City doing a video game voice-over. None of it made any sense."

Charley licked her fingers and doused the closest candle.

"And I drew all my strength from that."

ALLEGRA GOODMAN's novels include *Intuition, The Cookbook Collector, Paradise Park,* and *Kaaterskill Falls* (a National Book Award finalist). Her fiction has appeared in the *New Yorker, Commentary,* and *Ploughshares* and has been anthologized in *The O. Henry Awards* and *Best American Short Stories.* Her latest novel, *Sam,* was published in 2023.

$

ALLEGRA GOODMAN

In this family, you didn't talk about money—not even with euphemisms, the way you spoke of cancer (she is very sick) or feuds (they have been out of touch) or unforgivable behavior (it's not my business). When it came to money, nobody said anything. Dan and Steve were silent even to each other when they inherited equal shares of their mother Jeanne's estate. It was just the way they had been raised. Discussing such matters was rude, and also, somehow, dangerous.

Because of this, the brothers were surprised after Jeanne's death to learn of her many bank accounts and detailed bequests. She left generous sums to the Boston Symphony Orchestra, Jewish Family and Children's Services, and Mount Holyoke, her alma mater. Smaller gifts went to the YMCA in Brighton where she used to swim, and to the Longy School of Music where she had once taught. All good causes she had never mentioned. In her will, Jeanne left her piano to the All Newton Music School, and with some difficulty, her sons arranged this.

Jeanne also stated that her Vuillaume violin was to go to Dan's daughter, Phoebe, who would play it, but she left nothing to Steve's sons. "Well," Steve told his wife, Andrea, "she never liked boys."

After these donations, there wasn't much cash left—but Dan and Steve got the money from Jeanne's house. The big old Tudor in West Newton had sold for a fair amount, and after taxes and broker's fees, Dan and Steve each got a lump sum. A pretty decent lump, but the brothers didn't let it show. In fact, they were just as stressed as they had been before, and the reasons were not hard to guess. Dan was supporting his mother-in-law in memory care, and Steve was unemployed. With a salary, Steve would have felt differently—but Andrea did not make nearly enough to support the family, so they were burning through his inheritance.

Of course, Steve was trying to find work, but after twenty-five years editing composition textbooks, he was highly specialized. He had applied for jobs in publishing, and libraries, and research institutes, and nonprofits—but his skills were old-school, and his habitat had dwindled. His interviews were informational at best.

He was working intermittently with a cheerful tattooed head-hunter named Charlotte who specialized in creatives, as people like Steve were now called. The first time they'd met, Steve said, "I'm not sure I like being an adjective turned into a noun."

"Ha!" said Charlotte. "Good one!"

She was a creative too, a photographer with an unflinching eye. Her portfolio was mostly insects. Extreme close-ups of ants and iridescent flies and horrific praying mantises.

At their first meeting, they had talked about Steve's goals, and he had told her he would do anything, except teach high school.

"Any specific reason?" Charlotte asked.

Where do I begin? he thought, but he said, "I hate kids."

As the months passed, he had tried to think out of the box. He had even considered bookselling. "But those jobs are hard to come by," Charlotte admitted. "Would you consider tutoring, or, like, college counseling?"

"My wife does that," Steve said. "Conflict of interest."

258

$

Charlotte looked puzzled, but Steve explained. "It would cause conflict, because I'm not interested."

After several months of this, Charlotte told Steve, "Honestly, you're overqualified for most of this shit."

"I wonder if it's something else," said Steve. He had been brooding about certain former colleagues who might blackball him. Sworn enemies now alighting on whatever slender opportunities remained in publishing.

"Nah," said Charlotte. "You're a bad demographic."

"Too white," said Steve, but he thought too male.

"Too old," said Charlotte.

Old as he was, Steve tried networking the old-fashioned way. "Are you still in touch with Jeff?" he asked his brother on the phone.

"Jeff who?"

"Rosencrantz."

"Maybe once or twice a year. I think he's in Teaneck."

"And he's still married to Shira, right?"

"Yeah. Why do you ask?"

"Because he's in publishing."

"Really?"

"He's an indie publisher." Steve was standing at the picture window in his living room.

"I thought he was in advertising."

"No, he's got his own publishing house now."

"Wow. What's it called?"

Steve hesitated. Then he said, "Cloverleaf."

"What's that?" said Dan.

"Never mind." Steve gazed at his snowy walk. Andrea was working downstairs, and both the boys were off at Rutgers, so it was up to him to shovel and die of a heart attack. Not to be dramatic, but lately this had been his thinking. He had been out of work so long; he had spent so much time in New Jersey. He would perish in the most suburban way.

"I'll send you his email," Dan told him. "Is that what you want?"

"Maybe," Steve said.

Playwright, actor, beer pong champion, Jeff had been Steve's freshman roommate, and they had been close. It was only after marriage, college, kids, and the implosion of Steve's entire industry that reaching out began to feel humiliating. Steve thought, I cannot do this—but he started writing anyway.

He sat down with a yellow legal pad and drafted a preamble, in which he asked after Jeff and Shira and the whole family. Then fondly he recalled the days at Emerson, and nights at the radio station, WERS. After which he meditated on the passage of time, and the growing up of children.

Once he got all that out of the way, Steve spilled his guts, explaining what he had been through.

Andrea padded up the stairs with her travel mug of coffee because she still behaved like a commuter, even though she had been working in the basement for the past three years. "I think we should probably shovel."

"I'll get to it," growled Steve.

"What's wrong?"

"Nothing." He handed Andrea the yellow pad.

"You're writing to *Jeff*?"

"He's actually successful."

"Huh," said Andrea, as she leafed through the pages of Steve's letter.

"Are you reading?"

$

"At the time I left Hillier-Nelson," Andrea read aloud, *"I felt that the company was chasing new platforms instead of developing ideas, sacrificing the good for the expedient. We were selling our birthright—giving up on books and readers. It was terrible to watch. In fact, it was a tragedy. Even so, despite everything, I still believe that—"* Andrea looked up. "You sound like Anne Frank."

"Keep going."

"Books are not units. Content is not product. Good prose is vital, albeit increasingly rare, and we must resist the constant debasement and cheapening of words, and the thoughts they represent. This is a scared trust." She flipped the page. "When are you going to say you're looking for a job?"

"I don't know if there is a job," said Steve. "I'm reaching out."

"Oh, okay."

"You think it's too much."

She didn't answer.

"You think it's grandiloquent."

"I didn't say that!"

"You don't have to."

She turned the pages, scribed heavily in ballpoint. "This must be three-thousand words!"

"That's your comment?"

"I thought you wanted me to look this over."

"I didn't ask for a word count."

"I wasn't counting!"

"Then tell me what you think."

She kept leafing. "It's heartfelt."

"Heartfelt?" He snatched back his legal pad.

"I didn't mean it pejoratively."

"Oh, you meant it in a *heartfelt* way?"

"Steve!"

"I'm just asking what you think."

"It's too long."

"Fine! I'll cut it."

He said this, but he didn't cut anything. He typed just what he had written—not so much because it was good, but because it was true. *I still believe in art. I still believe in poetry. Cogent prose is the one resource we lack, and yet, clear writing is important as fresh water and clean energy.* He reread these words and sent the email—and then he went out to brave the drifts.

After shoveling the walk and driveway (he did not die) Steve checked his email. Nothing. No reply for several hours. He did not hear back from Jeff all day.

The next morning it snowed again, but just a little. Steve dug out the car for Andrea and touched up the driveway. Once he started, it felt good. He scraped off every bit of ice.

Then he stamped inside, took off his boots, and reread his credo. It was indeed grandiloquent, and it had a typo. Outage where he meant to say outrageous. His message did seem bloated, and he had not, in fact, asked Jeff directly about employment; he'd only suggested meeting sometime for coffee. It was all too long, too weird, and at the same time way too subtle. Jeff wasn't gonna answer this.

But no! That evening, Jeff Rosencrantz wrote back. *Hi Steve! Great to hear from you. Your email came at such a great time. Our little outfit is expanding!*

And lo, Steve woke early Monday morning, and drove to Panera Bread, where Jeff was waiting with his laptop and a stack of books and coffee.

"Hey!" Jeff stood and shook Steve's hand, and clapped him on the shoulder, and he was just as friendly as if no time had passed, although he had no hair left, and he was fifty pounds heavier than he had been in college. "How are you, man?"

"I can't complain," said Steve, although this wasn't true.

"Still writing poetry?"

"A little," Steve said, although this wasn't true either.

"I loved your stuff," Jeff told him.

"Really?"

"I still remember the one about the orange. The one that got all those awards."

Steve nodded, although the poem had been about an apricot. "Just one award."

"Oh, only one!" Jeff said good-naturedly.

Steve went up to the counter where he resisted a vanilla cinnamon roll. "Are you still writing plays?" he asked when he returned with coffee.

"No!" Jeff told him. "Work has been insane. Your message could not have come at a better time. I need good people. Desperately. We have so many books scheduled we cannot keep up."

Steve said, "Well, that's good to hear."

"Yeah, I know you think people aren't reading anymore," said Jeff, "and you're right. They're not. But everyone's writing like crazy. So, for self-publishing—we're riding a wave."

"What happens when it breaks?"

Jeff smiled. "I hear you. But that's just it! There's always another story coming. There is so much creativity out there it's scary. You've seen our website."

"Yes."

"So, you know what we're about."

"Quality."

"Yup. Our books are *beautiful*—and we do them all in-house, soup to nuts—from editing, to cover design, to marketing." Jeff pulled a glossy sample off the stack on the table. "This is a really smart vampire novel. And we're very proud of this. It's a collection of feminist oral histories. And here's a memoir. This guy is an obstetrician, and he's fascinating. He's a brilliant, brilliant guy. We vet all our authors, by the way."

Steve nodded, because he had indeed studied the Cloverleaf site. "They send you a writing sample."

"Right. We only take the most promising."

"But do you find that they're *all* mostly—promising?"

"No! Our potentials send us an excerpt and we do a sample edit on a thousand words and we talk about whether we're a fit. Then we match up author with editor—or writer."

"What's the writer for?" Steve asked uneasily.

"We're soup to nuts," Jeff reminded him.

"So, you not only edit, design, and market books but you . . ."

"Write them! Yeah!" Jeff said.

"Oh wow," said Steve.

"Look, everybody has a story," Jeff said. "But not everybody has the words." He held up the obstetrician's memoir, which was titled *Baby Doc*. "Production is such a small part of what we do. The writing is the most rewarding, and the most time-consuming."

"So that's why you're hiring."

"We need wordsmiths," Jeff said. "Frankly, we need poets, and novelists. Storytellers. People who can take the rough ideas and—"

"Spin straw into gold?" Steve ventured.

Jeff did not take offense. "Exactly!"

At home, Steve sat on the couch, opened his laptop and gazed at his first assignment. "It's a trial balloon," he told Andrea.

"What did they send you?"

Steve read the first paragraphs on his screen. "It looks like a family history of life in the old country."

"Oy. How bad is it?"

Steve read the opening silently. *Our family came from Bukovina in what is now Ukraine. We were descended from rabbis on both sides and naturally we were orthodox Jews (everybody in the village was very religious) and we spoke Yiddish. That was a given. It was a family where everybody loved each other but it was difficult because we were so poor. We had nothing except we had love which is everything. Along with Papa and Mama, there were seven brothers, Mendel, Yussel, Nachum, Dovid, Moisheh, Yitzchok, and Binyomin, and one sister (my grandmother Feygeleh) but at any moment the Tsar's men might come knocking on the door to conscript her brothers for his army after which they might never return. They lived in fear!*

"Well?" Andrea waited for the verdict.

"It's heartfelt."

"Steve!"

But he was reading Jeff's instructions. *So, this needs oomph. Author says it's nonfiction, i.e. don't change characters or incidents.*

Oomph. Steve began walking up and down. He poured himself a drink—but he could not unsee that first paragraph. The pronouns alone. He looked at Andrea and shook his head.

"Okay," Andrea said, but he caught the resignation in her voice, and he knew how hard she worked all day rewriting college essays—or, rather, helping high schoolers find their voices. How was this any worse than what she did? He wanted to share the load. But seven brothers? Mendel and Yussel and . . . Christ.

He stepped outside without his coat and stood in the freezing air. All was still. Only one neighbor was out walking her dog— and they were both elderly. Steve was glad he had shoveled to the pavement.

Do it. Do it, he thought. "Come on!" he shouted, as he did when he played tennis. Dog and neighbor turned around.

Steve waved. Then he retreated into his house, set himself up at the kitchen table, and started typing. *We live in fear. At any moment, the Tsar's men might ride up on their black horses. If they come and ask you for your sons, you cannot refuse. They must ride away to fight in the Tsar's army . . .*

He typed like this for half an hour and then he put the kettle on. *We only eat black bread*, he wrote, remembering something he had read. *Black bread with schmaltz if we are lucky. White bread is a delicacy—and in our village hard to find.* Steve thought for a moment and then he added, *We are always hungry.*

He worked and brewed some tea and worked some more. He looked up and thought about Sir Walter Scott, toiling by hand to pay his debts.

It was midnight when he sent his trial balloon back to Jeff. The house was still, and Andrea was already asleep. Back aching, Steve lay down on the living room floor. He'd done this thing. He had rewritten one thousand words. Maybe it wasn't straw into gold, but it was something.

In the morning, Andrea took her travel mug down to the basement, and Steve took the car in for service, since it was squeaking whenever he turned corners. He set up his laptop in the waiting room and plugged in his earbuds to block the sound on the wall-mounted TV. No response from Jeff—but it had only been nine hours since he sent in his trial balloon.

He watched the news on his computer, while different news played on the television above his head. The three other customers waiting were scrolling on their phones as Steve gazed at the Cloverleaf website. There was an old-fashioned typewriter on the homepage. *Yes, we publish first-time writers! Yes, we publish poetry.*

"Steve? Steve Rubinstein?"

It was the Subaru service person, Gary, coming to find him. "Yes!" Steve assumed his car was ready, but Gary knelt by his chair instead.

"So, we've got some issues," he said in a low voice, as though he was protecting the car's privacy.

"What kind of issues?"

Gary looked at him with regret and sympathy. "Steering column."

"What do you mean?"

"It's very unusual, but your steering column is cracked."

"How did that happen?"

"It's hard to say."

"How much would it be?"

Gary showed him the estimate on his diagnostic worksheet. "This includes parts and labor."

"Is it something we would have to do now?" Steve asked.

"Well frankly," said Gary, "at this point you might want to consider buying another vehicle."

Uh huh, thought Steve. With what? With your savings. With whatever you have left. Keep eating at it. Keep spending. And he sensed his mother's disapproval, her quick appraisal. Jeanne had always been quick. He said, "I don't want to buy another car."

"Understood," said Gary.

He was waiting for a decision, and Steve was staring at the enormous price of the repair. Wait, he thought. Wait, let me think! But just then his phone lit up. It was Jeff! A text! U NAILED it. sending contract asap

Steve felt a rush of affirmation, celebration. Pure adrenaline. "Let's do it!" he told Gary. "Let's fix this thing!"

"All *right!*" said Gary, springing to his feet.

Seven hours and a loaner car later, Steve drove home with his new steering column, and he felt efficient, productive. Solvent. No longer spending his inheritance, counting down to bankruptcy. He thought of texting Charlotte the headhunter. Hey, I did find employment despite my advanced age, in case you were wondering.

"I got it," he told Andrea, who had finished work and was now lying on the couch.

"What?" She sat up. "Amazing!"

"They're sending me a contract."

"For how much?"

"I mean, I don't know the details."

"I was just wondering what kind of job it is. Like do you get paid by the project, or do you get a salary?"

"I said I don't *know* yet!"

"You didn't even ask, did you?"

"They are very successful." Steve thumped into the kitchen and opened the refrigerator. With the kids gone, the shelves were almost bare. He saw condiments and leftovers and Greek yogurts.

"Don't stand there with the door open," Andrea said.

He closed it but he said, "I'm hungry." And he wanted to go out. He wanted a proper restaurant-cooked meal. Because he had done this. He had done this thing, and maybe it wasn't going to be a lot of money. Maybe it wasn't going to be his old salary, but it was work. It was living by his wits.

But he didn't want to jinx himself. He drove to the store for salmon and broccoli and cooked dinner. It was one of those sheet-pan recipes where you gave the broccoli a head start, and then you glazed the fish with a mix of soy sauce, mustard, and brown sugar, and you broiled everything together and it came out great.

$

Steve's father, Irving, had never cooked a meal in his life. He had left it all to Jeanne, who had been pretty angry.

But preparing food was not so bad. Neither was ghostwriting. It just took patience—and ingenuity.

"I actually think I did a pretty good job," Steve told Andrea as they sat together at the kitchen table.

"It's delicious," she said.

"I mean the memoir," he told her. "I think I captured the family's fear."

"What's that?" said Andrea.

His phone was buzzing. A text from Jeff. Call me?

"Uh oh." Steve's mood changed instantly.

"What happened?"

"Not good."

"You don't know that."

"Yes, I do know. Something's wrong." He called back and then he started pacing the living room while Jeff's phone rang.

"Steve!" Jeff said, as though everything was fine.

"Hi!" Steve answered, trying to match Jeff's tone.

"So, this is just a bump in the road."

Instantly, Steve thought, you charlatan, you con artist. You aren't going to pay me! But he said, "What is it?"

"The author," Jeff said, and suddenly he sounded like the Subaru serviceperson, Gary. "She has a few issues."

Steve's lower back tightened. "What do you mean?"

"Okay, listen. First of all, I want to reassure you this is very normal. It's just some questions. And they are all totally doable! The author wants to know why it is in the present tense, when this book happened in the past."

"It's the historical present!" said Steve.

"*I* know that, and *you* know that," Jeff said. "Next, she wants to know, why is it so harsh?"

"Because they were living in the shtetl in poverty."

"Yeah, but she says she wants the tone to be more cozy."

"*Cozy?*" Steve glanced at Andrea in the kitchen. "This is supposed to be nonfiction."

"I'm just talking about tone. She wants it sweet and cozy."

"Like sepia-toned, rose-colored glasses?"

"Exactly."

"Nonfiction, but not real either?"

"Bingo."

"Who is this person?"

"She's the author," Jeff said, "and this is what she wants."

How incredibly simple, Steve thought. How straightforward. No need for criticism. No need for theory. The author has knowable intentions—in case you're wondering. But then he thought, what about me? "I gave it my best shot," he told Jeff.

"Hey, this isn't the end!" Jeff said. "This is just the beginning!"

"You want me to rework this?"

"It's just tone," said Jeff. "It's rounding a few edges."

"What I did was good," Steve declared.

"No question," Jeff said. "But I don't have to tell you—there are a million ways to write a story."

Steve lay on the floor for his gentle back exercises. He lifted one leg just a few inches. Then the other.

"What did you decide?" Andrea was gazing down at him.

"You heard what I said."

"You'd think about it?" Her eyes looked bigger from this perspective.

"I'll find something else. I'll contact Charlotte and ask about switching to photography."

"Don't be that way," said Andrea.

"Don't look down on me."

"Fine!" She backed off, hurt.

Immediately, he sat up. "It was a joke!"

"You know what?" she said.

"Yes," he told her. "I know. I know. I know." Because he was not funny. He was not positive. His jokes sucked, as the kids would say. And in fact, he missed the kids, his sons who were big and loud with muddy cleats. Unlike his mother, Steve liked boys—okay he liked his own. Without them his house was deadly still. He could hear the slow leak of his line of credit.

"There are lots of things you can do," said Andrea.

"Yup." He sat up gingerly and then he stood on his own two feet. "There are a million ways to tell a story."

He drove to Joe's, which was an excellent bar, and he sat himself down at a nice table and set up his laptop and ordered a Rob Roy. "L'Chaim." He toasted Sir Walter and drank it up. He ordered another, and he began to feel cozy.

"Mama, mama," cried little Feygeleh, "I see horses."

"What horses? Let me see!" Mama held Feygeleh tight and together they looked out the small window of their little house.

The horses were black. The men were tall and grim. The Tsar's Cossacks! They were riding through the village!

"Oy veyismere, what will we do?" Mama whispered. "Here we are all alone while Papa and your brothers are at shul."

The horses passed the house and swept through the village like a wind, but Feygeleh began to cry. "Don't cry, little one," Mama said. "We will clean the house and make our Shabbos meal and tonight we will have white bread!"

Now, Mama took out her big broom, and Feygeleh took out her little broom and together they swept the floor. Then Mama took out her big bowl and Feygeleh took out her little bowl and together they kneaded challah. They braided a big loaf for Mama

*and a little loaf for Feygeleh. Soon the little house was filled with
the scent of baking bread.*

"Can I get you something else?" asked Steve's waiter, Jayden.

"Absolutely," Steve said.

"You're workin' it," Jayden observed.

"I'm in a state of flow."

Steve wrote until the bar closed, and then he drove carefully
to his own cozy house. The lights were off. Andrea had gone to
sleep, but she had cleaned the kitchen, and he sat down at the
table, and he reread his work, and then he wrote even more. He
wrote about the Shabbos candles shining. *They were shining on
all the faces of the family. Papa and Mama and all the brothers
and little Feygeleh. They shone in the window, and they shone
on falling snow.*

Toward dawn, the kitchen light flicked on, and he saw Andrea
standing in the doorway. "Steve?" She was wearing her pajamas
and her thick robe covered with stars.

"I'm a genius," he told her. "I am Laura Ingalls Wilder and
Fiddler on the Roof and *Dubliners* and Joan Nathan rolled into
one." He held up a cookbook Andrea's mom had given them
years ago. It was called *The Children's Jewish Holiday Kitchen.*

"Listen." Andrea sat down next to him. "This isn't worth it.
This is not the job for you."

"I was born for this job." Steve pushed his laptop toward her.

She sat there huddled in her robe and she began to read. "Oh
gosh," she said.

"What? Doesn't it scream rose-colored sepia glasses?"

She just shook her head at him. "I mean you can't send it,
but . . ."

"I already did."

And the strange thing was he did not regret it, not even later
in the cold light of morning. He felt creative. He felt free. He loved

$

his shtetl family. Their rosy cheeks, their flickering candles. Their warmth and their dirt floors. He loved protecting them from the Tsar's army. He was the writer, after all. He could do that, even if history did not. Was it art? Not at all. Was it satisfying? Totally. It was like assembling an entire breakfront with an Allen wrench.

However, he did not hear from Jeff all day, or the next day either. Two more days passed, and Steve began to understand something. The author might not find his work so charming. She might detect the tiniest bit of fakery and mania and drunkenness. Mockery! Clearly, this was the one thing you could not do. This was the unspoken rule. You had to take your author seriously.

He emailed Jeff—*just checking in!* No answer. He wrote again. *You know Jeff, I don't have time to write entire books on spec. If this is how you treat your so-called writers*—but he did not send that one.

Five full days passed. Andrea said, "Look, it's a blessing in disguise."

Steve set up a phone call with Charlotte to explore new options. "I'm ready to think out of the box," he said.

"Teaching?" she asked delicately.

"Bring it on."

"Even though you hate kids?"

"I don't hate them."

A moment of surprised silence. "Really?"

"It's adults I hate. It's just humanity."

"Okay cool!" said Charlotte. "I'll set you up with Emily."

"Another Brontë?"

"She does the private high schools."

"Only private?"

"I mean you'd have to get certified to apply to public. It's not too late to look into that!"

"Nah," said Steve. "I just want to start." He would teach American literature. He would take the veil, retreating to the classroom, which was practically the only place you could talk about poetry. Did he really like kids apart from his own? No. But maybe he would change a life or two. Maybe he would be the one his students remembered and looked back upon. Strict but fair. Tough but kind. Super smart (a little tragic). Weren't the best ones a little bit forbidding? He remembered his own English teacher, Mr. Spector, who had written his master's thesis on the works of Thomas Hardy. Maybe Steve would wear a tie.

"I'm going to do it," he told Andrea that night.

"You'd have to coach something," she said doubtfully. "They always make you do an extracurricular at these prep schools."

"Literary magazine."

"And you'd have to be . . ."

"Sensitive? Politically correct? What are you talking about?" said Steve, who had edited the Hillier-Nelson anthology of essays by women of color. "Diversity's my middle name."

He slept well and woke refreshed. Even as his coffee brewed, he sat down with his computer to rework his resume—and that was when he saw Jeff's message with two attachments. One was a contract. The other was the complete 352-page manuscript of GRANDMA FEYGELEH: A MEMOIR. Steve! Sorry about the delay! Author had cataract surgery, but we are good to go!

"Jeff?" Steve said when he reached his old friend on the phone.

"Hey!"

"I assumed when I didn't hear from you—"

"No, no, no. I'm sorry this took so long! I'm totally behind."

"She liked it?"

"LOVED. She is ecstatic. She says it's exactly what she was dreaming of."

"I'm not sure I can keep this shit up for three hundred pages."

"You're too modest," Jeff said.

"Listen, I'm starting a full-time job soon," Steve said.

"Not a problem! We are totally flexible. That's the beauty of this line of work."

Steve gazed at his computer with both memoir and contract on his screen. The contract to write the whole book was for almost exactly as much as his car repair. "I don't think I can commit just now."

"Take your time," said Jeff. "Just take a day or two! Meanwhile, I'll put you in touch with Ruth."

"Who's Ruth?"

"Your author. She's delightful. She's eighty-six and smart as hell."

"I just don't know if I can spread myself so thin," said Steve. What he meant by that was oy vey, how are you suggesting such a paltry sum of money for this kind of aggravation?

But Jeff did not take the hint. "It doesn't have to be either-or."

"Well," Steve countered.

"It can be both-*and*."

"Never say die," Steve said.

"Exactly. And here's the thing to remember. There's a lot more where this came from."

The waves, Steve thought. The stories rolling endlessly.

He should be fixing Subarus. He should have gone into insurance like his brother—but no, he had become a poet, contemplating different kinds of loss.

Not a problem! He could be a poet still. He could teach and he could write—poetry and prose. He could change lives and pay bills and cry out from the depths of his soul. Both and! Both and! Nobody was stopping him. Nothing was getting in his way.

Love List

MATT SUMELL

1. Helping turtles cross the street
2. Cleaning my shoes on escalator bristles
3. Running my hands on the clothes hanging in department stores
4. Breaking the little plastic thing holding new socks together
5. Taking my socks off in bed with my big toe
6. Pushing down all four bubble things on fountain soda lids (cola, diet, root beer, other)
7. Cracking everything on my body that's crackable
8. To-do list cross-outs
9. The free mini OJ containers that come with deli breakfast sandwiches
10. Spinning a dog on a linoleum floor
11. Shouting out random numbers when people are counting
12. Found money in pockets and dryers
13. Kicking pine cones
14. Kicking over standing objects on sidewalks (paper cups, soda cans, etc.)
15. Driving forward to get out of a parking spot
16. Homemade Halloween costumes
17. Poking holes in the plastic wrap around a new case of water
18. Poking packages of meat at the grocery store
19. Popping Snapple caps
20. Opening a new can of tennis balls
21. Making spiders less scary by naming them Jeff, Greg, and Denise
22. The cool side of the pillow
23. Controlling my own temperature in the car (heat on feet, windows open)
24. Peeling glue off my hand

25. Peeling the plastic off a new phone screen
26. Pushing down sprinkler heads
27. Getting packages in the mail
28. Getting a haircut while high
29. Spraying dirt off stuff with a hose
30. The micro mist when peeling an orange
31. The rattle of the ball bearing in a spray paint can
32. The sound of car tires on a wet road
33. Strangers returning lost wallets
34. Wiping dogs' eye boogers off
35. The smell of a hardware store
36. The smell of a new shower curtain/swim toy/tire shop
37. The smell of fresh cut grass
38. The smell of concrete/dirt after it rains
39. The smell of laundered clothes that dried on a line outside
40. The smell of gasoline
41. Gasoline rainbows
42. Rainbow sprinkles
43. The very end or tip of an ice cream cone
44. Small spoons
45. Pretty girls in dresses with pockets on bikes with baskets
46. When waitresses call me darlin'
47. When scissors glide
48. When the odometer hits a large round number
49. When dogs cross their paws
50. Dogs following a patch of sun
51. Lady chefs
52. Cracking into creme brûlée
53. Car eating
54. Clean car interiors
55. Crushing chocolate Easter bunny heads
56. Stovetop popcorn in a brown paper bag with salt and nutritional yeast
57. Taking the paper wads out of new shoes
58. Sliding down a wooden hallway with socks on
59. Crushed ice
60. The imaginary guy running next to the car
61. The matrix-like sound of racquetball
62. Watching lizards do push-ups
63. Watching chonky bumblebees fly stupid

64. Watching people struggle not to fall asleep
65. Watching raindrops race on the windshield
66. Watching a drop of water dance around a frying pan
67. Watching animals chew
68. Lightning bugs
69. Counting rabbits on Ocean Parkway
70. Hand-sharpening pencils
71. Riding a bicycle on a warm night
72. Swimming in the rain
73. Having correct change
74. Wiffle ball
75. Lighting and blowing out matches
76. Shit-talking flies I'm about to murder: "Shouldn't've come in here, bro."
77. Right turns
78. Gerbera daisies (long vase life and add color to any room or garden)
79. Burnt Cheez-Its
80. Beer in the shower
81. Movie previews
82. Right earbud in right ear, left in left
83. Getting off an airplane
84. Hotel living
85. Waking up to snow
86. Warm shaving cream on my neck at the barbershop
87. Messing with sleeping dogs
88. The wipe-wash feature
89. Vinyl record crackling sound
90. Croutons
91. New York pretzels
92. A boat on the Great South Bay
93. Mallard ducks
94. Peeing outside
95. Stepping on dry leaves
96. Hot sand/cold sand
97. Mispronouncing words on purpose
98. Throwing spikey tree seeds at people
99. Classic cars
100. Old motorcycles
101. Finding a Canadian coin in loose change
102. Howard Stern on the commute to work

103. No-work Sundays
104. Eggs over medium
105. Heated towels
106. Going through an automatic car wash stoned
107. Dog zoomies

LACY M. JOHNSON is a
Houston-based professor,
curator, activist, and is the
author of *The Reckonings*
and *The Other Side*—both
National Book Critics Circle
Award finalists—and *Trespasses*. She is editor, with
the designer Cheryl Beckett,
of *More City Than Water:
A Houston Flood Atlas*. She
teaches creative nonfiction
at Rice University and is
the founding director of the
Houston Flood Museum.

The Creek, the Wind, the Holly

LACY M. JOHNSON

L et's begin with a memory: it is winter and light drains from the forests and fields and the pasture—the movement and color freeze into variations of dull brown-gray. It is cold, so cold that the grass crunches under my feet on my way to the barn. Even the sound of the world is arrested in a dull gray blur. I hear only the noises I make: my feet in the snow, my breath in front of my face. I make a game of trying to see in all that sameness something else: the persistent green of a pine tree; the occasional orange of a sunset behind the cover of gray clouds. The hardest color to find is red: the taillights on my father's truck and the flag on our mailbox at the end of the driveway. What I really want to see is a berry, a bud, a wing flapping loud and bright as a siren. The whole time I do my chores I scan the pasture, the hedgerow, the edge of the forest. My eyes are hungry for it.

If I look long enough, stand still as stone, a rabbit might emerge from under a brush pile, or a deer might step into the open pasture, followed by her tentative fawns. I might hear the cry of a hawk, or crows cawing in warning, or just after the light fades, owls calling to one another as they begin hunting from the trees. In wintertime, I never wander past the barn, or into the pasture, or down to the pond. I might walk down the hill as far as the rabbit hutch, where I can see the tracks of one of the barn cats out hunting birds. I never go into the forest, though I sometimes follow the steps my father has left in the snow to the trees he's felled on the edge. I look for the thin chips of wood splayed on the ground, the axe marks he left on the stumps. The tree rings tell me a story about the good years and bad, how the present holds all the moments of the past, maybe even exists inside them.

One evening, just after my father has come home from work and my mother is inside getting dinner on the table, I am in the barn putting out fresh hay for the horses. They huddle together under the warm red light. I look from the steam that rises from their backs to the barbed wire, the bald strip of ground by the stock tank where they like to prance and nibble each others' flanks; I look to the tangle of branches along the property line, and then—a white tuft of ear hair, a tawny patch of forehead, a wet black nose. The shoulders come up higher than our bird dogs, the legs are more gangly, and the whole body moves along a seam between the grasses. The body is close enough to smell: a little like pepper and souring meat. The wind shifts and the eyes turn to look right at me: bundled in my hat and gloves and my sister's old coat and so terrified I hold my breath, though I have no reason to be. A long moment passes, both of us frozen, until I finally let my held breath go. A cloud escapes my lips, and when it clears, as quickly and quietly as it appeared, he is gone.

There's a photograph in an album somewhere of the old station wagon my parents used to drive, parked in a canyon carved between walls of towering snow. It's one of my favorite pictures because I have never seen snow like that in all my life, though my mother told me there used to be storms like that before I was born—that they were awful and beautiful and that she spent them freezing and terrified.

To me, snow means waking up to a thick white blanket that turns the ground and trees and even the roof of the barn into a source of light. It means pulling on coats and boots and gloves, and tumbling out the garage door into drifts large enough my sisters and I can dig holes underneath and crawl inside. Our mother watches us from the window. To her, snow means having to walk to the outhouse in the dark dead of winter, milk cows freezing in blizzards, and one blizzard so bad she had to cover the dining room table with a blanket and pull a mattress underneath, huddling together with my older sister so they could get warm enough to sleep.

In these winter memories, my father has already left for work, shoveling his truck out before anyone is out of bed, leaving a pile of snow clods and deep tire tracks down the driveway. He is both a farmer and an engineer, though I'm not sure which is his true vocation. He comes from a long line of farmers—at least seven generations, same as my mother—and from them he inherited pride in his work, a sense of belonging, a belief that working the land makes it your own. I inherited pride too—too much of it, he said. My mother tried many different jobs, though her occupation was pessimist; from her I inherited my belief that expecting the worst might actually prepare you for it.

The photograph of the station wagon in the snow canyon was under a cellophane sheet on one of the last pages of an album stacked among many in the corner of my grandmother's living room—photographs all the way back to the blur of strangers in horse-drawn buggies, the farmhands in their overalls squinting into the sun: all these people I'll never know, whose names I can't remember, whose choices shape mine like ghosts: to clear the land, to plant hay, to raise cattle, to be buried in the cemetery just up the road, to stay and keep staying. Photos of the one-room schoolhouse just around the bend, the children dressed for church and standing hand in hand. Somehow the people in the faded color photos—my father with his siblings, grown but young and sunburnt and smiling—seem more distant, though even as I hold their photos in my lap I hear their voices echoing through the house. There is an ease in their laughter, in the rhythm of their conversation that I never get to see for myself.

In these albums, my father is a man who smiles and laughs, who leans back in a chair to listen to the other side of a conversation. I have always known him as a man who leaves for work before I wake up and who comes home when it is time for dinner. He is a stranger who tells me he loves me every night before I go to bed.

Sometimes, when I am out walking in the field, I hear the ring of his shotgun, the echo of his voice calling the dogs as they flush a covey of quail. He comes back from the hunt with an armful of birds that my mother cleans and roasts in a pan. The table is set with her good plates; we sit and bow our heads for grace. My father thanks God for the food on our table and the clothes on our backs; he asks God to watch over us, to give him strength. The tiny bodies lie cross-legged on the plates. My mother warns us to be careful of the buckshot, to not chew too hard; she wouldn't want anyone to break a tooth. In the morning, out the back door, I find a pile in the snow: guts and skin and feathers.

Winter is a season of these surprises, of coming outside to find a deer carcass slashed from neck to navel, the entire torso made into a gaping wound, of my father and uncles going off into the woods before sunrise and staying gone until the late afternoon. Maybe they have something to prove. I have strict instructions:

286

to stay out of the forest, to stay by the house or inside it, to stay off the phone and the television; to answer when I hear some-one calling. My mother and aunts sit around the table in the dining room drinking pot after pot of Folgers, doing nothing but visiting. Sometimes the women let me stay upstairs, sitting in front of the couch on the floor, holding those albums in my lap. There are the faded color photographs of my father in a collared shirt, visiting from college, maybe, his arm around my mother: his young bride. Usually she shoos me downstairs, where I join my cousins and sisters pretending to be pirates or lions or dogs, singing and crawling around in circles, the red dye of the carpet rubbing off on our knees. When the men come home, their moods take the shape of antlers—each has forks and burrs and beams. They string the body up by the feet and let it swing from a tree.

Behind my grandmother's house stands a shed from which kittens emerge every spring. Behind that, a barn where my grand-mother keeps what remains of the farming equipment, a few saddles, and a riding kit for the horses. Weeds grow up around a decaying wooden cattle chute, the fence in which they were corralled, a corn silo that is empty but which I am forbidden to climb. A barbed wire fence keeps me out of the pasture; a swinging gate lets me inside. The pasture slopes down toward the woods and a small creek. I have just the slightest memory of the water's edge, the branches all tangled and covered in thorns. There is a tiny clearing where moss covers the ground; touching it makes a puddle in the shape of my fingers and hands and feet.

Spring has many wonders, but winter comes with its own kind, when the colors of the world fade and settle into browns and grays, or sometimes a brilliant, blinding white. The world I know recedes and another emerges out from behind: cardi-nals arrive to take sunflower seeds from the feeder outside my parents' bedroom window, the light glints off the metal roof of the barn—even the red door on the barn down the road becomes a kind of wonder. Suddenly the whole building seems to shudder in the wind before leaning into it: a recommitment to its weight, position, burden.

Both of my parents withdraw from my memory around this time. My father always at the power plant, where engineers like him burn coal to make the electricity that powers the lights, the kitchen stove, the radio in my bedroom; my mother, too, always leaving or about to return. I have one long memory of her streaking past, brilliantly perfumed, pulling on a jacket. She plants a kiss on my cheek, closes the door. I hear the engine start, the tires popping gravel down the driveway.

With both of them gone, nothing stops me from going into their room. I use their toilet and wash my hands in their sink. I try on my mother's jewelry, her lipstick. I look in their closet, find my mother's stash of cinnamon bears in a white paper bag. My father's shirts hang there; a few sweaters are neatly folded in his great uncle's dresser. My father's socks are in the drawer, his ChapStick in a dish with some pennies. There is hardly anything of him here.

Frost has formed all around the edges of their bedroom window: ferns and flowers that twist around and into themselves; out in the pasture grass grows crystal fur. Birds come to the feeder: a red cardinal, its pale, crested mate, a tiny dark-eyed junco, an occasional goldfinch. Time feels frozen and still: the birds at the feeder, the light on the barn, the expansiveness of the place and my time in it, as if all of this might go on forever. Thinking of that moment now, I feel a little chill: the shiver of a long gone feeling longing to return.

* * *

Maybe because farming is too much work, or because my parents don't want to do it, one day they sell the farm and move us to a house in town. There isn't a room for my older sister in the new house, so she never lives in it, though my parents each have separate rooms: my mom fills hers with craft supplies, a sewing table, skeins of yarn, spools of thread, piles and piles of fabric. My father has the living room, control of the television, his own personal recliner no one is supposed to sit in, even when he isn't there. When he is there, he puts on a golf tournament or the news or reruns of *M*A*S*H*, and sleeps in his chair until someone tries to take the remote from under his hand and he startles awake. Or sometimes he is already awake, eyes open and watching intently. These are the moments I try to talk to him, to tell him about my plans for the future, or to ask him about his own. He nods and blinks and seems to be listening but when I wait for him to respond he goes on blinking and watching the television. I say DAD loudly to get his attention. He startles, as if seeing me for the first time. "What?" he asks, a little surprised. I don't repeat myself. I leave the room, saying "never mind."

After I move away, and my younger sister moves away, my parents sell the house and each of them moves somewhere new. I never again sit in my grandmother's living room with albums in my lap, or climb the silo and look inside even though it is forbidden. The snowstorms stop coming, too. Or when they do come, they are not the same. I move farther and farther away and it is warmer each time I return. I can't even remember the last time I saw frozen grass, or an upside-down forest, or a snowdrift in a pasture. Now when I visit it's warm, even in winter.

My father and I don't talk about these changes. He cannot see them, or he refuses to. This is just one of the many unsayable things between us—like how he had wanted to be a father to at least one son but had only daughters, and how I in particular

289

have been a disappointing one. Or how it seemed he was always somewhere else and left before I arrived, how I've learned so much about him through a study of what he left behind. Now there are so many unsayable things between us that we do not speak at all.

L et's end with another memory: it is winter still but the light has started changing. The snow melts enough for me to follow a trail of green shoots through the pasture to the creek bottom, keeping my right shoulder to the fence, walking along the creek, all the way up to the culvert that passes under the road. I smell it before I see it: the tawny coat, the gray tail with its black tip, and all along one side of its body a shock of glistening red. He is dead: hit by a car or shot by a gun. These are the only witnesses: the water in the creek, the wind in the trees, and the bush by the drainage pipe with new glossy leaves. It has the reddest berries I've ever seen.

BARRY LOPEZ is the author of three collections of essays, including *Horizon*; several story collections; *Arctic Dreams*, for which he received the National Book Award; *Of Wolves and Men*, a National Book Award finalist; and *Crow and Weasel*, a novella-length fable. He contributed regularly to both American and foreign journals and traveled to more than seventy countries to conduct research. He was the recipient of fellowships from the Guggenheim, Lannan, and National Science Foundations and was honored by a number of institutions for his literary, humanitarian, and environmental work. He died in 2020. A final book of essays, *Embrace Fearlessly the Burning World*, was published in 2022.

A Short Manifesto

BARRY LOPEZ

Port Townsend, Washington, July 13, 1984

In our dealings with each other and with the natural world
we should cultivate an atmosphere of dignity and respect.

With regard to the land, we should defer to principles
of mutual obligation and courtesy. The power of the land is innate.
Its value, if it must be assigned, is deeper and more subtle than we know.
Its achievement does not require our permission,
nor does it depend upon our compliance.

We must announce that the economic dimensions of our
national problems are not paramount, that our physical
and spiritual well-being are of more enduring concern.

We must agree that among the greatest of wrongs we can effect
is to directly intervene in the process of biological evolution.
As heinous must be considered the manufacture
and deployment of nuclear weapons. These weapons
promise to incinerate our dignity utterly.

We need to discover that our grace resides in our generosity,
and our wisdom in a greater courtesy toward the mystery that contains us.

Contributor Notes

Ghaith Abdul-Ahad is an Iraqi journalist. Born in Baghdad in 1975, he trained as an architect before he was conscripted into Saddam Hussein's army, which he deserted. Soon after US-led coalition forces took control of Baghdad in April 2003, he began writing for the *Guardian*. He has won numerous awards, including the British Press Awards' Foreign Reporter of the Year and two News and Documentary Emmy Awards. *A Stranger in Your Own City*, his debut nonfiction chronicle of Iraq, was published in 2023.

Julia Alvarez has written novels, collections of poems, nonfiction, and numerous books for young readers. Best known for the novels *In the Time of the Butterflies* and *How the García Girls Lost Their Accents*, her most recent work is *Afterlife: A Novel*, and a new picture book for young readers, *Already a Butterfly: A Meditation Story*. The recipient of a National Medal of Arts, Alvarez is one of the founders of Border of Lights, a movement to promote peace and collaboration between Haiti and the Dominican Republic. She lives in Vermont.

Hannah Lillith Assadi is the author of *Sonora*, which received the Rosenthal Family Foundation Award from the American Academy of Arts and Letters and was a finalist for the PEN/Robert W. Bingham Prize, and *The Stars Are Not Yet Bells*, named a best book of 2022 by the *New Yorker* and NPR. In 2018, she was a National Book Foundation 5 Under 35 Honoree.

Lana Bastašić is a Yugoslav-born writer. She majored in English and holds a master's degree in cultural studies. She has published three collections of short stories, one book of children's stories, and one of poetry. Her debut novel, *Catch the Rabbit*, was short-listed for the 2019 NIN Award in Serbia and was awarded the 2020 European Union Prize for Literature.

Wendy Chen is the author of the poetry collection *Unearthings* and the novel *Their Divine Fires*, forthcoming from Algonquin Books. Her translations of Li Qingzhao's poems are also forthcoming from Farrar, Straus and Giroux in a collection titled *The Magpie at Night*. She is the editor of *Figure 1* and associate editor-in-chief of *Tupelo Quarterly*.

Sandra Cisneros is a poet, short story writer, novelist, and essayist whose work explores the lives of the working class. Her novel *The House on Mango Street* has sold over seven million copies, has been translated into over twenty-five languages, and is required reading in elementary schools, high schools, and universities across the nation. Her numerous awards include a MacArthur Fellowship, the PEN/Nabokov Award for International Literature, the National Medal of Arts, and the Ruth Lilly Poetry Prize. A new collection of poems, *Woman Without Shame*, her first in twenty-eight years, was published by Knopf in 2022. Cisneros is a dual citizen of the United States and Mexico. As a single woman, she chose to have books instead of children. She earns her living by her pen.

Kelsey Day is a poet from southern Appalachia. Their work has been nominated for the Pushcart Prize, the Penrose Poetry Prize, and Best of the Net. Their next poetry project, *Field Notes from the Anthropocene*, is a collection that explores the intersections of queerness, decay, and environmental violence in the rural south.

Dave Eggers is the author of *The Every* and *A Hologram for the King*, among other books. He is the founder of *McSweeney's*.

Omar El Akkad is a journalist and author based in Portland, Oregon. His first novel, *American War*, is an international bestseller and has been translated into more than a dozen languages. His second novel, *What Strange Paradise*, won the Giller Prize in Canada.

Sara Elkamel is a poet, journalist, and translator living between Cairo and New York City. She holds an MA in arts journalism from Columbia University and an MFA in poetry from New York University. Her poems have appeared in *Poetry* magazine, the *Yale Review*, *Gulf Coast*, *Ploughshares*, and the *Cincinnati Review*, among other publications. She is the author of the chapbook *Field of No Justice* (African Poetry Book Fund & Akashic Books, 2021).

Louise Erdrich, a member of the Turtle Mountain Band of Chippewa, is the author of many novels as well as volumes of poetry, children's books, and a memoir of early motherhood. Her novel *The Round House* won the National Book Award for Fiction. *Love Medicine* and *LaRose* received the National Book Critics Circle

Award for Fiction. Erdrich lives in Minnesota with her daughters and is the owner of Birchbark Books, a small independent bookstore. Her recent novel, *The Night Watchman*, won the Pulitzer Prize.

Allegra Goodman's novels include *Intuition*, *The Cookbook Collector*, *Paradise Park*, and *Kaaterskill Falls* (a National Book Award finalist). Her fiction has appeared in the *New Yorker*, *Commentary*, and *Ploughshares* and has been anthologized in *The O. Henry Awards* and *Best American Short Stories*. Her latest novel, *Sam*, was published in 2023.

A. Kendra Greene began her museum career marrying text to the exhibition wall, painstakingly, character by character, each vinyl letter trembling at the point of a bone folder—and then fixed. Her first book, *The Museum of Whales You Will Never See*, was published by Penguin Books.

Since retiring from her academic post, **Celia Hawkesworth** has been working as a freelance translator and has to date published over forty titles. She has won several awards including the Oxford Weidenfeld Translation Prize in 2019 for her translation of Ivo Andrić's *Omer Pasha Latas*. Her translation of Daša Drndić's *EEG* won the Best Translated Book Award in 2020 and the AATSEEL Best Literary Translation Prize in 2021.

Aleksandar Hemon is the author of *The Lazarus Project*, which was a finalist for the National Book Award and a *New York Times* bestseller, as well as *The Question of Bruno*, *Nowhere Man*, *Love and Obstacles*, *The Book of My Lives*, *The Making of Zombie Wars*, and *My Parents*. He received a MacArthur award, cowrote the script for *The Matrix Resurrections*, and produces music as Cielo Hemon. He teaches at Princeton University. His latest novel, *The World and All That It Holds*, was published in 2023.

Andrew Holleran's first novel, *Dancer from the Dance*, was published in 1978. He is also the author of the novels *Nights in Aruba* and *The Beauty of Men*; a book of essays, *Ground Zero* (reissued as *Chronicle of a Plague, Revisited*); a collection of short stories, *In September, the Light Changes*; and a novella, *Grief*. In 2022 he published a new novel, *The Kingdom of Sand*.

Tania James is the author of *Atlas of Unknowns, Aerogrammes*, and *The Tusk That Did the Damage*, which was shortlisted for the Dylan Thomas Prize and longlisted for the Financial Times Oppenheimer Fund Emerging Voices Award. Her most recent novel, *Loot*, was published by Alfred A Knopf in 2023.

Honorée Fanonne Jeffers is a fiction writer, poet, and essayist. She is the author of six books, including the National Book Critics Circle Award for Fiction winner *The Love Songs of W.E.B. Du Bois* and the poetry collection *The Age of Phillis*, both longlisted for the National Book Award, among numerous other honors. She is currently writing a biography of the great poet Lucille Clifton. She teaches creative writing and literature at the University of Oklahoma.

Denis Johnson (1949–2017) was the author of *Jesus' Son, Train Dreams*, a finalist for the 2012 Pulitzer Prize, and several novels, including *Tree of Smoke*, the 2007 National Book Award winner and finalist for the 2008 Pulitzer Prize. His last short story collection, *The Largesse of the Sea Maiden*, was published by Random House in January 2018 and was nominated for the National Book Critics Circle Award for Fiction.

Lacy M. Johnson is a Houston-based professor, curator, activist, and is author of *The Reckonings* and *The Other Side*—both National Book Critics Circle Award finalists—and *Trespasses*. She is editor, with the designer Cheryl Beckett, of *More City Than Water: A Houston Flood Atlas*. She teaches creative nonfiction at Rice University and is the founding director of the Houston Flood Museum.

Mona Kareem is the author of three poetry collections and the trilingual chapbook *Femme Ghosts* (Publication Studio, 2010). She is a recipient of a 2021 NEA literary grant, and has held fellowships and residencies with Princeton University, Poetry International, the Arab-American National Museum, Norwich Writers' Center, Forum Transregionale Studien, and the Center for the Humanities at Tufts University. Her work has been translated into nine languages. She holds a PhD in comparative literature from the State University of New York at Binghamton.

Mieko Kawakami is the author of the internationally best-selling novel *Breasts and Eggs*, a *New York Times* Notable Book of the Year and one of *Time*'s 10 Best Fiction Books of 2020. Her other novels, translated by Sam Bett and David Boyd, include *Heaven* (2021), shortlisted for the 2022 International Booker Prize, and *All the Lovers in the Night* (2022), a finalist for the 2023 National Book Critics Circle Award for fiction.

Rachel Khong is the author of the novels *Goodbye, Vitamin* and *Real Americans*, forthcoming from Knopf. She lives in California.

Li Qingzhao (1084–1151) is considered the greatest female poet in Chinese history. During her lifetime, she defied cultural expectations for women by writing and persevering through war, exile, imprisonment, and the loss of her fortune. Li Qingzhao is renowned particularly for her ci (lyrics), poems set to music with predetermined meters and tones.

Barry Lopez is the author of three collections of essays, including *Horizon*; several story collections; *Arctic Dreams*, for which he received the National Book Award; *Of Wolves and Men*, a National Book Award finalist; and *Crow and Weasel*, a novella-length fable. He contributed regularly to both American and foreign journals and traveled to more than seventy countries to conduct research. He was the recipient of fellowships from the Guggenheim, Lannan, and National Science Foundations and was honored by a number of institutions for his literary, humanitarian, and environmental work. He died in 2020. A final book of essays, *Embrace Fearlessly the Burning World*, was published in 2022.

Rebecca Makkai's novel *The Great Believers* was a finalist for both the Pulitzer Prize and the National Book Award, and won the ALA Carnegie Medal and the LA Times Book Prize among other honors. She is also the author of the novels *The Borrower* and *The Hundred-Year House* and the story collection *Music for Wartime*. A 2022 Guggenheim Fellow, she is artistic director of StoryStudio Chicago. Her new novel, *I Have Some Questions for You*, was published in 2023.

Colum McCann is the internationally best-selling author of seven novels, including *Apeirogon*, *TransAtlantic*, *Let the Great World Spin*, and *Dancer*, as well as three critically acclaimed story collections and the nonfiction book *Letters to a Young Writer*. His fiction has been published in over forty languages. He has received many honors, including the National Book Award, the International IMPAC Dublin Literary Award, a Guggenheim fellowship, the Pushcart Prize, and an Oscar nomination for his short film *Everything in This Country Must*. He is a member of the American Academy of Arts and Letters, as well as the Irish association of artists Aosdána, and he has also received a Chevalier des Arts et des Lettres award from the French government. He is the co-founder of the global nonprofit story exchange organization Narrative 4. *American Mother*, a non-fiction account of the life of Diane Foley, mother of journalist James Foley, will be published in March 2024.

Semezdin Mehmedinović was born in 1960 in Kiseljak near Tuzla. He studied comparative literature at the Faculty of Philosophy in Sarajevo. A poet and essayist, he has also been the editor of newspapers and magazines, and been involved in radio and film productions. He is the author of *Sarajevo Blues*, *Nine Alexandrias*, and *My Heart*, among other works. He lived in the United States for many years before returning to Sarajevo.

Sayaka Murata is the author of many books, including *Earthlings* and *Convenience Store Woman*, winner of Japan's Akutagawa Prize. She was chosen for inclusion in *Freeman's: The Future of New Writing* and was a *Vogue* Japan Woman of the Year. Her latest book is a story collection, *Life Ceremony*, published in 2022.

Chinelo Okparanta was born and raised in Port Harcourt, Nigeria. Her debut short story collection, *Happiness, Like Water*, was nominated for the Nigerian Writers Award, longlisted for the Frank O'Connor International Short Story Award, and was a finalist for the New York Public Library Young Lions Fiction Award, as well as the Etisalat Prize for Literature. Her first novel, *Under the Udala Trees*, was nominated for many awards, including the Kirkus Prize and Center for Fiction First Novel Prize, and was a *New York Times Book Review* Editor's Choice. She received her MFA from the Iowa Writers' Workshop, and she is currently associate professor of English and creative writing at Swarthmore College. Her most recent novel is *Harry Sylvester Bird*.

Tommy Orange is the *New York Times*–best-selling author of *There There*, winner of the 2018 Center for Fiction First Novel Prize, and longlisted for the National Book Award for fiction 2018, the Aspen Words Literary Prize, and the Carnegie Medal for Excellence in Fiction 2019. It was deemed a Top Five Fiction Book of the Year by the *New York Times* and won the John Leonard Award for Best First Book and the PEN/Hemingway Award for Debut Novel. *There There* was also a finalist for the Pulitzer Prize. His next novel, *Wandering Stars*, will be published by Alfred A. Knopf in 2024.

Matt Sumell is the author of the linked collection *Making Nice*, developed for a comedic series by Warner Brothers, and his short fiction has appeared in the *Paris Review, Esquire, Noon, McSweeney's*, and elsewhere.

Ginny Tapley Takemori is the award-winning literary translator of Japanese authors Sayaka Murata and Kyoko Nakajima, among others. Her most recent translation is *She and Her Cat*, by Makoto Shinkai and Naruki Nagakawa. She lives in Japan.

Hitomi Yoshio is associate professor of Global Japanese Literary and Cultural Studies at Waseda University. She specializes in modern and contemporary Japanese literature with a focus on women's writing. Her translations include *This Is Amiko, Do You Copy?* (Pushkin Press, 2023) and Mieko Kawakami's forthcoming short story collection, *Dreams of Love, Etc.*

About the Editor

John Freeman was the editor of *Granta* until 2013. His books include *Dictionary of the Undoing*, *How to Read a Novelist*, *Tales of Two Americas*, and *Tales of Two Planets*. His poetry includes the collections *Maps*, *The Park*, and *Wind, Trees*. In 2021, he edited the anthologies *There's a Revolution Outside, My Love* with Tracy K. Smith, and *The Penguin Book of the Modern American Short Story*. An executive editor at Knopf, he also hosts the California Book Club, a monthly online discussion of a new classic in Golden State literature for *Alta* magazine. His work has appeared in the *New Yorker* and the *Paris Review* and has been translated into twenty-two languages.